Introducing Systems Development

Introducing Systems Development

Steve Skidmore and Malcolm Eva

First published 2004 by
PALGRAVE MACMILLAN
Houndmills, Basingstoke, Hampshire RG21 6XS and
175 Fifth Avenue, New York, N. Y. 10010
Companies and representatives throughout the world

PALGRAVE MACMILLAN is the global academic imprint of the Palgrave Macmillan division of St. Martin's Press, LLC and of Palgrave Macmillan Ltd. Macmillan® is a registered trademark in the United States, United Kingdom and other countries. Palgrave is a registered trademark in the European Union and other countries.

ISBN 0–333–97369–0

This book is printed on paper suitable for recycling and made from fully managed and sustained forest sources.

A catalogue record for this book is available from the British Library.

10   9   8   7   6   5   4   3   2   1
13   12   11   10   09   08   07   06   05   04

Printed in China

Contents

Contents

Preface

Introduction

Introducing Systems Development provides an introduction to contemporary systems development.

The book is divided into three parts. Part 1 looks at issues concerned with the **inception** phase of systems development – getting the project off the ground. This part looks at how Information Systems (IS) may be delivered, organised and accounted for. The strategic selection of projects is examined in the context of Critical Success Factors (CSF) and the Soft Systems Methodology (SSM), before being subjected to a formal Feasibility Study.

Part 2 looks at the key techniques in the **elaboration** phase of development, developing the detailed requirements of the project. The principal models in this phase are from the Unified Modeling Language (UML). However, because a toolkit approach to systems development is suggested, they are complemented by structured techniques (such as Entity Life Histories) and traditional methods (for example, Structured English and Decision Tables). The aim of this part of the book is to equip the reader with a wide range of tools and techniques to model the user's information systems requirements.

Part 3 focuses on the external elements of the **construction** phase and the **transition** to the new system. Emphasis is placed on external design: how the design is experienced by the end user. Hence inputs, outputs, interfaces and controls are considered. Appropriate legislation, quality assurance, testing and implementation are also explicitly considered in this part of the book. Finally, many organisations now fulfil their information system requirements through selecting a commercially available software package. This is recognised throughout the book, but in this part the advantages and disadvantages of this approach are discussed, together with a suggested method for effective software package selection.

Changes to previous editions

This book replaces the second edition texts of *Introducing Systems Analysis* and *Introducing Systems Design*. Most of the text has been rewritten, but key points are:

▶ A focus on Unified Modeling Language (UML) models, techniques and vocabulary. Some structured and traditional techniques are retained as part of the analyst's toolkit.

▶ A recognition of the role of quality assurance and testing in the systems development process.

▶ A recognition that many organisations now fulfil their information system requirements through purchasing software packages. This book looks at the advantages and disadvantages of this approach and presents a method for selecting between competing solutions.

The book no longer considers the internal design of databases, files and programs. There are many excellent books on this subject, which provide a variety and coverage that cannot be provided here. For example, see *Data Analysis for Database Design* (Howe, 2001) for database and file design and *Software Design Using Java2* (Lano *et al.*, 2002) for program design, using Java as the teaching language.

The book is primarily aimed at

▶ Students undertaking an introductory module in information systems development

▶ Students undertaking professional examinations, such as ACCA and CIMA

▶ Trainee analysts studying for professional qualifications or following professional development schemes, such as the ISEB Business Systems Development scheme; in particular, the certificates in

  – Analysis and Design Techniques
  – Business Systems Investigation

▶ Practising systems analysts

Introduction

In this chapter you will learn about:

▶ The structure of systems development within the context of this book

▶ The case study used in certain sections and exercises

1.1 Introduction

This book is concerned with information systems development in organisations. The focus is on the identification, analysis and implementation of computerised business systems to support the management, control and administration of an organisation. Virtually all organisations now depend upon such systems, so the identification of appropriate systems and their successful analysis and implementation are now key activities in most organisations. The case study company, Woodland Transport, is an example of such an organisation. The company is keen to develop an information system that will help it to continue the effective administration and management of its business. Like many organisations it currently has a computerised information system, but it is keen to develop a more sophisticated successor.

Information systems development usually passes through, to varying degrees, four main phases of systems development. These are:

▶ **Inception** – identifying potential projects, assessing their feasibility and getting them off the ground

▶ **Elaboration** – analysing in detail the requirements of the user

▶ **Construction** – building the system specified in the elaboration phase

▶ **Transition** – implementing the system developed in the construction phase

The main focus of this book is inception and elaboration. However, significant areas of construction are also considered, together with a brief look at transition.

1.1.1 Inception

This stage is concerned with getting the project off the ground. Normally organisations are faced with competing demands on their resources. They undertake strategic studies, which are concerned with defining possible Information Systems (IS) contributions to the objectives of the enterprise. This is the focus of Chapter 2, which introduces two different approaches to establishing a limited number of candidate applications that will then be subjected to detailed feasibility studies. Each candidate area is examined and outline business and technical solutions suggested. A comparison is undertaken in the context of economic, technical and operational issues, culminating in a feasibility report, which recommends a possible solution and comments on whether detailed analysis should commence. Candidate areas are compared within the organisation to see which are worth investing in, and from this the detailed analysis of system projects is initiated. These feasibility studies are the focus of Chapter 3. Organisations must also decide how they are going to organise and deliver information systems. This is the focus of Chapter 4.

In determining the feasibility of the project the inception phase will also use some of the techniques used in the next phase, elaboration. The typical end of the inception phase is shown in Table 1.1.

Table 1.1 The end of the inception phase (adapted from Arlow and Neustadt, 2002).

Conditions of satisfaction	Commentary/deliverables
The stakeholders have agreed the project objectives	A document that states the project's main requirements, features and constraints. Usually formally stated in a Project Initiation Document
System scope has been defined and agreed with the stakeholders. Key requirements have been captured and agreed with the stakeholders	Using use cases and perhaps an initial class model, supported by Requirements Catalogue
Cost and schedule estimates have been agreed with the stakeholders. A business case has been raised by the project manager	The business case is presented in a feasibility report, which may also include the initial project plan
The project manager has performed a risk assessment	Risk assessment document
Confirmation of feasibility through technical studies and/or prototyping	Throwaway prototypes may be constructed to show proof of concept
An outline architecture	An initial technical architecture may be presented in the feasibility report

1.1.2 Elaboration

Elaboration is concerned with building up a detailed model of the requirements using appropriate fact-gathering techniques. These techniques are described in Chapter 5, but they underpin the rest of the book. Detailed requirement models are described in Chapters 6–9. These models are concerned with defining functional system requirements: what the user wants the system to do.

The default models are from the object-oriented environment using the Unified Modeling Language (UML), the *de facto* standard for this perspective. Use cases (Chapter 6), class models (Chapter 7), interaction diagrams (Chapter 8) and statechart diagrams (Chapter 9) are all from UML. However, because this is not solely a book about UML, representative models are also taken from other approaches. For example, the structured approach contributes data flow diagrams (Chapters 6 and 8) and extended entity life histories (Chapter 9). The Entity Relationship Model (Chapter 7) is also often identified with the structured techniques, although it was described long before in the context of database design. Traditional, ubiquitous techniques are also offered in Chapter 6 (process maps) and Chapter 8 (Structured English and decision tables). Our idea here is to offer a toolkit of techniques that the analyst can use to reflect different circumstances and requirements. UML offers a rich vocabulary, but it is interesting to see how older techniques compare and complement, and this is the focus of several exercises. The outcomes of the elaboration stage will also be affected by whether a bespoke or software package solution is envisaged. The latter will probably require a subset of models, with less detail than would be required for a bespoke development.

The typical end of the elaboration phase is shown in Table 1.2. (adapted from Arlow and Neustadt, 2002). In certain circumstances the elaboration phase may also consider issues that might be predominantly associated with the construction phase. You will notice that a real, executable system is envisaged. However this would not be required if an off-the-shelf software package is to be selected and it may also not be applicable if the application is going to be a bespoke development by an external software company. The customer may wish to build a complete model of their requirements before putting this out for competitive tender. This book focuses on the model building aspects of elaboration, although elements of prototyping are considered and a more integrated analyse, design and build cycle is reviewed in Chapter 10: Rapid Application Development (RAD).

1.1.3 Construction phase

The construction phase is concerned with building the system described at the end of the elaboration phase. Further analysis and design work will be required, but essentially this is the build phase of development. This is represented in this book by Chapter 10 (rapid application development) and the external design chapters: 11 (usability), 12 (controls) and 13

Table 1.2 The end of the elaboration phase (adapted from Arlow and Neustadt, 2002).

Conditions of satisfaction	Commentary/deliverables
A resilient, robust executable architectural baseline has been created	This will include appropriate function, static and event models. In a UML environment it may be a class model, use cases and interaction diagrams supported by a real, executable computer system
The vision of the product has stabilised	Scope of the product has been agreed
The risk assessment and business case have been revised	Updated risk assessment and project plan agreed with stakeholders
A detailed project plan has been produced for the next phase	Updated project plan
Agreement has been reached with the stakeholders to continue the project	Sign-off document

(testing). In general, construction requires both internal and external design. Internal design is concerned with the detailed specification, design and coding of programs together with the design and implementation of detailed data structures. These are major subjects in their own right and they are not considered in this book, although their place in development is identified within the chapter on rapid application development. However, the parts of the design that the end user experiences – inputs, outputs, interfaces, controls – are covered. The construction phase ends with a software product that is sufficiently stable and of sufficient quality to be deployed to the end user community. Hence testing is also considered within this stage, although the aspects of quality assurance introduced in this chapter also apply to both the inception and elaboration phases.

Finally, there may be no construction. The software solution may be a software package, and although usability, controls and quality will be taken into account in selecting such a package, they are just part of the process described in Chapters 14 and 15. Many organisations now prefer to implement their information system requirements through software packages, and this emphasis is reflected in the book.

The typical end of the construction phase is shown in Table 1.3.

1.1.4 Transition phase

The transition phase is concerned with the deployment of the new system. Aspects of this phase are described in Chapter 16. The typical end of the transition phase is shown in Table 1.4.

Table 1.3 The end of the construction phase (adapted from Arlow and Neustadt, 2002).

Conditions of satisfaction	Commentary/deliverables
The software product is sufficiently stable and of sufficient quality to be deployed in the user community	The software product and its design is complete and system tested
The stakeholders have agreed and are ready for the transition of the software to their environment	User manuals Description of this release of the software product
The actual expenditure versus the planned expenditure is acceptable	Updated project plan

Table 1.4 The end of the transition phase (adapted from Arlow and Neustadt, 2002).

Conditions of satisfaction	Commentary/deliverables
User acceptance testing is complete, necessary changes have been made, and the users agree that the system has been successfully deployed	User accepted software product
The user community is actively using the product	
Product support strategies have been agreed with the users and implemented.	User support plan User manuals

It has to be recognised that each of these phases is not self-contained. For example, inception will require analysis techniques (described in the elaboration phase) and perhaps also programming (from the construction phase). However, it provides a handy structure for taking a system from the first glimmer of a proposal through to its formal acceptance by the user community. The chapters describe the major preoccupations of each stage in the context of the scope of this book.

The potential roles of employees in an information systems department are considered in Chapter 4. Within this book the terms *analyst*, *designer* and *developer* are used interchangeably for textual variety. It just represents the people who do the work! Similarly, the term *user* is usually employed with a broad definition encompassing the people who require the work being done and who get to use the software when it is delivered.

1.2 Woodland Transport case study

At appropriate times during the book, reference is made to the following case study. This sometimes forms the basis of examples and sometimes the focus of exercises. The requirements are presented in this chapter, although obviously they would not emerge in such detail until some time during the elaboration phase.

1.2.1 Background

Woodland Transport Limited was established in 1980 by the multinational holding company United Logistics. It was set up to provide an exclusive contract to the large Kronenhalle Brewery plant in the East Midlands. Under the terms of the contract, Kronenhalle Brewery agreed to move all of the lager it produced in Woodland Transport vehicles, while in return Woodland Transport agreed to undertake no work outside the Kronenhalle contract.

Woodland Transport currently has 80 tractors (the cab part of an articulated lorry), 170 trailers and 70 drivers. The contract with Kronenhalle is reviewed every three years. Kronenhalle Brewery is currently reviewing its contract arrangements prior to the renewal of the next transport contract.

A seven-day, two shifts per day work pattern is followed. Forty drivers are allocated to the early shift and 30 to the late shift. Work is also carried out on Saturdays and Sundays in emergency circumstances. The workload is spread evenly over the year, with the exception of late October/November when delivering stocks for Christmas leads to volumes up to 50% higher than the rest of the year. This increases Saturday and Sunday working and also leads to the employment of subcontract drivers and tractors as well as agency drivers from local employment agencies.

The trailers are operated and serviced by Woodland Transport. The offices of Woodland Transport occupy a self-contained ground floor suite within the main brewery block.

1.2.2 Strategic issues

Woodland Transport is at risk because it is a one-contract company. The future existence of the company depends upon the renewal of the contract. At the time of the last contract renewal, Woodland Transport implemented a bespoke computer solution using a local software house. This system (CLASS) allowed the company to reorganise internal procedures and to automatically create and update the roadsheets used by the drivers when they make their deliveries.

The system is written in a character-based programming language. It is used over a five-user network, with three PCs in the Traffic Office, one in Administration and one on the Managing Director's desk.

Unfortunately, the software house that wrote the CLASS system has now gone into receivership. As a result it has been decided to completely rewrite the CLASS system. The replacement software should offer:

▶ Improved functionality. A number of issues and new requirements have arisen in the Traffic and Administration departments since the original implementation.

▶ A Windows-based interface. It has been decided to write the new system in Visual Basic with a SQL Server database. These are the standards used throughout the United Logistics Group.

▶ An increased scope, to reflect the planning activities undertaken in the Logistics department. This was specifically excluded from the scope of the original CLASS system.

1.2.3 The operational system

The current operational system is administered in four departments.

▶ **Logistics/planning**
This department is responsible for the production of the Loading and Delivery Schedules for each shift. Tractor and trailer unavailability is received from the workshop, and driver unavailability (holidays and planned sick leave) from Administration. Dorn Taylor, who is assisted by two full-time clerks (one per shift), heads the section.

▶ **Traffic Office**
Traffic is responsible for the production and confirmation of the roadsheets. Kim Watson heads the department, assisted by four clerks (two per shift).

▶ **Administration**
Jerry Brand, the Administrative Supervisor is the only employee in this section. He is responsible for the production of all payment and absence information and the resolution of personnel issues.

▶ **Workshop**
The workshop undertakes the servicing of both tractors and trailers. Arthur Lovick heads it. The Workshop is responsible for ensuring that all tractors and trailers receive regular maintenance and for keeping records of their availability.

All the department heads report to Stuart Talbot, the General Manager.

Traffic Office
The Traffic Office is responsible for the operational control of drivers. This is essentially a two-phase process.

1. The first phase is producing roadsheets and despatching the drivers at the start of the shift.

2. The second phase is confirming that deliveries have been completed when the drivers return.

Figure 1.1 The create pre-delivery roadsheet function.

FUNCTION NAME: Create Pre-Delivery Roadsheet
General description This function allows the creation of the pre-delivery roadsheet.
Business logic The system automatically allocates the next **Roadsheet Number**. This value cannot be overwritten by the user. The system automatically displays the current system date as the **Roadsheet Date**. This may be overwritten by the user. The user enters the **Driver Number**. A pull-down list of valid driver numbers and names is available at this point. The system displays the **Driver Name**. The user enters the **Start Time**. The value for **Shift** is automatically derived from the start time. The system now requests leg information. As the user provides information about each leg, the system allocates the leg number automatically. For each leg, the system requires the user to enter the start point of the journey (the **Source Code**). A pull-down list is provided at this point showing valid depot codes and their names. The user then enters the end point of the journey (the **Destination Code**). A pull-down list is provided at this point showing valid depot codes and their names. If the leg concerns a delivery, then the user enters the **Delivery Note Number**. **This is not validated by the system**. Any **Special Instructions** associated with the destination depot are displayed in the appropriate column.
Operational issues Once roadsheet information has been entered, two copies are printed. One remains in the Traffic Office, the other is given to the driver.

Phase One

1. Traffic receives a delivery schedule from Logistics the day before a given shift. Traffic stores this schedule until delivery notes for the schedule arrive.

2. The delivery schedule identifies which driver (number) and tractor will deliver which loads.

3. Logistics receives delivery notes from the brewery (Kronenhalle) and checks that they are correct before passing them to the Traffic Office.

4. The delivery note is a three-part set. Each part is identified by its colour. The customer's copy is white (delivery advice). The red copy is signed by the customer and will be returned by the driver to the Traffic Office. The blue copy remains in the Traffic Office as a control copy (see below).

5. The create pre-delivery roadsheet (see Figure 1.1) in the CLASS software creates the Phase One roadsheet. Two copies are printed. One goes with the driver, while the other is retained in the Traffic Office along with the blue copies of the delivery note.

Figure 1.2 The confirm post-delivery roadsheet function.

FUNCTION NAME: Confirm Post-Delivery Roadsheet
General description   This function allows the entry of details filled in on the roadsheet by the driver as he or she makes the daily deliveries.
Business logic   The user enters the **Roadsheet Number** and the system retrieves the information entered in the function Create Pre-delivery Roadsheet. A pull-down list of valid roadsheet numbers is available at this point.   The user enters both **Start Mileage** and **Finish Mileage**. It rejects the value of Finish Mileage if it is before the Start Mileage.   The user enters any **Fuel Drawn**.   The user enters the **Finish Time**. The system checks that the finish time is after the start time.   The user enters any **Oil Drawn**.   The system now requires the completion of leg information.   For each pre-specified leg, the user enters (where relevant) the **Trailer Number**. A pull-down list of valid trailer numbers is available at this point.   For legs specified while the driver was already on the road, this function uses the same logic as the creation of the pre-delivery roadsheet leg, except that special instructions are not displayed.   The user enters delay information noted by the driver at the bottom of the roadsheet into a **Delay Information** field.   If the delay information requires an action, then this is recorded in an **Action** field.
Operational issues   A completed copy of the roadsheet is kept in Traffic. The other pre-delivery roadsheet is destroyed.

Phase Two

1. When the driver returns, Traffic checks that the roadsheet has been completed properly. Details are then entered into the CLASS software using the confirm post-delivery roadsheet function (see Figure 1.2).

2. There are two reasons why a driver may fail to make a delivery (see below). In either event the driver will return with both the white and red copies of the delivery note.

3. If a delay occurred and there was not time to reach the destination, the blue copy of the delivery note is reattached to the white and red and the three-part set is sent to Logistics for rescheduling.

4. If the depot has refused delivery (due to incorrect delivery), the three-part set is returned to the brewery.

5. Finally, after the roadsheet has been processed, the Traffic clerk signs it on the bottom and files it. The copy of the pre-delivery roadsheet retained in Traffic is destroyed. The red copy of the delivery note is sent to the Brewery. The blue copies remain in Traffic.

1.2.4 Reports currently produced by the CLASS system

Delivery Exceptions Report
Week beginning: 19 May

Date	Roadsheet number	Driver name	Delivery note number	Reason	Action
20/5	70165	Mulligan	9121-142	Delay on M25	Rescheduled for 22/5
22/5	70191	Sachs	9121-165	Lost Copy 3	Photocopy to KBL
23/5	70206	Barber	9121-159	Delivery rejected	Referred to KBL
23/5	70215	Adamson	9121-209	Delay at the brewery	Rescheduled for 24/5

Delivery Report
A record of all the deliveries made on selected day(s).

Delivery date	Delivery note number	Depot	Roadsheet number
20/5	9121 – 23	Northampton	70183
20/5	9121 – 36	Melton Mowbray	70183
20/5	9121 – 206	Bedford	70183
20/5			
20/5			
20/5			

Daily Driver Listing
A list of the hours and miles covered by drivers on a selected day.

Day: 20 May

Driver no.	Driver name	Roadsheet number	Hours worked	Mileage
38	Sams	70182	09:30	175
37	Collins	70183	11:15	301

Tractor Efficiency Report

Tractor number	Total mileage	Total fuel used	Miles/gallon
237	2100	287.7	7.3
238	1908	293	6.5
239	1600	242	6.6

Depot Location Report

Depot	Name	Address	Phone	Contact	Special instructions
MEM	Melton Mowbray	38 High Street Melton Mowbray Leicestershire MM8 7RT	01669-78788	Tom McGable	Closed 12.00–13.00
HUL	Hull	Farmington Road Membury Hull	01804125129	Terry Jack	Tanks to gate 3 only

Driver Details Report

Driver no.	Initial	Surname	Address	Phone number	Shift
037	E	Collins	8 Ash Lane Thorbury Northants	01604 412847	Early
038	P	Samms	22 Pimms Road Pearly Heath Northants	01604 290112	Late
039	E	Mulholland	53 Bushey Lane Ishinham Northants	01605 331018	Early

Driver Weekly Hours Report

Week beginning: 6 May									
		Hours Worked							
Num	Name	Sun	Mon	Tue	Wed	Thu	Fri	Sat	Total
23	A.T.Thompson	0.0	11.0	9.0	13.0	8.5	10.0	0.0	51.5
24	E.G.Swanwick	0.0	8.0	12.0	10.0	0.0	9.5	0.0	39.5
25	R.S.Jones	8.0	9.0	10.0	13.0	12.0	8.5	0.0	60.5
26	J.Clay	0.0	10.0	9.5	10.0	9.0	8.5	0.0	47.0
27	T.F.Jones	0.0	9.5	11.5	10.5	0.0	0.0	0.0	31.5
30	A.S.Stephens	0.0	10.0	9.5	9.0	10.0	9.5	0.0	48.0
31	R.T.Yorke	0.0	9.5	12.0	12.5	9.5	11.5	0.0	55.0
32	I.B.Squires	0.0	10.0	10.0	9.5	7.0	9.0	0.0	45.5
33	C.B.Dale	8.0	0.0	12.5	11.5	11.0	9.0	0.0	52.0
34	D.J.Sams	0.0	10.0	10.0	9.5	8.0	10.0	0.0	47.5
35	I.J.D.Lindley	0.0	0.0	13.0	9.0	9.5	10.0	0.0	41.5

Driver Weekly Pay Hours Report

Week beginning: 6 May					
		Hours			
Driver	Name	Standard time	Time × 1.5	Time × 2	Pay hours
23	A.T.Thompson	50.0	4.0	0.0	56.0
24	E.G.Swanwick	40.0	2.0	0.0	43.0
25	R.S.Jones	50.0	5.0	8.0	73.5
26	J.Clay	50.0	0.0	0.0	50.0
27	T.F.Jones	30.0	2.0	0.0	33.0
30	A.S.Stephens	50.0	0.0	0.0	50.0
31	R.T.Yorke	50.0	6.0	0.0	59.0
32	I.B.Squires	50.0	0.0	0.0	50.0
33	C.B.Dale	40.0	5.0	8.0	63.5
34	D.J.Sams	50.0	0.0	0.0	50.0
35	I.J.D.Lindley	40.0	3.0	0.0	44.5

1.2.5 Requirements for the future

1. The facility to code delays by an appropriate delay type and to produce reports analysed by such codes. For example:

Delay type	Brewery delay		
Date	Roadsheet number	Destination	Reason
99/99/99	12345	Hull	Trailer not loaded
	12366	Acton	Await load
99/99/99	12407	Melton Mowbray	Trailer damaged
Delay type	Customer delay		
99/99/99	12350	Northampton	Queue to unload
99/99/99	12508	Warminster	Order dispute

2. To produce a last known trailer location report. This shows the last reported location of trailers.

Date: 99/99/99	Trailers not used since: 99/99/99		
Trailer number	Location	Roadsheet number	Date
101	Leeds	12345	99/99/99
108	Hull	12501	99/99/99
114	Melton Mowbray	12506	99/99/99

3. To produce tractor utilisation statistics.

Fleet	Monday		Tuesday		Wednesday		Thursday		Friday		Utility
No.	E	L	E	L	E	L	E	L	E	L	
123	Y		*Y*	*Y*	*Y*	*Y*	*Y*		*Y*	*Y*	80%
124		*Y*	*Y*	*Y*	*Y*	*Y*	*Y*	*Y*	*Y*	*Y*	90%
125	*Y*	*Y*		*Y*	*Y*	*Y*	*Y*	*Y*	*Y*	*Y*	90%
126	*Y*		*Y*	*Y*	*Y*	*Y*	*Y*		*Y*	*Y*	80%

4. To analyse movements by movement type. This shows the number of legs analysed by movement type. Five movement types are envisaged:

Deliveries, Collections, Empty running (trailer empty), Tractor only and Other.

Date	Deliveries	Collections	Empty running	Tractor only	Other
99/99/99	150	100	50	45	5
99/99/99	175	150	10	15	0
99/99/99	160	175	35	10	2

5. To enter delivery notes earlier in the system so they can be verified in the first process. This would allow the system to report on delivery notes not yet allocated to roadsheet legs.

Delivery note information is not currently verified by the CLASS system. It would be useful to enter this information earlier in the business process, so that the values can be verified when roadsheet information is entered.

1.2.6 Administration

The administration function produces the Driver Pay Hours Report and the Driver Hours Worked Reports (see previous reports). These are sent to the United Logistics headquarters in Swindon, where they are used to produce the payslips for the drivers. Most of the information contained in these reports is derived from the roadsheets entered in the CLASS system. However, two further functions are used to complete the information required to produce the correct output. These are described below.

Maintain pay rules
The current rules are that, on Monday to Friday, drivers are paid a standard, guaranteed ten-hour day for each day they work. Any time worked over ten hours is paid at time and a half.
For example:

Worked hours	Paid hours
8	10
9	10
10	10
11	11.5
12	13

On a Saturday there are no guaranteed hours and all hours worked are paid at time and a half. For example:

Worked hours	Paid hours
4	6
5	7.5
6	9

On a Sunday, there are no guaranteed hours and all hours worked are paid at double time. For example:

Worked hours	Paid hours
4	8
5	10
6	12

The pay rules are defined held in a DAY database table with the following structure:

Day, guaranteed-hours, standard-rate, overtime-rate

Enter absence details

Drivers are also paid for certified sickness and holidays. The following absence types are defined on the system and pay rules are associated with them.

Absence type	Rules	Comment
Certified sickness	Paid up to a maximum of 30 days	Sickness certified by a medical practitioner
Self-certified sickness	Paid up to a maximum of 3 days per sickness	Sickness self-certified by the driver
Uncertified sickness	Unpaid	
Holiday	Paid	Subject to a maximum of 23 days per year

Requirements

The system needs to distinguish subcontractors and agency drivers from full-time staff. This was not fully appreciated when the CLASS system was specified.

Subcontractors are self-employed drivers. They may be employed on a temporary basis and may or may not have their own tractors. Subcontractors submit invoices for their work, which may include the use of their tractor.

Agency drivers work for a particular agency (such as StaffPower). At the end of each week, the agencies send in invoices covering the work of their drivers. Agencies do not have tractors.

Woodland Transport needs to distinguish between Agency drivers, Subcontractors and full-time staff on the CLASS system. The following two reports should also be produced.

Sub-contractor	Tony Brown		
Date	Roadsheet number	Destination	Comment
99/99/99	12345	Hull	Tractor
		Park Royal	Tractor
	12362	Leeds	
99/99/99	12401	Glasgow	Tractor
	13456	Melton Mowbray	

Agency	StaffPower		
Date	Roadsheet number	Destination	Driver
99/99/99	543231	Leeds	Alcock
	654323	Melton Mowbray	Brown
		Northampton	Brown
	435621	York	Dearden

1.3 Summary

This chapter has introduced systems development within the context of this book. It has also presented a case study, which will be used selectively in subsequent chapters and exercises.

References

Arlow, J. and Neustadt, I. (2002). *UML and the Unified Process.* Reading, MA: Addison-Wesley.

Booch, G., Rumbaugh, J. and Jacobson, I. (1999). *The Unified Modeling Language User Guide.* Reading, MA: Addison-Wesley.

Information systems strategy

This first part of the book looks at strategic issues in organisation, delivery and identification of projects. There are two dominant themes:

▶ Projects must be properly identified and justified before detailed work can commence.

▶ The structure and maturity of the organisation affects the types of project that are selected as well as the formality of how these projects are subsequently specified and developed.

As mentioned in Chapter 1, this part is primarily concerned with the inception phase of systems development.

Chapter 2 looks at the organisational structure in which information systems delivery takes place. The way that information systems are organised and paid for will have a significant effect on the application of the techniques and issues described in the rest of this book. The growth of cross-charging arrangements and outsourcing has led to a more formalised approach to requirement specification. It is now common for relatively formal arrangements to exist between the customer and the provider of the information systems, even when that provider is only a different department in the same organisation. Clearly, this becomes particularly important and significant when the information systems provider is an external company participating in an outsourcing arrangement.

Chapter 3 focuses on the identification of worthwhile projects for potential computerisation. Two contrasting approaches are presented. The first is a 'top-down' business approach based on business objectives, critical success factors and key performance indicators. In this approach the overall mission of the enterprise is progressively elaborated until it can be defined in terms of candidate information systems projects. In contrast, the Soft Systems Methodology provides a less clinical approach, providing a framework for exploring the messy reality of organisations. In this approach, the comparison of conceptual models with how the systems actually work provides a basis for projects, which may or may not include computerisation. This chapter also includes a review of the stages of IS growth as the enterprise's IS/IT maturity also affects the way that projects are selected.

It is unlikely that an organisation will have sufficient time and resources to pursue all the worthwhile projects identified using the techniques examined in the previous chapter. Consequently, projects have to be compared and prioritised and projects selected that provide the best 'payback' to the enterprise, however that 'payback' is defined. This is the theme of Chapter 4. It looks at feasibility and feasibility studies, culminating in a consideration of the likely structure of a feasibility report. The feasibility report ends with a recommendation. If it suggests that the project should go ahead, then the project may be subjected to the detailed techniques described in the next two parts of this book.

Information systems delivery

In this chapter you will learn about:

▶ The participants in an Information Systems department
▶ The advantages and disadvantages of a centralised Information
  Systems department
▶ The principles of cross-charging for Information Systems delivery
▶ The advantages and disadvantages of outsourcing.

2.1 Introduction

This chapter examines how the Information Systems (IS) function might
be structured and accounted for. The comparative advantages of
centralised and decentralised departments are discussed, along with how
costs may be redistributed in a centralised arrangement. Some
organisations have chosen not to retain their own IS function at all, but to
outsource systems development and maintenance to an external third-
party supplier. The advantages and disadvantages of this approach are
discussed, together with some of its implications for requirements
gathering and specification.

2.2 The structure of the Information Systems department

Many organisations have specialist information systems departments,
where the employees who do the sort of work described in this book (and
much more!) are located. One of the debates over the last two decades has
been whether it is better to **centralise** the information systems activity or
to **decentralise** it across the user departments. This is one of the decisions
that an organisation must make about its information systems provision.
This section looks at the advantages and disadvantages of the two
approaches.

The existence of a separate information systems department normally reflects a centralised approach to information systems development. In this approach, there is a specialist department serving all other functional departments (such as marketing and manufacturing), headed by an information systems manager or director. Within the department there are normally a number of different roles. For example, **systems analysts** are responsible for interviewing users, analysing and documenting current systems and designing their replacement. Their work usually culminates in the specification of the proposed system. **Programmers** are usually the people who take the analyst's specification and turn it into a working system. Sometimes the roles of analysts and programmers are merged to create the role of **analyst/programmer**, a term that many organisations have now replaced with the generic name of **systems developer**.

Employees in the **Operations** section undertake a critical but unglamorous role in the information systems function. They are concerned with job scheduling, computer room operation, input and output, data preparation and control, as well as other important infrastructure tasks. The increased importance of networks means that many organisations also employ **network specialists** who maintain this important aspect of the company's technical infrastructure.

In some organisations the job of the systems analyst is distinguished from those of the data analyst and the business analyst. In general, **business analysts** are concerned with exploring business solutions and are usually associated with projects prior to and including feasibility. **Data analysts** are at almost the other end of the development process. They are largely concerned with specifying, designing and building databases. Organisations are increasingly employing specialist **web designers** for their e-commerce applications, and many organisations have also seen the advantage of employing specialist **systems testers**, whose job it is to thoroughly test software before it is released from the department to the end users.

The centralised approach to information systems delivery has a number of perceived advantages over the decentralised approach:

▶ It allows the organisation to establish a coherent information system strategy, making sure that compatible hardware and software are used across the whole of the organisation. It is difficult to maintain and exploit fragmented systems written in different programming languages and running on incompatible hardware platforms.

▶ The use of standard hardware and software allows the organisation to build up a large and skilled specialist workforce. Not only does this mean that most technical problems can be solved fairly quickly, but also that the loss of one or two key staff may be borne more easily.

▶ The large number of people in the IS department and the different roles available make for a motivating environment where individuals can see a professional career path. Such individuals are more likely to stay in the organisation to fulfil their career aspirations.

▶ The centralised operation means that the department can achieve economies of scale in the purchase of hardware, software and consumables. Its size gives it a powerful platform for negotiating special deals and discounts.

▶ The centralised employment of staff recognises that demand for information systems development is variable. Work tends to be organised into projects, which begin and end. In a centralised organisation a large pool of multi-skilled systems developers may be moved around projects as required. This very flat organisational structure allows the company to deploy its workforce flexibly as well as providing a highly motivating environment for employees.

In contrast, some organisations prefer to decentralise their information systems function giving the budget, people and resources to the individual departments. Hence, for example, IS employees may be distributed through marketing, production, distribution and research departments. The perceived advantages of this approach are:

▶ It is easier for the end user department to control information systems development and expenditure because the user department controls the whole of the budget. There are no unforeseen and unpredictable overhead costs associated with decisions made outside the department. Budget responsibility is very clear, so this approach is particularly attractive to organisations with devolved profit centres.

▶ Information systems specialists begin to build up intimate knowledge of the application areas they are working in. They become used to the jargon, culture and business processes of the department and hence can contribute more to the successful computerisation of these processes.

▶ In a decentralised arrangement the best hardware and software fit can be purchased for each department. There is no need for them to buy into expensive corporate-wide information systems strategies, which they see no need for.

▶ Information systems specialists are offered a broader business career path giving them opportunities that would never have arisen within the confines of a small information systems department.

▶ Finally, there is a feeling that departmental solutions are less complex with fewer people to please. Hence projects can be undertaken quicker and cheaper, delivering solutions that provide immediate payback to the department and the organisation as a whole.

In reality, most organisations still have a centralised structure, largely, we suspect, because of the difficulty of recruiting, monitoring and motivating specialist staff. Furthermore, the need to maintain increasingly diverse and complex technical infrastructures has encouraged centralisation, because these are impossible to manage in a piecemeal fashion. However, like many management theories, these things go in cycles. At the time of writing, a large services group known to us has decided to dismantle its large centralised IT and IS department and redistribute its resources back to the companies within the group. This reorganisation will be expensive as they dismantle the (also expensive) centralisation strategy of the now departed IT director.

2.3 Accounting for information systems delivery

In a centralised information systems department, accounting for the cost of information systems resources and development can become a major issue. This section focuses on looking at different ways in which this can be handled.

For example, an organisation may have five departments: marketing, manufacturing, distribution, research and development, and warehousing. A specialised information systems department services the IS/IT requirements of these core departments. The problem that the organisation faces is how to share the overhead of the IS/IT costs between the other five departments. One option is to divide the cost equally between the five departments, irrespective of use. This might be improved by using a formula based on the relative sizes, perhaps using the number of employees in each department as a measure of that size. Examples are given in Table 2.1 for an Information Systems budget of €500,000.

Alternatively, the organisation may wish to distribute the cost based on the relative use of technology, resources and staff. This would include the cost of hardware and software as well as the cost of using information systems staff and resources. For example, three analysts may be required for five days to specify a system for the distribution department. This means that 15 staff days will have to be charged for at some agreed rate per staff day. Setting a charge rate per day is usually achieved by dividing the cost of the IS department by the number of days work it can offer. In some instances, the cost of the IS department includes notional costs for office rent, essential services (such as electricity) and other overheads, such as cleaning and security. In other cases it is just the employees' salaries of the IS department that have to be recouped. Whatever the basis of setting the charge rate, it is clear that under this approach IS becomes

Table 2.1 Allocating IS costs.

Department	Allocated equally (€000)	Number of employees	Allocated in proportion to number of employees (€000)
Marketing	100	5	25
Manufacturing	100	50	250
Distribution	100	30	150
Research and Development	100	5	25
Warehousing	100	10	50

an important cost centre, cross-charging its services to other departments.

Although the principle of cross-charging is relatively simple, in practice it raises a number of important issues. In the first instance, it is often difficult for the user to understand and control the amount of hardware resource that their applications are using. Furthermore, there is often no viable alternative if the cost is perceived as too high. It is possible on some discretionary processes, such as management reports, for the software to calculate the cost of producing the report before the user actually runs it. This allows the user to weigh up the value of the information contained in the report against the cost of obtaining it. Indeed, such an approach may lead to a much more careful use of computing resources. However, in non-discretionary processes, such as running the payroll or producing a picking list, the cost of the processing has to be accepted, even if the user thinks that the charge is too high.

The cost of using information systems staff is also a particular problem for both the user and the information systems department. Many cross-charge rates are less than commercial software house rates because the internal cost does not have to take into account many of the overheads, such as sales and marketing, that the commercial company has to meet. Furthermore, the internal department does not have to make a profit. However, despite the relatively low unit charge, many users find that the number of days quoted for a particular job often appears to be excessive, giving a high overall cost for a particular requirement. And, because the information systems department is often a monopoly supplier of such services within the organisation, there is very little the user can do about this charging problem.

This problem of cost per staff day and the number of days taken for a particular job is a further issue in major projects. There is also a fundamental problem surrounding the estimates produced for information systems development and the cost–benefit analysis undertaken in the feasibility study. In bespoke systems development, a significant amount of the costs (documented in the feasibility study) will concern the time taken to analyse requirements, specify a solution and design and program the software solution. At the time of the feasibility study these estimates are notoriously difficult to predict accurately. Even in organisations where there are established software estimating methods these figures are still likely to be very imprecise.

The implication of this imprecision becomes clear when the project progresses. For example, if the information systems department predicts 300 days of work at, say £300 per day, then £90,000 can be budgeted for in the cost–benefit analysis at the feasibility study stage. However, when the work actually takes place there are three possibilities that can occur. Firstly, the work can take less than 300 days. This has a very low probability of taking place, but if it does then the user will be very happy and the cost–benefit analysis even more favourable. The IS department may be less happy, as it will now have to find more internal work to cover its costs. Secondly, the work takes exactly 300 days. In this case everybody is happy! Finally, and most likely, the work takes more than 300 days. In this instance the organisation has to decide whether:

▶ The internal IS department still only charges for 300 days. The user will be happy with this. There may be a delay in delivery of the software, but the cost–benefit analysis will remain valid. Unfortunately, the IS department now has a problem in recouping its cost. This may lead to it distributing the uncovered cost across the five departments, who consequently receive an unwanted and unexpected bill.

▶ The internal IS department charges for the actual days taken to produce the software. For example, it may have taken 360 days, rather than 300. If this approach is adopted then users are unlikely to be happy and the original cost–benefit analysis will be invalid. However, the IS department will be able to recoup its costs.

Clearly it is possible for the IS department to factor in an estimating error into its cross-charging fee. However, many user departments are unhappy about this and often counter by declaring that they wish to be able to approach external software houses for competitive quotes. Indeed, this is the strategy that many organisations have taken: forcing the internal IS department to compete for internal tenders against external companies. This is again a simple principle, but it must be recognised that if the internal department does not successfully compete for enough tenders, it will again be unable to cover costs, and these will have to be recharged across the organisation. The same problem can occur if there is simply not enough work for the IS department to do.

The problems of defining and administering a fair and acceptable cross-charging system have led to some organisations simply setting up their internal IS department as a separate company profit centre. This company can charge market rates for the work they undertake, but they also take the risks associated with poor estimating and lack of work. Normally this profit centre is a legally separate corporate entity that can now take in work from other sources to help it meet its profit objectives. In essence this is the beginning of an outsourcing arrangement (see below), but it is an arrangement where the customer still has a vested interest in the success of the supplier. Consequently, the original host organisation must make sure that any newly created software company is economically viable. It must also recognise that the company should have sufficient entrepreneurial skills to succeed in the marketplace. And, finally, it must make sure that the company does not become too successful elsewhere, so that work for the host organisation becomes uneconomic and unattractive.

The trend for organisations to set up their information systems departments as separate cost or profit centres has led to more formal agreements between the information systems and the user departments. These often require user departments to sign off specifications as well as setting up formal Service Level Agreements between the user department and the information systems department. Furthermore, changes in requirements are then subjected to formal change control procedures and may lead to extra charges being made to cover the cost of making such changes.

Most organisations dabble, at one time or another, with cross-charging. It is usually in response to a need to make users feel responsible for the money they are spending. It also provides the information systems department with an economic framework to work in. It is an attempt to prevent solutions that are 'over-engineered' and 'providing a Rolls-Royce solution to a Mini requirement'. However, although it has certain advantages, cross-charging has to be thought through, or else it can create more problems than it solves.

2.4 Outsourcing

Outsourcing has become an acceptable and fashionable way of providing services in both public and private sector organisations. Many companies that have traditionally employed their own cleaning, catering and security staff now subcontract or outsource these to specialist suppliers. Appropriate employees of the organisation are usually transferred to these suppliers and hence become employees of the specialist contractor. This contractor then provides an agreed service to the host organisation for a specified contract period. At the end of this period the host organisation is able to evaluate competing suppliers before placing the next contract. The specialist supplier assumes profit and loss responsibility for the delivery of the service as well as taking on the employment and employment rights of the employees.

Outsourcing is a significant trend in the delivery of information systems and services. 'Executives are advised by many practitioners, academics and consultants to outsource their IS services along with their cafeteria, mail delivery and custodial services' (Lacity and Hirschheim, 1993). In some instances, this is further encouraged by government policy demanding Compulsory Competitive Tendering (CCT) for public sector contracts.

In this section the term *outsourcing* is used (following Lacity and Hirschheim) to imply 'total outsourcing' where the supplier is in charge of a significant proportion of the IS work. In its most extreme form the complete hardware supply and maintenance and software development and support is turned over to an external supplier. This is often termed Facilities Management (FM) in the United Kingdom.

The perceived advantages of outsourcing include:

▶ **Cost reduction**

Lacity and Hirschheim reported that the overwhelming reason an organisation explores outsourcing options is to identify opportunities for cost reduction. The perception is that outsourcing vendors can provide IS services more cheaply due to economies of scale. Elliot McNeil, Southland's IS Manager, claims that IS is largely a utility – rather than pay for the entire plant, why not just pay for the energy used? 'It's like the electric company; you use less, you pay less.'

Many organisations have been prepared to publicly claim outsourcing savings of between 10% and 50% of the IS budget, although this seems rather optimistic. Most IS departments are accounted for as an overhead function and senior managers tend to evaluate such departments on cost efficiency. Consequently they are always seeking opportunities for cost savings in the IS department.

▶ Emphasis on core business

The principle of outsourcing is that specialists are brought in to provide the supporting functions, allowing the management of the company to concentrate on its core business. This may be to provide insurance, distribution channels or biscuits – it is less usual to provide information systems. Thus outsourcing means that the management of the company can focus on its reason for existence, rather than being diverted into time-consuming tactical issues concerning its support services which it neither understands or values. Indeed, IS is the core business of the outsource supplier and so should benefit from that organisation's concentration on its core business.

▶ Access to new resources and technical expertise

Organisations may decide to outsource to efficiently access technical resources and expertise that may be both expensive and time-consuming to develop and provide in-house. For example, an outsourcing vendor may have expertise and experience in converting systems from mainframe to PC-based client–server applications. It may be more cost-effective, and certainly quicker, for an organisation with a similar project, but with no internal expertise in that area, to outsource the project to the experienced supplier.

▶ Variable staffing requirements

The development of information systems is a project-based activity. The demand for staff, even within a project, will fluctuate through the life cycle of the project. It is difficult for many organisations, organised along traditional line management arrangements, to support variable staffing requirements effectively. This problem is compounded in some countries by employment laws that make it difficult to employ, make redundant and re-employ staff. Outsourced arrangements allow a much more flexible employment structure for the host organisation. The supplier provides staff to meet varying requirements and is much more likely to be able to redeploy employees on other projects at times when the host organisation does not want them.

▶ Internal political problems

There is evidence to suggest that some organisations use outsourcing to solve internal political problems. In such instances the management of the enterprise has usually become boxed into a corner with an unwieldy and inflexible IS department with ambitious staff who need the IS department to expand to further their individual careers. Outsourcing IS resolves the political problem overnight because it effectively becomes somebody else's problem. The justification for outsourcing can be further supported by the suggestion that career and training opportunities will be greater for staff working in an organisation where the product is software – not insurance or biscuits. Staff may gain from being able to transfer to other projects, so opportunities open up for them that would never have occurred in an internal department faced by constant cost-reduction pressures.

The perceived disadvantages of outsourcing include:

▶ **Contract length**

Most of the outsourced IS contracts are for a relatively long period. This is because of the high cost of transferring assets and employees as well as maintaining technological investment. The long period of the contract causes three particular problems.

(a) Difficulties in getting out of a contract if the supplier turns out to be unsuitable.
(b) Problems in foreseeing what the business will need over the next five or ten years (typical contract lengths), hence creating difficulties in establishing an appropriate contract.
(c) The almost insurmountable problem in re-forming an internal IS department after the contract period is finished (see below).

▶ **Competitive edge**

Many writers believe that effective and innovative use of IS can give an organisation a competitive edge over its rivals. Some commentators believe that this will be lost in an outsourced arrangement. They claim that a competitive business advantage can only be provided by an internal IS department that understands the organisation and is committed to its goals. In an outsourced arrangement, IS staff are striving to achieve the goals and objectives of the outsourcer, which may conflict with those of the host organisation. Consequently, the host organisation may fail to take advantage of technological opportunities that could have been identified by internal employees.

▶ **Contract renewal**

In some outsourced services it may be relatively easy to change suppliers at the end of the contract, or indeed to go back to an in-house operation. For example, a large organisation has recently reappointed internal cleaning staff after six years of outsourcing to two external companies. However, this may be difficult to do in IS, as Ray Perry, vice president at Avon Products, recognised. 'It is difficult to disengage a contract. You've eliminated dedicated people. Three or four years later you have to start at ground zero.' In other words, it is difficult to rebuild an information systems department after you have systematically closed it. Hence the host organisation is at a disadvantage in contract renewal because the option of returning to an in-house operation is so daunting.

▶ **Confidentiality**

In some organisations the information stored in the computer systems is central to the enterprise's success or survival. For example, there may be information about pricing policies, product mixing formulas or sales analysis. There are examples of companies deciding against outsourcing for fear of placing confidential information in the hands of vendors, particularly if those vendors offer services to companies competing in the same market-place. Although the outsourcing companies usually dismiss this threat, because it is covered by confidentiality clauses in the contract, there are recorded instances of companies not choosing a particular supplier because competitors were already being supported.

▶ **Scope definition**

Most IS projects suffer from problems associated with successfully defining the scope of the system. The same problem afflicts outsourcing arrangements. Many difficulties are due to contractual misunderstandings between the client and its supplier. In such circumstances the client believes that the service it requires is within the contract scope, whilst the supplier is sure it is outside and so is subject to extra charges. Contractual disagreements often lead to tension and mistrust.

In some instances the scope of the original contract has been purposely restricted to justify the outsourcing agreement and award the contract. Unfortunately, this leads to significant extra charges to cover variations and this again contributes to customer/supplier tensions as well as under-use of technology as the customer strains to keep the contract within the bounds of the budget.

Organisations that enter outsourcing arrangements for information systems development soon realise the importance of formal specifications as part of the contract of supply. They recognise that these define the scope of the application and any misunderstandings causing changes in that scope will lead to unwanted delay and extra costs. Much of this formality is also concerned with making the specifications as unambiguous as possible. This is particularly important if the outsourcing arrangement uses 'offshore' developers: programmers employed in a nation where labour costs are lower. For example, a few years ago we were involved in a project where the analysts were in Belgium, the customer in eastern Europe and the programmers in India! Lack of ambiguity in the specification was essential. Hence the models described in the second section of this book become especially significant in outsourced systems development.

2.5 Information systems delivery at Woodland Transport

Although outsourcing is an option for most large organisations, for small or medium sized enterprises (SMEs), like Woodland Transport, it is a necessity. Specialist expertise may be available from a holding company (in this case, United Logistics). However, in general, the company is on its own, relying on pockets of informal expertise within the company supported by external consultants and suppliers. Similarly, many SMEs are just not large enough to use or justify cross-charging, and this is the case at Woodland Transport, where the costs are justified on a company-wide project basis.

The absence of specialist staff to develop, maintain and support the information systems is an issue. Many SMEs do not realise that problems have to be analysed before they are solved (the usual role of business and systems analysts) and so blunder into inappropriate solutions. The relatively high cost of these solutions (to the turnover of the company) can seriously damage the financial health of the company and in some instances has sent it spiralling into bankruptcy. Furthermore, the absence of employees with a responsibility for testing means that system and user acceptance testing is performed informally. Consequently, incomplete and faulty solutions are accepted and implemented, with unpredictable effects on the business operations of the company.

The two main alternatives for Information Systems delivery at Woodland Transport are:

1. To commission external software houses to develop solutions that meet their specific information system requirements. These are usually termed **bespoke** solutions because they are made to special order to exactly fit the requirements of the company.
2. To identify commercially available software packages that appear to fulfil their information systems requirements.

However, in both cases the company will need to identify potential projects, assess their feasibility and then define the detailed requirements of each project. A software package or a bespoke solution will then fulfil these requirements. The next two chapters look at assessing potential projects and their feasibility. Subsequent chapters introduce techniques for analysing and defining requirements. The appropriate use of these techniques will depend on whether Woodland Transport pursues the bespoke or software package approach.

2.6 Summary

This chapter has considered how the information systems department may be structured and accounted for. A number of options are available, all of which should be considered in an organisation's information systems strategy. In practice, organisations are constantly monitoring and experimenting with these options, leading to expensive and time-consuming reorganisations. The implications of this chapter for small and medium size enterprises, such as Woodland Transport, must be considered. Outsourcing and the purchase of commercially available software packages are features of such sized companies.

EXERCISES

1   Investigate the structure of a real-life Information Systems department. Draw an organisation chart of this department and document the roles shown on the chart.

2   List three advantages and three disadvantages of centralising the Information Systems department.

3   Investigate how the cost of Information Systems is accounted for in a real-life Information Systems department you can gain access to. Comment on the advantages and difficulties experienced by the department in administering and managing this system.

4   List three advantages and three disadvantages of outsourcing information systems delivery.

References

Bocij, P., Chaffey, D., Greasley, A. and Hickie, S. (1999) *Business Information Systems: Technology, Development and Management.* Upper Saddle River, NJ: Prentice Hall.

Gibson, C. F. and Nolan, R. L. (1974). Managing the four stages of EDP growth. *Harvard Business Review*, Jan–Feb, 76–88.

Lacity, M. and Hirschheim, R. (1993). *Information Systems Outsourcing.* New York: John Wiley.

O'Brien, J. (1996). *Management Information Systems*, 3rd edn. London: Times Mirror.

Project identification and selection

CHAPTER OVERVIEW

In this chapter you will learn about:

▶ A model for assessing the maturity of Information Systems (IS) in an organisation

▶ An approach to project selection based on Critical Success Factors

▶ An approach to project selection based on Soft Systems Methodology

3.1 Introduction

To be effective, Information Systems (IS) development projects should be aimed at supporting the business mission and be designed and implemented in accordance with the overall business strategy of the organisation.

This chapter looks at the early stages of a project, examining some of the issues that can be encountered and considering approaches to initial project selection. The detailed assessment of the feasibility of a project is considered in the next chapter.

It is vital that the selected projects should reflect and support the business priorities of the enterprise rather than reacting to *ad hoc* requests for local developments. In order to ensure that costly IS developments are focused on business needs we need to have methods to examine the relative priorities of competing projects. This chapter explores how IS development projects can be derived from the business objectives, which in turn come from the company's stated business mission.

3.2 Stages of IS growth

The selection and prioritisation of IS developments is strongly influenced by the level of Information Technology (IT) *maturity* that an organisation has reached. Consequently, this is one of the first issues that must be determined for understanding effective project selection.

This concept of maturity stems from a model originally put forward in 1974 by Nolan and Gibson, which traced the path of a company's adoption of IT. They proposed a six-stage model to chart the level of assimilation of technology, from a maverick champion of IT to the final stage of maturity. This final stage represents the point where all IT/IS developments are part of a larger IS strategy that supports the business objectives of the enterprise.

The stages of the model are:

▶ **Initiation:** This stage concerns the introduction of computer technology into the company, usually in order to make cost savings. This stage focuses on simple data processing tasks designed to speed up work and reduce staff levels. Initiation is often due to a champion of IT who wishes to introduce new technology, often to great scepticism and suspicion from some, but also in the light of interest from others in the company.

▶ **Contagion:** This is usually the result of successful initiation, which encourages other members and departments of the organisation to search for uses of IS/IT. The result of this enthusiasm is generally an expensive investment in technology and software on a first come, first served basis with minimum planning and management. The divide between user management and the technical experts becomes accentuated during this stage. This leads to senior business management giving the technical developers a lot of scope for initiatives, largely because the business managers have little or no understanding of what is happening. Despite notable IS/IT failures, IS budgets grow very quickly in this stage.

▶ **Control:** This refers to the control upon the proliferation of new applications. At this stage requests for systems are vetted for cost-effectiveness; procedures are put in place for developing systems and project management methods are established. However, the focus is still on using IS/IT to reduce costs. At this stage systems are still seen as ways of controlling company costs and IS/IT is viewed as a cost centre rather than an aid to fostering business growth.

▶ **Integration:** The focus of this stage is to produce a shared infrastructure that user departments use to run their own applications. During this stage innovation is encouraged among the IS staff, so controls and standards are eased. Furthermore, it is likely that the IS function itself will be devolved, with its members now working more closely with the business. IS now becomes more of a service department and Management Information Systems (MIS) are more readily available.

▶ **Data administration:** This stage represents the first time that the prime motivation for IS systems is not concerned with cost savings and routine data processing. Information, not automation, becomes the focus of system development. Access to shared company data and managing all the risks associated with that are the key drivers for IS activities. Corporate data models and databases are developed and most project developments are intended to support and exploit these. With access to corporate data, the possibilities of developing Executive Information Systems (EIS) and Decision Support Systems (DSS) are increased. Information systems are no longer considered as just supporting the business activities but are major factors in influencing business direction.

▶ **Maturity**: This is the highest level of usage and assimilation of IS technology. At this level IS is represented at Board level and all IS developments are explicitly aligned with the defined business strategy of the organisation. Some of the strategies will be business-led and the IS strategy devised to help implement them, while other strategies, particularly in the realm of e-trading, will be technology-led. In both instances, business management and IS management cooperate in a team. They are no longer rivals for resources, or client and provider, as in the earlier stages of the model.

The first two stages, at least, now belong to history. Most organisations are between Stage 3 and Stage 6. Small to Medium Enterprises (SME) are the organisations likeliest to be still at Stage 3, while in the current technology-driven environment large companies must have achieved at least level 5 or 6 to compete successfully.

The level of maturity that a company has reached in its use of IS/IT is most significant at the later stages of the model. These stages recognise that information systems have more to contribute than reducing staff numbers or saving costs. It is acknowledged that they may be a major tool and resource for gaining and keeping market share. It also has to be recognised that the cost of IS/IT at this stage is now a significant part of a company's expenditure. Targeting this expenditure towards the goals of the company in a coherent manner is a better way of ensuring that it is a wise investment. It is too easy to allow money to be frittered away on *ad hoc* developments that suit disparate sets of users and user departments but contribute little to overall business objectives.

What is also clear from the six-stage model is that the types of project selected for development will be affected by the organisation's level of maturity. Projects defined in a *mature* organisation will be different in character and be undertaken very differently from projects in an organisation still in the third stage of the model. Hence an analysis of the technical maturity of the organisation is an important first step in project identification and selection.

3.3 Woodland Transport – maturity

Woodland Transport has clearly gone beyond both the Initiation and Contagion stages. The CLASS system was designed to support some of the core business activities of Woodland rather than to meet the *ad hoc* local needs of individual managers.

The terms for the proposed replacement IS system suggest that it is to:

▶ Provide a standard platform for the organisation

▶ Provide compatibility with the parent company

▶ Incorporate extra functionality to meet new business requirements

These factors place it at least at level 3 (Control) or level 4 (Integration). However, the work is to be outsourced as Woodland Transport does not have its own IT department and there is no indication that it has an IT manager. Without specialist IT staff available responsible for responding to users' concerns and ideas and without any IS representation at board level, Woodland Transport's use of IT is below the level of full maturity. The new IS requirements appear to be driven in part by the need to produce more reports rather than simply to automate procedures and this implies a possible level of data administration. However, no mention is made of corporate data models or databases. Executive Information Systems and Decision Support Systems do not seem to be considered for development so it seems that Woodland Transport is not fully at the Data Administration stage after all.

We can conclude that the company is currently at the stage of Integration and possibly ready to move towards Data Administration. However, it is not equipped to move towards the Data Administration stage without the help of outside consultants and a readiness for internal reorganisation.

3.4 Strategic alignment

This section looks at the importance of aligning information systems with business strategy. This is a long-established problem. Kit Grindley and John Humble made it a central part of their *Effective Computer* approach (Grindley and Humble, 1973). They observed that 'the only valid objective for computers is to assist in achieving defined business improvements which would be impossible or uneconomic without the computer'. This remains true three decades later.

Two different approaches are taken. The first is a top-down rational approach, culminating in projects that support Critical Success Factors. The second is a more holistic approach exploring the problem situation from different perspectives.

3.4.1 Business objectives

Organisations exist to achieve a particular purpose. This might be to make a profit, to provide a return on investment for shareholders or to serve specific community needs. Organisations define a series of objectives that should assist them in achieving their overall purpose. Such objectives must be identifiable and measurable and are intermediate steps towards the primary purpose, or *mission*, of the organisation.

It is possible to look at this mission in a three-stage hierarchy of objectives culminating in Critical Success Factors (CSFs).

1. *A primary economic objective*

This is an overall target for the company established in advance of how the target is to be achieved. Examples might include:

▶ To treble after-tax profits from £250,000 to £750,000 by the end of the fifth year of the plan.

▶ To provide a £90,000 per year income package for each of the partners by the end of the second year of the plan.

Many writers argue that most primary objectives will be established in terms of profits (revenues in excess of costs) or profitability (return on investment). This is because even if the company has other objectives it must ultimately make a profit or return on investment or sooner or later it will cease to exist.

2. *Secondary objectives that describe the intended corporate identity*

These objectives give a picture of the company's aims in terms of the nature and scope of the business, its trading and staff relations, and intended developments, expansions and locations. In this respect it is a statement of how the chief executive, chairman or directors perceive the future of the company. The narrative objectives are a method of trying to communicate and share that perception with the rest of the company.

These social and non-economic objectives reflect the needs of the firm's stakeholders, such as employees and shareholders and they serve to influence and constrain management's pursuit of the primary economic objective. Many secondary objectives are also expressed explicitly in the mission or vision statements produced by the organisation.

3. Goals or intermediate business objectives

Goals are milestones on the way to the overall economic target. A network of compatible goals or business objectives leads to the achievement of the primary objective.

Objectives might be established for:

▶ The capture of a certain market share

▶ An absolute value of sales

▶ A minimum figure for customer complaints

▶ Cost reduction targets

▶ A minimum time for answering an emergency call

▶ A date by which a product launch will take place

It is a major task to set the objectives and ensure that they support the mission. It is unlikely that an information systems analyst will be involved at this level but the objectives will have a major impact on what the analyst can achieve.

Once the objectives have been set, they have to be met. There are a number of methods to help achieve this. This chapter looks at just one, Critical Success Factors, and how they cascade down to identifying individual information systems projects.

3.4.2 Critical Success Factors

Critical Success Factors are defined as: 'The limited number of areas in which results, if they are satisfactory, will ensure successful competitive performance for the business'. They relate to the key objectives of the organisation. This definition, with its reference to 'competitive performance', implies a commercial organisation but in fact CSFs can apply to commercial, public sector or non-profit-making organisations.

For example, one of the objectives of a school might be to attain a high pass rate at the highest grades in public examinations. There are a number of factors in the running of a school that are crucial to achieving this objective. For example, the quality of teaching at the school may be a significant factor. Consequently, one CSF might be to appoint teachers of certain experience supported by another CSF that will ensure the quality of their teaching. Another factor associated with this objective might relate to pupils' ability at the time that they are due to sit their examinations. CSFs to support this element might be concerned with ensuring that only pupils of a certain academic ability will be entered for the examinations (and possibly enrolled in the school). Further CSFs may be concerned with ensuring that pupils have reached the expected education level for their age when they are enrolled and that they have covered the appropriate syllabus in their lessons.

If any of these are not in place the school is in danger of not achieving one of its major objectives; this is what makes them *Critical* Success Factors.

CSFs derive from the work of John Rockart of MIT. Their purpose is to help identify the real information needs of managers rather than build systems that seem like a good idea but which actually commit resources and time without advancing the business.

When CSFs are specified they should meet certain criteria if they are to be useful. At the most basic level, a CSF must be specific rather than general; it should be measurable and it must be achievable. By these criteria, the school's CSFs should include, for example, '80% of pupils must have reached a preset standard by the end of their pre-exam year', rather than simply, 'Most pupils must be well-prepared for their examinations'.

As part of the objective-setting exercise of the organisation it is useful to identify and specify the CSFs. Once identified the strategist now needs to understand how to measure them. As long as each one has been stated in a measurable format it provides its own Performance Indicator (PI). The PIs should indicate the information requirements to support them, which in turn identify the information systems needed to meet the requirements. For example, the CSF '80% of pupils must have reached a preset standard by the end of their pre-exam year', sets a PI as well as suggesting an information system that records and analyses coursework and other appraisals.

To be achieved CSFs will prompt key decisions from managers responsible for those areas. Once the key decisions to be made are known,

Figure 3.1 The interrelationship of business objectives, Critical Success Factors, Key Decisions and information systems (from Robson, 1997).

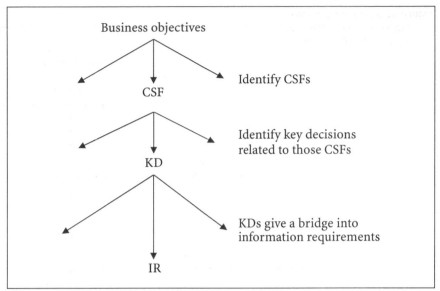

a bridge can be made to the information requirements a manager will need to make those decisions. Figure 3.1 illustrates the interrelationship between the business objectives, corresponding CSFs, key decisions and information systems.

As the diagram implies, CSFs act as a bridge between the information user (management) and the information provider (IS). This gives us a further set of desirable requirements for a CSF; they must be:

▶ Meaningful to senior managers

▶ Meaningful to IS managers and staff

▶ Feasible

By providing a common language that centres on the business objectives, CSFs enable client and provider stakeholders to focus their joint attention on aligning the IS and business strategies. This definition and explanation of CSFs is not expected to be a straightforward exercise. Its value lies in helping IS staff and managers keep their eye on the critical areas for development in the context of the company as a whole.

3.4.3 Critical Set Factors

Critical Set Factors are an extension of the Critical Success Factors. The extension is achieved by adding the elements of Critical Assumptions (CA) and Critical Decisions (CD) to the Critical Information (CI) that affect the Critical Success Factors.

The IS strategy can be determined by identifying the assumptions and decisions that follow from the Critical Success Factors and examining them to pick out the scope for IS support. The Critical Success Factors themselves will, as always, derive from the business objectives. These will translate from a strategy, which will cascade for implementation to a set

37

Figure 3.2 Critical Success Factors – assumptions, information and decisions (from Robson, 1997).

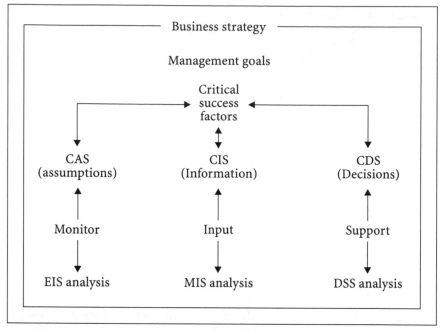

of shorter-term goals. Each objective will have CSFs for completion, supported by input systems (information) and, where appropriate, monitoring systems (to test assumptions) and decision support systems. Hence each CSF contributes to IS strategy by providing opportunities for information, monitoring and support systems. This is shown diagrammatically in Figure 3.2. The information elements of Critical Success Factors lead to Management Information Systems (MIS). The assumptions that underpin the CSFs are monitored in Executive Information Systems (EIS). Finally, the decisions required within the CSFs are taken with support from a Decision Support System (DSS). In many practical implementations this balance is not explored or pursued. Hence the systems concentrate on providing information that is ill suited to decisions and is based on assumptions that are rarely tested.

From the three prongs at the bottom of the diagram, it is possible to identify and prioritise the candidate information systems to support the CSFs. The analysis to enable the prioritisation will study such factors as:

▶ The stability of the assumptions and their importance to the business strategy

▶ The scope for IS to enhance the decision making

Using Critical Success Factor and Critical Set Factor analysis as a basis for identifying projects for development helps to ensure that what is included in the programme for new IS developments is aligned with the business direction and business priorities. It assumes a high level of maturity in the organisation. It cannot be carried out where expansion is uncontrolled or where rigid budget controls and inappropriate procedural standards have been imposed.

3.4.4 Critical Success Factors at Woodland Transport

Woodland Transport is in an unusual, although not unique, position in that it is tied to one and only one customer and to a limited product range. This restricts its business objective to renewing its contract with the customer. If it fails in this objective it will cease to exist. This restricts the goals and CSFs that could apply, but some can still be formulated.

Business strategy: To provide integrated information support for planning and operations activities.

Critical Success Factors:

The CSFs for Woodland Transport relate to three particular domains: deliveries, vehicles and drivers.

▶ *Deliveries*
The successful renewal of the contract will be considerably influenced by Woodland's ability to make deliveries on the dates requested by Kronenhalle.
 – Successful deliveries
 – Unsuccessful deliveries

▶ *Vehicles*
The profitability of the contract will be greatly influenced by the efficiency of the tractors and the effective utilisation of trailers.
 – Reliability and efficiency of tractors
 – Knowledge of trailer whereabouts

▶ *Drivers*
The profitability of the contract will be greatly influenced by the availability and effective use of drivers.
 – Availability of drivers

To make these general observations into SMART CSFs (Specific, Measurable, Realistic, Testable), they can be expressed in the following terms:

▶ Over a period of a calendar month a minimum of 99% of all deliveries must be made on the delivery date requested by Kronenhalle.

▶ A minimum of 95% of the company tractors and trailers must be available in sound condition every working day.

▶ Tractors must achieve an average fuel consumption of 7 miles per gallon over the period of the contract.

▶ All trailers that have been deposited at client sites must be collected within 3 working days.

▶ There must be sufficient drivers available on each shift for the day's planned deliveries.

The CSFs can be supported by such Key Performance Indicators as:

▶ Percentage of deliveries made on the required delivery date

▶ Daily percentage availability of tractors and trailers

▶ Fuel economy of tractors

▶ Number of days trailers have been left over 3 days at client sites

▶ Number of cancelled deliveries due to lack of drivers

In order to achieve these CSFs, Woodland Transport must have information on:

▶ Successful and unsuccessful deliveries. The reasons for unsuccessful deliveries must be reported, analysed and appropriate action taken.

▶ The service history of each tractor and trailer. This must be maintained, together with anticipated service dates, as this affects availability.

▶ The fuel efficiency and utilisation of tractors.

▶ The location of each trailer to arrange timely collection.

▶ How many tractors will be required for each shift and the number of available drivers to drive them. This will include an awareness of expected absences such as leave and long-term sickness. Contact details for substitute drivers will also be required.

This information may be provided within the scope of one or more development projects.

3.5 Soft Systems Methodology

Setting business objectives and defining Critical Success Factors presents a rather clinical and idealistic image of the planning process. This approach also represents a managerial perspective of the organisation and although this is clearly an important one it is not the only valid viewpoint. Not all employees concerned with information systems change will share this perspective of the company. Furthermore, management's perspective of reality may differ considerably from what is actually taking place. The Soft Systems Methodology is a framework for exploring the messy reality of organisations and is a potential starting point for identifying information system projects that can deliver value to the organisation.

Soft Systems Methodology (SSM) derives from the work of Peter Checkland. It is important to recognise that its focus is not on the detailed specification of user requirements for immediate implementation. Rather, it is concerned with *understanding* the organisational issues and ill-defined problems experienced by the organisation. Its job is not so much to suggest specific solutions as to identify what the actual problems are that need to be resolved. It is a common tendency for many managers in organisations to push for a quick computer solution to a perceived problem. This is understandable, as they want to see progress and quick results. However, in many instances treating the perceived problem or *symptom* makes the underlying problem worse. SSM uses a set of techniques to explore the symptoms as the different stakeholders perceive them. It emphasises a thorough exploration of the problem situation. The Soft Systems framework is primarily concerned with tackling the ill-structured problems of the real world and suggesting solutions that may, or may not, include computers. The framework was developed and presented by Peter Checkland (1981) and variations appear in Wilson (1984) and Wood-Harper *et al.* (1985). Practical applications have been documented by David Patching (1990).

For example, a company we are aware of recently identified that it was losing customers. The marketing director suggested that the problem was poor customer contact management and he suggested that the company should buy a Customer Relationship Management (CRM) software package. 'That should do the trick', he asserted.

SSM would recognise that the loss of customers is not the problem, but a symptom. It would suggest a wide-ranging exploration of the problem situation that may identify that the problem lies in:

▶ Poor after sales service

▶ Inadequate product range

▶ Poor quality control on the production line

▶ Inefficient distribution

▶ Inaccurate invoicing

▶ Personality clashes in the company

It is better, says SSM, to explore and clarify the areas related to the symptom than to quickly identify a possible underlying problem and suggest an inappropriate solution.

The premise underlying SSM is that the system and its environment need to be viewed in a *holistic* rather than a *reductionist* way. That is, to recognise that all the components in a system are interconnected so that an intervention in one area will have an effect in other areas which were initially thought to be irrelevant.

In contrast, the reductionist view, also known as Hard Systems thinking, suggests that the elements of a system are discrete and can be adjusted by themselves with minimal effect on other parts of the system. If a problem is clearly defined and bounded a Hard Systems approach is as likely to succeed as any other. For example, if the problem is to increase the number of invoices to be printed off in one day there are a number of straightforward options that are relatively simple to implement. For example, the company could simply buy a faster printer. However, in the case of the loss of customers there are many potential issues. Some of these issues are not specifically technological but to do with:

▶ Workflow

▶ Morale

▶ Work culture

▶ Management expectations and style

▶ Human interaction

The traditional Hard Systems analysis only addresses workflow and technology.

Checkland is particularly concerned with what he terms the Human Activity System (HAS). Computer systems are concerned with data, processes and transaction handling, but often the designers overlook the impact that IT will have upon the working practices of the users and their interaction with each other and the organisation. Whichever part of the customer-loss situation an analyst decides to focus on, the HAS must be considered and included.

3.5.1 Two strands

There are two broad streams of enquiry that run through SSM:

▶ The examination of the 'real' world, whether that is in terms of workflow, relationships between tasks, relationships between the people, the management procedures that govern the departments or the opinions and emotions of the actors involved in the system.

This is a problematic strand because the act of observing and expressing this real-world activity has an effect upon it. This is one of the tenets of the holistic approach: that to observe people is to change how they behave. Another difficulty is that capturing information about opinions and emotions is difficult for an outsider. Analysts/consultants tend to be given a 'front view' rather than a 'back view' of a workplace and it is the 'back view' – the situation as it really is, rather than a sanitised view for public consumption – that they really need to understand.

▶ The conceptual modelling of the systems under discussion. While the first strand of enquiry is continuing this next strand is likely to begin. The modelling taking place is concerned with the HAS rather than modelling, say, data structures or process flows. It is modelling the stakeholders' views of the system.

This approach involves the analyst switching from one mode of thinking to the other, as the conceptual activities will clearly relate to the real-world situation.

3.5.2 Framework

Although it is termed a methodology, with the implication of a prescribed sequence of steps, SSM is more of a framework of thinking processes that the analyst needs to apply. In broad terms seven stages are suggested, which combine examination of the 'real-world' situation with more conceptual modelling or, as Checkland terms it, 'systems thinking'. Figure 3.3 illustrates Checkland's suggested shape for the framework.

Above the line are the 'real-world' activities, while below are the 'systems thinking' elements of modelling the system from the point of view of the stakeholders.

The real world is examined initially (1) to observe the processes, people, culture and so on. In 2, the findings are expressed in a drawing

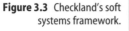

Figure 3.3 Checkland's soft systems framework.

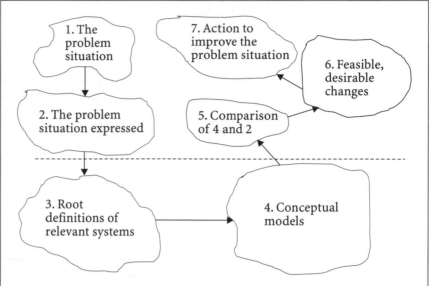

called a Rich Picture. It is 'rich' because it tries to capture all the nuances of the HAS as well as formal details of document flow and process. Rich Pictures are explained further in Section 3.6. After the systems thinking elements, the ideal picture of what the system should be like is compared with the findings of 1 and 2. The next step (staying above the line), in 6, is to propose changes to the current working system to bring it in line with the ideal. SSM does not specify how Stages 5 and 6 are to be carried out, just that the analysts must find some way forward that is acceptable to the stakeholders. This way forward should be in line with the desired company culture and address existing conflicts and political difficulties.

The last part of the method is the identification of the actions to take to meet the proposal. This action may be in the form of a Project Initiation Document for a further hard study of the area under concern, with the objectives and constraints being the result of the soft proposals.

The 'systems thinking' sector, below the line, comprises two parts, each of them relating to individual roles within the system. Stage 3 proposes a Root Definition for each of the roles. The Root Definition will be explained and illustrated in Section 3.6. Its purpose is to understand the *perspective* of the actors involved in the workings of the system. For each Root Definition, the analyst will draw a Conceptual Model of what should be done in the system to meet the perspective expressed in that Root Definition.

Although the term 'analyst' has been used here, Soft Systems brands the person or team making the intervention as 'problem solvers', as the term *analyst* carries the implication that a computer-based solution will follow the study. SSM is concerned less with a solution as with understanding the problem. That is why Stage 7 can lead to a hard study, with the boundaries clearly defined, where a solution is the objective rather than the objective being a full understanding of the problem domain.

3.6 SSM techniques

3.6.1 Rich Pictures

Rich Pictures are a form of drawing to visualise the problem domain. They do not have a stipulated notation but are intended to model the Human Activity System by including the following aspects:

▶ Boundaries between different departments or work areas

▶ Work and data flows (but only at a high, broad-brush level)

▶ Attitudes of actors involved

▶ Sources of conflict and disagreement

▶ Criteria for monitoring activities

▶ Relationships between actors and tasks and between tasks

Rich Pictures can be drawn either by the problem solvers or by the actors themselves for their own part of the system. They should take up a side of A3 or flipchart paper and be easy to read.

Although they do not have a standard notation any symbols that the drawer includes should be easy to understand. There is sometimes a temptation for people using them for the first time to treat them as challenges or cryptic crosswords that need several hours to decode. This defeats their object. An example of a Rich Picture is given in Figure 3.4. The context is of a hospital theatre booking, and the actors shown are: Doctor, Theatre Sister, Admin Clerk, Hospital Administrator and Patient.

The symbols used in this example are shown in Figure 3.5.

Figure 3.4 A Rich Picture of a hospital operating theatre booking system.

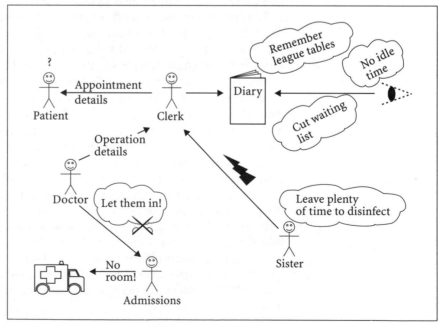

Figure 3.5 Rich Picture symbols.

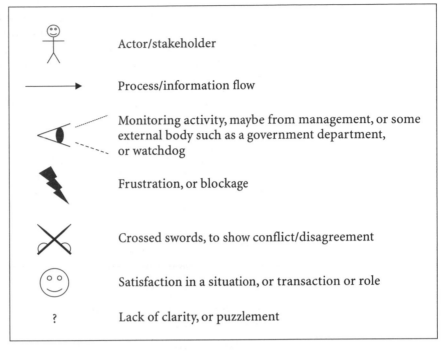

Rich Pictures focus as much on the Human Activity System as on the more formal function processing/task aspect of the environment. That is what gives them their richness. How they will be used will depend very much upon local circumstances. A graphical medium like this can be popular with non-technical users who are suspicious of technological solutions (and this suspicion can be included in the picture). However, managers may be dismissive of a 'cartoon' being submitted as part of the project documentation. Also, if the conflicts are too significant in the workplace, talking through the picture may just exacerbate the situation rather than clarify it. It is up to the project team to make a judgement on whether to use it just for their own purposes or to let the user team see and comment upon it.

Ways to use the Rich Picture
▶ The problem-solving team draw one for their own understanding of the situation.
▶ The picture is submitted to the users for their comments and corrections.
▶ The picture is drawn up by the problem-solving team and presented to management and the project sponsor as a part of their findings.
▶ The actors in the situation draw up a Rich Picture together in a workshop facilitated by one of the problem-solving team.

3.6.2 Root Definitions

A Root Definition is completed for each actor in the Rich Picture. It represents that actor's perspective about what the system is to do. A Root

Definition encapsulates in as few sentences as possible what the actor perceives to be the function and responsibility of the system.

There is an acronym to help ensure that important ingredients of the perspective are included in a well-formed and complete Root Definition. The acronym is CATWOE:

▶ C – Customer: who will be the client or beneficiary of the system

▶ A – Actor: who will carry out the activities or transformations of the system

▶ T – Transformation: the core activity/transformation of the system, the central process that the system is to achieve

▶ W – *Weltanschauung* (or Worldview): the underlying outlook or belief that gives meaning to this system

▶ O – Owner: the person or body that has the power and authority to control, approve or stop the system.

▶ E – Environment: the environment that will impose constraints on how the system is executed

An example of a CATWOE set and Root Definition for the hospital scenario might be:

C – Healthcare purchasers, patients
A – Doctors
T – Optimise usage of operating theatre resources
W – The Trust must meet its targets in reduction of waiting lists
O – Hospital Trust
E – Waiting list targets set by Department of Health and critical media attention to underperforming hospitals

Root Definition:

'A system run by the Hospital Trust where doctors respond to demands from healthcare purchasers by dealing with patients with minimal or no delay, in line with targets set by central government.'

The Root Definitions are likely to be very different between the actors, particularly those on different levels of the organisation. A doctor's Root Definition might be more concerned with the quality of healthcare for the patients and less about targets. Doctors might disagree with the Administrator about optimising usage of theatre resources because one of their concerns might be that reduced time between operations leads to a higher chance of cross-infection.

The problem solvers' role is partly to help with the formulation of the various Root Definitions and partly to help reconcile conflicting ones. This latter task is frequently very difficult because of local politics or self-interest, so the role then becomes one of facilitating a way forward for the study.

3.6.3 Conceptual Models

Each Root Definition takes a view of what the system *should* be achieving, through the transformation and *Weltanschauung*. The next step is to explore, in Stage 4, what should happen in the system in order for this to be achieved. The model used for this is called a Conceptual Model and it shows the activities needed to make the Root Definition a reality. While, again, there is no prescribed notation for it, a bubble chart is usually used to show *high-level* activities, rather than detailed task descriptions. There will be one Conceptual Model for each Root Definition.

Conventionally, the Conceptual Models show the operational activities and also any monitoring and control activities. They will always begin at an overview level, but individual activities may be subsequently decomposed to show greater detail. Figure 3.5 shows a Conceptual Model to support the Hospital Administrator's Root Definition of the hospital system.

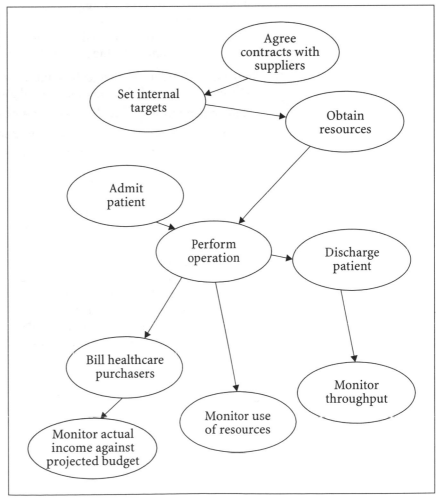

Figure 3.6 Conceptual Model to support the Hospital Administrator's Root Definition.

Although the Root Definitions may be quite different from each other, the Conceptual Models that support them will have many features in common. After drawing up each of the Conceptual Models to be considered, the task is to present them to the users to agree on a composite model that meets the company's intentions for the system. This will involve a lot of negotiation over both the Root Definition and the Conceptual Model.

There are a number of issues to consider with Conceptual Models:

▶ At this stage, we are looking only at the logical activities that are expected to be needed, not a description of tasks.

▶ The activities are not those activities for the project, but for the operational running of the system environment.

▶ The outcome of the study will be a recommendation for information systems support; building the system is not a part of the model (unless the business is a software supplier).

These techniques are the only ones specified by Checkland for SSM. The remaining stages are in the framework, but with no recommended techniques for carrying them out.

When the models are compared with the real-world situation (as it is now), there are a number of dimensions to explore.

▶ Activities and processes themselves and how well they map to requirements identified in the Conceptual Model

▶ Reporting, monitoring and decision support procedures

▶ The appropriateness of the organisation structure in place

▶ The skills and attitudes of the staff currently in place

▶ Whether or not the culture of the company suits the system defined in the Conceptual Model

From the conclusions come the searches for the acceptable solutions. From this point onwards, the Soft Study hardens into a programme of developments. These will be to provide information support for those candidate activities on the conceptual model that are to be carried forward to implementation.

In this way Soft Systems analysis can help with the identification of projects to be developed. It also adds richness in that the *collateral* systems that support the focal system are also identified and built into the programme. These collateral systems include the planning and reporting systems, which can be shown as activities on a decomposed Conceptual Model.

The soft systems approach tends to lead to projects that are wider in scope and less focused on information technology solutions than the top-down business objective-based approach.

3.7 Application of Soft Systems at Woodland Transport

3.7.1 Rich Picture

Most of the issues that concern Woodland Transport can be regarded as Hard System problems with a clearly defined boundary. The Human Activity System does not present many problems to explore but a Rich Picture can still yield information to help express a fuller understanding of the environment. Figure 3.7 represents the areas of Woodland Transport that are expected to be covered by the proposed information systems.

3.7.2 Root Definition

There do not appear to be conflicting views regarding Woodland Transport's role or purpose, so in this case it is not necessary to derive multiple Root Definitions. The CATWOE elements can be inferred as:

C – Kronenhalle Brewery
A – Logistics, Traffic, Administration, Drivers
T – Deliver lager to designated locations
W – Service must be reliable and cost-effective
O – United Logistics
E – Renewable contract

The Root Definition to encapsulate these elements could be:

'The company, owned by United Logistics, provides reliable and cost-effective deliveries of Kronenhalle Brewery products to locations designated by the brewery, under the terms of a renewable contract. The deliveries are managed by the Logistics, Traffic and Administration functions and executed by full-time, contract and agency drivers.'

3.7.3 Conceptual Model

The Conceptual Model to express the Root Definition is shown in Figure 3.8.

3.7.4 Analysis

The Conceptual Model is the final part of systems thinking analysis. In order to move forward to diagnosis and project selection, the model must be compared to the current operations in order to identify any mismatch. The Rich Picture gives suggestions for one or two corrections:

▶ Locating trailers is currently haphazard and unsatisfactory.
▶ There is no evidence of reporting on absenteeism or failed deliveries. Reports may be produced, but it is unclear – the problem solver must consult Dorn, Jerry and Kim to clarify this.

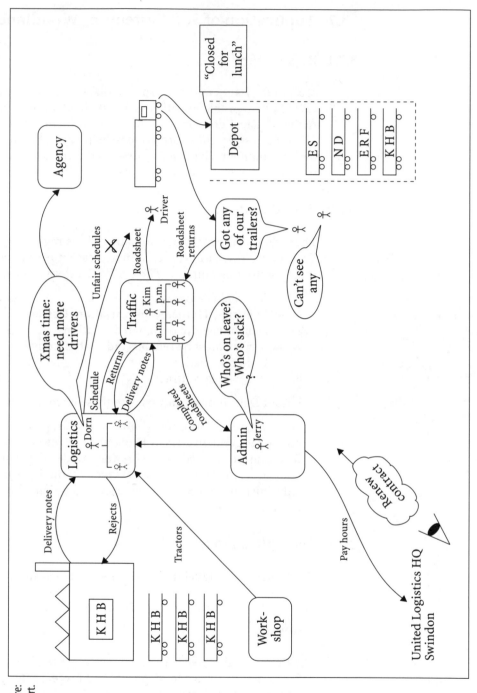

Figure 3.7 Rich Picture: Woodland Transport.

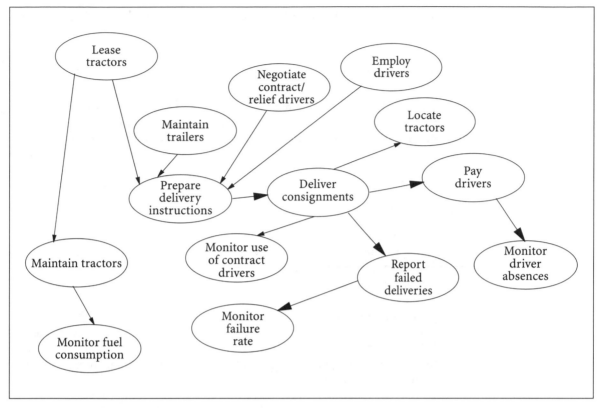

Figure 3.8 Conceptual model: Woodland Transport.

It can be seen that there are procedures in place to provide contract drivers, to service vehicles and to deal with failed deliveries, but there is no indication of how effective they are – again, the users must be consulted.

A valuable approach to finding the mismatches in the system will be to discuss each element on the conceptual model with the managers of the relevant sections, asking them whether or not those activities are currently performed and, if they are, how effectively. This provides a gap analysis between what the system should achieve and what it actually does achieve right now. The gaps identified represent a possible need for an information system.

The SSM products have identified a number of systems and information outputs needed and these correspond closely with the systems identified through the Critical Success Factor analysis (see Section 3.4). In this project the requirement for new systems is not as a result of problems in the Human Activity System but simply due to a need to replace an obsolete technology. However, the soft analysis has still provided useful insights into Woodland Transport's needs. If the project at Woodland had been undertaken because of soft, fuzzy problems then SSM would be the method of choice. However, because it has come about because of an agreed business objective, SSM can be used to complement a broader CSF-based study, playing a subordinate part in the analysis.

3.8 Summary

Business Information Systems were, in their early days, mostly simple data processing activities that initially saved headcount and therefore money. As computers have become cheaper and more powerful, they have come to play a different role in the company. Instead of being a cost they are now used to implement company strategy and are widely regarded in 'mature' organisations as a tool to exploit opportunity, enlarging the business and providing new business initiatives. However, any development is a large investment, and to protect that investment it is important that any development projects are aligned with the business strategy. They are only undertaken because it is recognised that they further that business strategy.

Critical Success Factor analysis is one powerful tool to help identify and then prioritise the IS development portfolio. An alternative or complementary method of ensuring that developments meet business requirements, rather than an individual user's wish list, is through the Soft Systems study. This produces a portfolio of developments designed to meet a specific perspective on what a business, or a part of a business, is aiming to achieve.

EXERCISES

STAKIT-HI plc

STAKIT-HI plc is a quoted company that owns and maintains 42 large supermarkets throughout the country. Each supermarket sells a wide range of food and household goods to the general public. The organisation is split into geographical regions, each with one depot responsible for keeping the individual branches stocked with goods. In some regions, stock levels continue to be too high, being three days for perishable goods like milk and fresh fruit/vegetables and up to 30 days for tinned goods. This has resulted in a high stock-holding cost for the company as a whole.

STAKIT-HI plc is in a market where there is significant competition from other supermarket groups.

Historically, STAKIT-HI plc has tended to trail the industry in computerisation. It did not introduce Electronic Point of Sale (EPOS) systems into most of its supermarkets until the mid-1980s, after all its main competitors had already adopted this technology. Furthermore, each region was encouraged to buy its own systems, rather than have Head Office dictate platforms and processes. A small IT department was established, but this was mostly responsible for operating Head Office systems and producing appropriate Management Information Systems (MIS). Regions were given their own IT staff responsible for operating the local systems and maintaining the networks that linked the supermarkets to the regional depot.

The Board of the plc has decided to standardise the operations of the different regions and install a central IT/IS facility to control stock management and distribution. The company is also considering an investment of over £200 million to integrate all its EPOS systems and Customer Relations Management (CRM) systems in an attempt to improve its market share. The databases associated with the system will be able to store information relating to stock levels of each product line, cash and receipts and sales to individual customers. STAKIT-HI's competitors are, again, slightly ahead of them, but it is not taking so long for the company to realise it must catch up. For the first time, it is looking for new ideas in IS/IT to give it a competitive edge over its rivals. Because STAKIT-HI plc has already produced the initial feasibility study and systems specification, the company hopes to implement its integrated systems within 10 months.

Required:

1 State where you think STAKIT-HI fits on Nolan and Gibson's maturity model. Justify your answer.

2 Suggest, and justify, the Critical Success Factors you think that STAKIT-HI must consider if its new integrated system is to give it the advantages its seeks.

3 Derive a Root Definition for STAKIT-HI, and draw a Conceptual Model.

GDL Timber Distribution
GDL is a timber distribution agency based at Goole docks. The company handles the physical importation, storage and distribution of timber on behalf of the multi-national shipping agents Escarbe–Laroche (E/L). The timber on the boats is sold by the shipping agents to companies known in the trade as 'receivers', who are based in all parts of the UK. Goods may be sold prior to shipment, while they are at sea, or after they have been unloaded in the UK on to the timber berth at the docks.

The receivers, in turn, may sell to 'end customers' who are usually local timber merchants or housebuilders. A receiver may also be an end customer.

Timber stored on the quay at Goole attracts quay rent after a certain period of time and hence it is in the interests of receivers and end customers to move the goods to their depots and yards as quickly as possible. The intent to move goods is known as a 'call-off' and these are usually faxed through to GDL, specifying the timber required and also the location it has to be delivered to. It is GDL's responsibility to arrange for the hauliers to make specific deliveries and usually many loads are required to completely deliver the 'call-off'.

Personnel and responsibilities
Charlie Bradley is the General manager of GDL and he has three staff reporting directly to him; Vinnie Smith, Eric Black and Tony Shaw.

Vinnie is primarily responsible for processes that take place before 'call-off' of the timber. Eric Black is primarily responsible for the processes of call-off and Tony Shaw for arranging and rating deliveries. However, the demands of a small office means that all staff members should be competent in all areas.

System overview: technical position

GDL has a single-user PC-based system developed and implemented five years ago. The system has helped GDL achieve its original business objective of increasing market share from 30% to 50%. However, there are now technical and business limitations to this system. It has been decided to redevelop the system in a multi-user environment and to revisit business requirements to fit in with current needs. A new shipping agent – Intraland (I/L) also wishes to use GDL's services and this expanded business requirement must be reflected in the new system.

System overview: operational procedures

GDL receives initial shipping documents from the shipping agent. These documents provide initial information about the voyage (such as vessel name and expected arrival date).

Once the ship has set sail from its departure port, GDL receives a faxed copy of the finalised ship's manifest from the shipping agent. This lists all the timber on the ship bound for GDL. Information is grouped into Bills of Lading. Each Bill of Lading is divided up into Marks and each Mark comprises sets of timber of different Mark Lengths. A Mark is a actually a physical mark made on the side of a set of timber.

For example:

▶ Bill of Lading 1023 may comprise Marks LOT1, LOT2 and LOT3.

▶ LOT1 may comprise 10 packs of 7 metre wood, 12 packs of 9 metre wood etc.

▶ LOT2 may comprise 5 packs of 5 metre wood, 3 packs of 7 metre wood etc.

Once the voyage has arrived the GDL staff note the actual date of arrival of the voyage. Customs and Excise then inspect the timber before clearing it for despatch from the quay. This date of 'customs clearance' is also noted on the voyage details as soon as the Cleared Customs notification is received from Customs and Excise.

Once the timber has cleared Customs, it can be 'called-off' by the Receivers who have imported the timber into this country. Call-offs are faxed to GDL and they refer to specific Mark Lengths within a Mark within a Bill of Lading. Call-offs can be modified up until the date of delivery.

Deliveries are arranged by GDL staff for each Call-off. Deliveries are arranged with local hauliers and usually several deliveries are required to deliver one Call-off. Each delivery has a separate Delivery Note with information about the end Customer where the goods have to be delivered to.

Delivery Notes do not carry financial information. However, a copy of the Delivery Note is rated using a prescribed formula and sent to Head

Office for invoicing out to the Receiver. The difference between the rated value and the cost of distribution through local hauliers represents the income of GDL.

Some timber is imported into the country 'on spec' by an Agent and is not bought by the receiver until it is on the ocean or the dockside. Hence this timber needs to be identified and Receivers allocated to it later in the process, when the Shipping Agent is able to notify GDL of the Receiver.

System overview: reports and documents
It is expected that the system will produce:

▶ All procedural documents (such as Delivery Notes)

▶ A restricted set of standard reports will be supported (five maximum)

▶ A restricted set of standard enquiries will be supported (five maximum)

The Landlocked Group, based in Dagenham, Essex, owns GDL. It undertakes all invoicing and credit control on its AS/400 minicomputer running standard accounts packages. A direct link is required between Goole and Dagenham to allow the daily downloading of delivery notes to allow invoice production.

Receivers usually import timber through a number of shipping agents. GDL is keen to undertake 100% of a receiver's business. To achieve this it wishes to offer a remote enquiry, call-off and reporting facility that it can offer free of charge to receivers. Each receiver will be able to

▶ View its current position

▶ Call-off stock

▶ Raise certain stock reports

It is expected that 'tying-in' of receivers will increase market share to 65%.

Required:

4   Suggest, and justify, the Critical Success Factors you think that GDL must consider if its new system is to give it the advantages its seeks.

5   Draw a Rich Picture of the GDL problem situation.

6   Derive a Root Definition for GDL from the perspective of Charlie Bradley and draw a Conceptual Model

References

Checkland, P (1981). *Systems Thinking, Systems Practice*. New York: John Wiley.
Grindley, K. and Humble, J. (1973). *The Effective Computer*. New York: McGraw-Hill.
Patching, D. (1990). *Practical Soft Systems Analysis*. London: Pitman.
Robson, W. (1997). *Strategic Management and information Systems*, 2nd edn. London: Pitman.
Wilson, B. (1984). *Systems: Concepts, Methodologies and Applications*. New York, John Wiley.
Wood-Harper, A. T., Antil, L. and Avison, D. E. (1985). *Information Systems Definition: The Multi-View Approach*. Oxford: Blackwell.

Feasibility study

In this chapter you will learn about;

▶ An approach for assessing the feasibility of a project

▶ An economic approach to choosing between competing projects

▶ The structure of a feasibility report

4.1 Introduction

The previous chapter made the case for identifying projects from an organisational perspective. This was illustrated using Critical Success Factors and the Soft Systems methodology. Both approaches are likely to identify a number of likely projects or project areas.

However, it would be unusual for an organisation to have the resources to pursue all worthwhile projects. Consequently, projects have to be compared and prioritised. This comparison is usually undertaken by looking at costs and benefits, leading to the selection of the project that offers the most financial payback to the organisation, using some agreed way of defining this payback.

This can be illustrated using the Woodland Transport application. The Critical Success Factors approach has suggested that the company needs information about:

▶ Successful and unsuccessful deliveries. The reasons for unsuccessful deliveries must be reported, analysed and appropriate action taken.

▶ The service history of each of tractor and trailer. This must be maintained together with anticipated service dates, as this affects availability.

▶ The fuel efficiency and utilisation of tractors.

▶ The location of each trailer to arrange timely collection.

▶ The number of tractors for each shift and the number of available drivers to drive them. This will include an awareness of expected absences such as leave and long-term sickness. Contact details for substitute drivers will also be required.

These Critical Success Factors could be divided into three potential project areas:

▶ Recording vehicle movements:
  - Successful and unsuccessful deliveries. The reasons for unsuccessful deliveries must be reported, analysed and appropriate action taken.
  - The fuel efficiency and utilisation of tractors.
  - The location of each trailer to arrange timely collection.

▶ Recording vehicle history:
  - The service history of each tractor and trailer. This must be maintained together with anticipated service dates, as this affects availability.

▶ Planning vehicle movements:
  - The number of tractors required for each shift and the number of available drivers to drive them. This will include an awareness of expected absences such as leave and long-term sickness. Contact details for substitute drivers will also be required.

Each of these project areas may be subjected to a more rigorous examination in a feasibility study. The analyst will, of course, already have formed some ideas about the application from the preliminary work. However, the feasibility study represents an opportunity to firm up knowledge of the system and to form ideas about the scope and cost of possible solutions. In many respects the feasibility study is a quick and dirty mini-systems analysis with the analyst being concerned with many of the issues and using many of the techniques required in later detailed work and covered in the following chapters of this book.

Feasibility studies are usually undertaken within tight time constraints and normally culminate in a written and oral feasibility report. The content and recommendations of such a study will be used as a basis for deciding whether to proceed, cancel or redefine the scope of the project. Thus, since the feasibility study may lead to the commitment of large resources, it is important that it is conducted competently and that no fundamental errors of judgement are made. This is easier said than done.

This chapter examines three different aspects of feasibility and the compromise that eventually has to be made between them. The results of this compromise are eventually presented in a feasibility report, which recommends whether a project should progress to the detailed investigation stage.

4.2 Three types of feasibility

In the conduct of the feasibility study the analyst will usually consider three distinct but interrelated types of feasibility.

4.2.1 Technical feasibility

This is concerned with the technical performance criteria that the system will have to meet to be accepted. For example:

▶ The ability to produce defined outputs in a given time-scale; for example, 20,000 examination certificates in three weeks.

▶ The ability to provide certain response times under certain conditions; for example, no more than a two second response time at each terminal when there are 120 terminals being used simultaneously. This might be particularly important in a call centre application.

▶ The facility to input a large number of documents in a limited time-scale; for example, 400,000 gas readings in one day.

▶ The ability to process a certain volume of transactions at a certain speed; for example, to report on seat availability and record airline reservations without a significant delay to the passenger.

▶ The facility to communicate data to distant locations; for example regional sales figures transmitted to an American Head Office.

▶ The facility to interface with other software already used by the organisation. This might include the ability to use data mining tools on the application.

▶ The ability to fit into pre-defined technical constraints; for example, the system must run on the existing local area network (LAN).

In examining technical feasibility it is the configuration of the system that is initially more important than the actual hardware make. The configuration should show the system's requirements: how many workstations are provided, how these units should be able to operate and communicate, what input and output speeds should be achieved and at what print and screen quality. This can be used as a basis for the tender document against which suppliers and manufacturers can later make their equipment bids. Specific hardware and software products can then be evaluated in the context of these technical needs.

At the feasibility stage it is possible that two or three different configurations will be pursued which satisfy the key technical requirements but which represent different levels of ambition and cost. Investigation of these technical alternatives can be aided by approaching a range of suppliers for preliminary discussions. The technical performance and costs of rejected alternatives should be documented in the feasibility report.

It is also possible that the required system is not technically possible; for example, secure data communications are needed in a geographical region that does not have the necessary infrastructure, so the system requirements have to be re-thought.

4.2.2 Social and operational feasibility

Social and operational feasibility is concerned with social, human, organisational and political aspects. Among the issues examined are:

▶ What job changes will the system bring? Most people react unfavourably to change. Planned job changes must be carefully handled so that those affected are seen to gain in the way that they feel is acceptable. This may be through job enrichment or simply through raising wages.

▶ What organisational structures are disturbed? The suggested system may cut across accepted organisational relationships and threaten the status of individuals and their promotional expectations.

▶ What new skills will be required? Do the current employees possess these skills? If not, can they learn them? How long will they take to learn?

It is unlikely that the project will be rejected solely on the grounds of social or operational feasibility, but such considerations are likely to critically affect the nature and scope of the eventual recommendations. A preliminary understanding of these factors should be available from the Rich Picture.

It must also be recognised that although the computer brings significant alterations to an organisation, it is not the only source of change. The way that an organisation manages and implements changes in other areas should be considered when computer-related changes are planned. Agreed procedures for discussing proposals – staff consultative committees, trade union agreements and employee forums – should be identified and followed.

4.2.3 Economic feasibility

Many organisations evaluate projects on an economic basis – they must show a financial return that outweighs the costs. For this reason management tends to give more weight to economic feasibility than to technical and operational considerations. A number of approaches to assessing the cost of solutions have been suggested. Approaches include the following.

Least cost
This is based on the principle that costs are easier to control and identify than revenues. Thus it assumes that there is no income change caused by the implementation of a new system or that competing project opportunities offer the same benefits. In such an evaluation only the costs are listed and the option with the lowest cost is selected. The approach could be used across projects; Table 4.1 is from the Woodland transport application.

Table 4.1 Least cost approach: Woodland Transport.

		Cost
Project 1	Recording vehicle movements	£60,000
Project 2	Recording vehicle history	£20,000
Project 3	Planning vehicle movements	£90,000

Hence the *Recording vehicle history* project (Project 2) will be selected for development using this technique.

However, the approach is more usually used *within* projects when looking at alternative ways of providing a solution. It assumes that all potential solutions offer the same functionality and quality and that price is the only thing that differentiates them. Hence the cheapest solution is chosen. Such a simplistic approach is often used in public sector tendering, usually with disastrous results.

Time to payback

The time to payback method of economic evaluation is an attempt to answer the question 'How long will it be until we get our money back on this investment in systems?'. This requires data on both cost and benefits. The net cash flow for each year is calculated by subtracting the value of benefits from the cost.

In the time to payback method, the alternative which repays the initial investment the quickest is selected.

In the example given in Table 4.2, Project 1 pays back during year 4, Project 2 during year 5 and Project 3 in year 3. Hence Project 3 would be selected, despite its lower return (than Project 1) in the long term. This method of evaluation has two significant disadvantages.

▶ The example shows how the approach only considers the time taken to return the original investment and ignores the system's long-term profitability. Thus options that are more profitable in the long run are not selected.

▶ The method does not recognise the time value of money. Benefits that accrue in the distant future are not worth as much as similar benefits that occur more quickly, but the time to payback method fails to recognise this. Payback provides a crude measure and weighting of project cash flows.

Table 4.2 Time to payback: Woodland Transport.

Year	Project 1		Project 2		Project 3	
	Net cash flow	Cumulative cash flow	Net cash flow	Cumulative cash flow	Net cash flow	Cumulative cash flow
0	−40,000	−40,000	−15,000	−15,000	−80,000	−80,000
1	−20,000	−60,000	0	−15,000	10000	−70,000
2	10,000	−50,000	5,000	−10,000	50,000	−20,000
3	30,000	−20,000	5,000	−5,000	20,000	0
4	30,000	+10,000	3,000	−2,000	10,000	+10,000
5	30,000	+40,000	3,000	+1,000	5,000	+15,000

However, the approach:

▶ Is simple to calculate and understand.
▶ Favours quick return projects that may produce faster growth for the company and hence enhance liquidity.

Furthermore, choosing projects that pay back the quickest tends to reduce corporate risk.

Net present value

This is a well-defined and practised method of economic evaluation. It builds in an allowance for the time value of money, represented by the Present Value Factor. In this method the net cash flows are reduced in value by applying this factor, so reducing the value of a cash flow to its present worth. For example, a cash flow of £30,000 planned for 10 years time will actually only be worth £4,800 if a present value factor of 20% is used. Thus benefits that appear later in the project's lifespan contribute little to its economic feasibility. This may make project selection a little conservative. In many computer-based projects positive cash flows appear late in the project life and heavy discounting of these benefits may lead to the selection of a less ambitious project which yields a quicker return.

The principle of time preference is represented by discounting future cash flows with an appropriate discount rate. These discount rates can be calculated or taken from published discount tables. The present value of cash flows using a discount rate of 10% is shown in Table 4.3.

The total present value (Net Present Value or NPV) of the project is less than zero, and this indicates that the project is probably not worth doing.

The approach can be used for the three project options facing Woodland Transport (Table 4.4). In this instance the discount rate is set at 4%.

In this case, Project 1 is now clearly the best option. Hence any of the three options could have been selected, depending on the economic evaluation method!

Table 4.3 Example of Net Present Value.

Year	Net cash flow	Discount factor	Present value
0	−15,000	1.0000	−15,000.00
1	500	0.9091	454.55
2	5,500	0.8264	4,545.20
3	5,550	0.7513	4,169.71
4	2,500	0.6830	1,707.50
5	3,000	0.6209	1,862.70
		Total	−2,260.34

		Project 1		Project 2		Project 3	
Year	Discount factor	Cash flow	Present value	Cash flow	Present value	Cash flow	Present value
0	1	−40,000	−40,000	−15,000	−15,000	−80,000	−80,000
1	0.962	−20,000	−19,240	0	0	10,000	9,620
2	0.925	10,000	9,250	5,000	4,625	50,000	46,250
3	0.889	30,000	26,670	5,000	4,445	20,000	17,780
4	0.855	30,000	25,650	3,000	2,565	10,000	8,550
5	0.822	30,000	24,660	3,000	2,466	5,000	4,110
			26,990		−899		6,310

The Internal Rate of Return (IRR) is a related measure. The IRR is the discount rate that yields an NPV of zero for the project. This IRR can then be compared with the cost of capital, the interest rate, to see if the project is worth doing. If the yield from the project is less than the cost of capital then it is probably not worth proceeding with the project.

Breakeven analysis
Breakeven analysis is particularly useful when the benefits accruing from the system vary with different workloads. It distinguishes between fixed and variable costs and fixed and variable benefits. Data is plotted on a graph where the vertical axis is the amount of cost or benefit, and the horizontal axis is the increasing level of the workload. The fixed costs are plotted first, with the variable costs plotted above them to show the increase in total cost as the workload increases. The same is done for benefits. The crossing point of the total benefits line with the total costs line indicates the breakeven point. Workloads to the left of this point do not justify the use of the system, while workloads to the right of the breakeven point do. Breakeven analysis does not give the full picture needed for the economic evaluation of systems, but its emphasis on volumes can be useful in certain instances.

There are various methods that may be used for the economic evaluation of projects. These methods may give contradictory advice, as we have seen in the Woodland Transport example, and none of them enjoys universal acceptance. However, whichever economic evaluation is adopted, apart from the rather simplistic least cost model, there will be a need to predict and quantify benefits. This is typically more difficult than quantifying costs and there are several reasons for this:

▶ Uncertainty about the timing and amount of benefits
▶ Problems of expressing certain benefits in direct monetary terms. For example, what is the value of not having to apologise for as many order

errors? Many benefits will often appear as intangibles; better management information, improved management controls etc.

▶ The benefit is often due to a joint effort of a number of departments in the organisation. In such cases it is very difficult to assess the computer system's contribution.

The difficulty of partitioning benefits should be explicitly recognised by ensuring that all costs and benefits incurred in a systems project should be included, not just those concerned with hardware, software and IS staff. This is a further justification for taking a top-down approach to project selection through first seeking business benefits. The advantage not only lies in the inclusion of all costs but, more importantly, the benefit itself is defined by the business objectives. The significance of this must not be missed. Many conventional projects are subject to a set of costs, which must be offset by scrabbling around for presumed benefits. These costs are often set in an inappropriate way; for example, someone decides that the project should have a budget of £50,000 because this sounds a reasonable figure. All subsequent costs and benefits have to be squeezed into this framework. Benefits may be hard to find, so intangible gains such as better control and up-to-date reports are introduced to make the project financially more attractive, but actually they are 'fixed' to make the project viable.

However, if the alternative perspective of defining objectives and benefits before cost is adopted, the framework for systems development immediately becomes more realistic. For example, the overall ambition of the project should become clearer. The budget for computer hardware and software can be set within the benefits that are likely to accrue. If savings of £50,000 per annum are envisaged, then it is probably unrealistic to restrict thinking to £10,000 systems. The recognition of this will permit more innovative technical solutions and operational strategies.

4.3 The feasibility report

The feasibility study will culminate in a formal written report and an oral presentation. The possible structure of a feasibility report is set out below.

Introduction
Background to the project

Management overview
A summary of the content and recommendations of the report

Terms of reference
This is likely to include reference back to preliminary analysis and an explanation of how the system under discussion was selected as a candidate for investigation. It will also include details about the scope, resources, time-scale and client of the study. It is important that these are

established and agreed at the outset. Possible terms of reference for a sales support project might be:

> To undertake a feasibility study of the sales support function identified in the corporate strategic plan study (see Section 2.5). The study will commence on 1 August 2003 and be undertaken by one senior and two junior analysts. A formal report will be presented to members of the information systems planning group on 11 November 2003, followed by a presentation at the group meeting on 24 November. The feasibility report will adhere to company standards (see ref 45/23/65) and evaluation criteria (ref. 45/23/141). The client for this project is Keith Freeman, Sales Manager – Northern Division.

Terms of reference should state what is expected, by when and what resources are available to achieve this. The intended outcome from this project stage is important. Many products are blighted by unfulfilled expectations: 'We expected to see a system, not a report'.

The term *deliverable* is often used to describe these outcomes. Terms of reference should always include the intended deliverables. In the example given above, these are a report and a presentation. In other instances they might be system, a program, a memorandum etc.

Existing system

This is a description of the relevant systems currently operating in the organisation. These will have to be investigated using the fact-finding techniques described in the next chapter and presented using appropriate models. These models will be less complete than in the subsequent analysis, but special attention must be paid to important operational requirements, for example the production of the roadsheet in the current Woodland Transport system. Particular problems will be highlighted and the implications of these discussed.

System requirements

These will be derived from the existing system (outputs currently produced may still be required when the system is replaced) and from discussion with system users and operators who have identified requirements that are not presently fulfilled. Critical performance factors must also be covered (e.g. the need to produce 5,000 invoices per day or to process transactions in less than five seconds) because these will have an important bearing on the hardware selection. Audit, security and data protection implications may also have to be discussed.

Proposed logical system

A number of business system options may be developed to reflect different combinations of requirements. The project client selects one of these options and required models can subsequently be developed to reflect the agreed business scope. This outline logical system design may be supported by definitions of key inputs and outputs described more in terms of their content than in layout and display. The differences and advantages of the proposed system over its predecessor will be highlighted, together with its effect on other systems currently operating in the organisation. The new system may impose certain constraints in operation (e.g. all input documents must be submitted by 4 p.m.) and these should be clearly described and discussed. The possible effects on staff must be identified and a strategy for staff training, reduction or redeployment suggested or requested.

Proposed physical system

A number of outline technical solutions may be evaluated and a preliminary technical implementation agreed.

The extent to which this can be done depends upon the current resources of the organisation. If the firm already has a large computer, then any extra hardware required is likely to be additional terminals, more secondary storage and perhaps more memory. It is likely that these will not be required until the system becomes operational, so the technical specification may be altered as detailed analysis and development clarifies the nature of the system.

In contrast, large projects and organisations without significant computer resources will have to invest in hardware before development can get under way. As a result, there are significant pressures to select and purchase the hardware very early in the project's life, before many of the detailed implications of the system been discovered.

Development plan

This will define a suggested project definition and plan for the detailed analysis and design phases, which will follow the acceptance of the feasibility report. A complementary plan will also be needed for hardware and software evaluation, purchase and installation. In effect, the feasibility report establishes the terms of reference for succeeding projects.

Costs and benefits

These have already been discussed. They will clearly vary in detail and accuracy, as will the techniques used to evaluate them.

Alternatives considered

In the process of arriving at a suggested system the analyst usually considers and rejects a number of options. It is important to record these considerations for two main reasons. Firstly, it may nip a number of time-consuming 'Have you considered?' discussions in the bud. Secondly, it permits the sponsor of the study to examine the legitimacy of the reasons for rejection. For example, the analyst may have rejected a certain option because, in his impressions gained from the preliminary analysis, it appeared to be too costly. However, the information contained in this study may now persuade the sponsor to change her mind about the level of ambition of the project, so that the rejected alternative becomes feasible. This alteration would be unlikely if details of rejected alternatives were not included.

Conclusions and recommendations
The report would normally end with conclusions, recommendations and relevant appendices. In general the recommendation will be:

▶ To proceed with the project

▶ To abort the project and invest elsewhere

▶ To review the scope of the project and hence redefine costs and benefits until it becomes justifiable

4.4 The feasibility compromise

The three ways of approaching feasibility are likely to conflict. In general, better technical solutions cost more money, while robust, helpful, user-friendly software is time-consuming to write and hence incurs higher development costs. Such software may also mean larger programs, so the system has to carry a much larger software overhead, which may begin to conflict with performance requirements. In many instances technical and economic factors become paramount; the system must have a two-second response time and return its investment in three years, so the operational factors become devalued. This often has unfortunate consequences.

The feasibility study differs from analysis proper in its level of detail. It is difficult to give general advice on what constitutes an acceptable depth of feasibility analysis because this will vary with the organisation and application. There is always the nagging worry that the detailed analysis work will uncover a hitherto overlooked fact that now makes the project infeasible. This is further complicated by the difficulty of reconciling the three feasibility criteria, particularly with the insistence of many organisations on an economic cost benefit analysis. The restricted time-scale of a feasibility study also makes it difficult to comprehensively evaluate and offer sufficient options at different levels of cost and ambition.

In SMEs using PC applications there are special difficulties in conducting feasibility studies. In large organisations the task may be given to a senior analyst, but in smaller firms there is no equivalent person. Thus the enterprise is very dependent upon its own non-specialist staff and the integrity of possible suppliers. In most instances the suppliers of PCs will not have the necessary resources, skill or time to perform a proper feasibility study. It is difficult to justify even one day of analysis on a job with a very small profit margin. Thus the preparation for computerisation may be less than ideal.

Prototyping may have an important role to play in this early stage of the project. Two examples must suffice.

In one instance the analyst was concerned about meeting technical output requirements identified in preliminary discussions with the main user. If these could not be attained using relatively simple technology, then the cost of purchasing and maintaining a new, advanced printer would render the project economically infeasible. This problem was resolved by creating a set of test programs that produced and timed representative output. The quality and speed of the printing were checked with the user who agreed that they met his requirements. This impressed the user as well as eliminating one of the analyst's doubts.

In another project the analyst was faced by a set of operators who had already suffered from a poorly planned computer installation. They seemed sceptical of his plans until he used a commercially available package to demonstrate the opportunities that existed. The operators made detailed criticisms, but their attitude towards the whole project became more positive as the session progressed. This simple idea changed aspects of the operational feasibility of the project within one hour.

4.5 Summary

Once possible business areas of application have been identified they should be subjected to a feasibility study. This chapter has identified and described three feasibility criteria and introduced four approaches to assessing economic feasibility. It has provided an outline of the contents of a feasibility report as well as recognising the compromise necessary between the three feasibility criteria. Finally, it has recognised the possible role of prototyping in arriving at that compromise. Financial information from the Woodland Transport case study has shown how a different strategy might result from adopting different economic evaluation methods.

EXERCISES

1   Briefly describe the relative advantages and disadvantages of the following approaches to economic feasibility:
    ▶ Least cost
    ▶ Time to payback
    ▶ Net Present Value

2   A company is currently looking to replace part of its computer network. Two suppliers have been asked to tender for the project. The relevant costs of each project are given in the table overleaf.

Required:
    (i)   Which solution would be selected using the *least cost* approach to selection? Justify your answer.
    (ii)   Which solution would be selected using the *time to payback* approach to selection? Show the calculations that justify this selection.

Year	Solution A		Solution B	
	Costs	Savings	Costs	Savings
0	100,000	0	75,000	0
1	0	20,000	25,000	0
2	0	30,000	0	60,000
3	0	30,000	0	40,000
4	0	40,000	0	40,000
5	10,000	50,000	5,000	40,000

(iii) If a discount rate of 10% is selected, which solution would be selected using the Net Present Value approach to selection? Show the calculations that justify this selection.

(iv) If the discount rate is changed to 5%, would this change your decision? Show the calculations that justify this decision.

3   A university wishes to install a new information system. Research has suggested that one-off costs for the project will be £120,000, while recurring costs are estimated at £50,000 per year. The Finance Department has suggested that a discount rate of 8% should be adopted. Benefits are estimated at £100,000 per year. The lifetime of the system is expected to be five years.

(i)   Calculate the *time to payback* of the project.
(ii) Calculate the Net Present Value of the project.
(iii) On financial grounds alone, what would be your recommendation on the proposal to the university? Explain your recommendation.

4   The chapter defines three types of feasibility. In the context of the Woodland Transport projects (recording vehicle movements, recording vehicle history and planning vehicle movements), define issues that might be considered under the headings of technical, social and operational feasibility.

5   An examination body usually distributes its examination results by surface mail. The candidates normally receive their results three days after they have been posted. There are approximately 100,000 examination results for each six-month sitting of the examination. The examination body is now considering allowing candidates direct access to their results held on the examination body's mainframe computer system.

(i)   How could such direct access technically be achieved?
(ii) What benefits would such direct access bring to the examination body?
(iii) What benefits would such direct access bring to the candidate?
(iv) What factors would have to be considered under the following headings?

– Technical feasibility
– Operational feasibility
– Social feasibility

6 A government department handles payments to building contractors. Each payment normally goes through the following stages:

1. Receipt of Invoice from contractor
2. Matching of Invoice against Order
3. Authorisation of Payment of Invoice
4. Raising Cheque
5. Despatch of Cheque to Contractor

Other stages (alternatives to above):

2a. Unmatched Invoices
3a. Rejected Invoice

During this process, many contractors phone up asking about the progress of their Invoice and its subsequent Payment. Bought Ledger Clerks respond to these queries by accessing their accounts system, which identifies the current status of all Invoices and Payments. The department is now considering putting this information online so contractors can access this information via the Internet.

(i)   What benefits would such direct access bring to the government department?
(ii) What benefits would such direct access bring to the contractor?
(iii) What factors would have to be considered under the following headings?

– Technical feasibility
– Operational feasibility
– Social feasibility

	Discount rate		
Year	10%	8%	5%
1	0.9091	0.9259	0.9254
2	0.8264	0.8573	0.9070
3	0.7513	0.7938	0.8638
4	0.6830	0.7350	0.8227
5	0.6209	0.6806	0.7835

References

Earl, M. J. (1996). *Information Systems Delivery Accounting for Information Systems.* Oxford: Oxford University Press.

Willcocks, L. (1996). *Investing in Information Systems: Evaluation and Management.* London: Chapman & Hall.

Defining systems requirements

The second part of this book examines the detailed investigation and modelling techniques that can be applied to the selected information systems projects. The approach is to provide a 'toolkit' of techniques and models, which can be applied as appropriate to the specific project situation. As the chapters progress, the models become less about modelling requirements and more about specifying how those requirements will be implemented. These techniques and models are fundamental to the elaboration phase of systems development.

Chapter 5 considers fact-gathering techniques and focuses on how the analyst will find out about how the current system works and what requirements users have for its successor. These techniques underpin the models defined in Chapters 6–9. So, for example, to develop the class model described in Chapter 7, the analyst will have to interview users, run workshops, analyse documents etc. A wide range of fact-gathering techniques are presented in this chapter, which concludes with a suggested mapping of these techniques on to the development circumstances.

Chapter 6 begins our consideration of modelling the facts gathered during investigation. The models presented here usually associated with the earlier stages of a project, where the analyst is still trying to get to grips with the application area. *Use case diagrams* from the Unified Modeling Language (UML) are introduced, supported by *use case specifications*, based on the approach of Alistair Cockburn. The second model, the *process map*, is a simple diagram of the business process and represents a long tradition of flowcharting in systems development. Finally, *data flow diagrams* are introduced as a specific way of modelling the detail of the current system when understanding that level of detail is felt to be important.

Chapter 7 looks at the fundamental concepts of class modelling. *Object and object class modelling* is applicable to a wide range of applications, although in this book the examples are from business information systems. In the early stages of the project, analysts may only be able to identify certain classes, tentative associations between those classes and some attributes in each class. However, as understanding improves, the class model will develop; with more classes, associations are better understood and expressed, and a complete set of attributes and a list of operations that affect that class are identified. In this way the class model provides a basis for subsequent design. The model becomes elaborated and adorned as the understanding of requirements improves. This chapter also introduces the *Entity Relationship Model* (ERM) as a well-established basis for understanding the static data structures of the organisation. The ERM only considers data (not operations) and is hence a more specialised model, more suitable where it has already been established that the application will be implemented with a relational database management system. The concept of normalisation is also examined in the context of the ERM.

Many users perceive systems from a functional perspective, and this is the viewpoint taken in Chapter 8. Users take a Course Booking or plan a Delivery or raise an Invoice. Such functions may be expressed in use cases (Chapter 6), but their actual realisation will normally require several classes to collaborate. This realisation is explored through *Interaction Diagrams* (the *sequence diagram* and the *collaboration diagram*). Drawing such diagrams will allow us to prove the class model and may lead to the addition of new classes and associations. Such diagrams assume a class model where the classes have responsibility for operations. A more restricted diagram, such as the ERM, will require a specification method for the functions, which are responsible for accessing and updating the data structures. This chapter looks at the data flow diagram for providing such a perspective, underpinned by *Structured English, Data Action Diagrams* and *Decision Tables*. The last three models can also be applied in an object-oriented approach to systems development.

The event models defined in Chapter 9 define a level of detail that provides a detailed specification of the system requirements and are hence associated with the later stages of analysis. *Statechart diagrams* or *State Transition Diagrams* are used in UML, and these are presented here. However, *entity life histories* (ELHs), although associated with structured techniques, provide a worthy alternative. In many respects the two perspectives (object-oriented and structured) can be brought together in the event model. ELHs can be applied to class models as they show how an object can be created, modified and deleted.

The elaboration phase of systems development (Chapter 1) may be supported by a real executable software product. As identified in Chapter 1, the prototyping approach is mentioned a number of times throughout the book. Chapter 10 looks at it in more detail in the context of Rapid Application Development. Elements of RAD are introduced and their effect on requirements gathering techniques (Chapter 5) is discussed. However, the focus of this part is very much on techniques of model building, rather than on system construction.

Fact-gathering techniques

In this chapter you will learn about:

▶ Problems of requirements gathering
▶ Problems of dealing with users
▶ Fact-finding for existing systems
▶ Requirements gathering for new systems
▶ Techniques for fact-finding
▶ Mapping of techniques to the development situation

5.1 Introduction

The first stage of most systems developments is known, variously, as investigation, fact-finding, elicitation or requirements gathering. Whatever name is given to this activity, it is a necessary part of the analysis phase of the development project.

There are a number of different situations that could face a developer. For example, the proposed system may be a replacement system, an enhancement of a current operational system or a completely new development. The business domain may be common (therefore standard, such as payroll) or a specialist area. The developers may have experience in the business domain or it may be new to them. The current system may be well documented or the result of an uncharted evolution. The requirements for the proposed system may be clear and precise or may be vaguely formulated and expressed.

This chapter explores a number of techniques for eliciting 'facts' about current working and new system requirements and suggests a framework to map these techniques on to the various circumstances listed above.

5.2 What facts?

Facts have to be supported by evidence. It sounds like a fact when a user claims that they handle 500 documents in a day but until samples of daily transactions have been counted it cannot be accepted. It may *feel like* 500 but turn out, after all, to be just 85.

A fact, therefore, is a **verified** piece of data.

Everything must be verified in one form or another. This may be done by interviewing someone else, watching the interviewee perform the task or searching through transaction logs or filing cabinets of documents.

During the investigation stage, the analysis will explore two broad interconnected paths:

1. What is the system to do/achieve (Functionality)?

2. What data is needed to support these functions (Data)?

These paths will be expressed in the form of diagrams: functions and processes can be modelled with Use Cases, Data Flow Diagrams, Structured English, Decision Tables and Trees. Data can be modelled in Entity Relationship Models, while data and functionality together can both be represented in Class Models. These diagrams are the subjects of later chapters.

If the system under investigation is a replacement of a current operation then the first diagrams will model the current processes and data. These are the first sets of facts, therefore, that will need to be uncovered. If there is no current system then the facts will be in the form of the required processes and data that the system will have to support.

While producing these diagrams and models the analyst will also prepare a Requirements Catalogue listing and describing the requirements for the new system.

An important point to make here is that during the investigation process facts and requirements will rarely emerge tidily and complete. They tend to emerge over time and often in a piecemeal fashion. This is one reason why it is so important to have a clear standard for **recording** the facts in terms of process, data (or classes) and requirements, so that they can be refined and elaborated throughout the investigation stage.

5.3 Techniques for fact gathering

This section examines a number of different techniques available to the analyst for uncovering details of the current system and its workings, together with requirements for its successor. The techniques covered are:

▶ Interviewing
▶ Questions and questionnaires
▶ Observation
▶ Protocol analysis
▶ Document analysis
▶ Workshops
▶ Prototyping

5.3.1 Interviewing

Interviews are a standard investigation technique. The interview consists of a face-to-face meeting between the analyst and an individual stakeholder in the system under investigation. These interviews are especially important in the early stages of the development. After all, how better to understand the workings of a system than to ask those who actually use it?

The purpose of these early interviews is to:

▶ Understand the business background behind the development

▶ Understand the technical context and constraints in which the development is set

▶ Understand the detailed procedures and data used in the current operations

▶ Identify any shortcomings in the current system

▶ Identify the requirements of the new system beyond its current operation.

Another very important reason for conducting interviews is that it gives the end users an opportunity to meet the analysts responsible for the new system and to ask them questions. An analyst must have the confidence of the users and a one-to-one interview gives the opportunity for the analyst to establish a rapport with them.

Interview techniques

An interview is not the same as an unstructured chat over coffee. An analyst preparing an interview needs to take a number of issues into account.

Who to interview

It is usually recommended that interviewing takes place top-down through the organisation. Hence managers are interviewed before supervisors and supervisors before clerks or operatives. The first interview is usually with the project sponsor, who can help identify the objectives, the deliverables and the scope of the application. The sponsor can also describe the business context and imperatives that drive the development. It is likely that only coarse-grained facts and requirements will emerge at this stage and more detail will be found from interviewees lower down the organisation. However, it is important to carry out high-level enquiries first, else the detail may have little meaning. It is also the project sponsor's requirements that will usually carry most weight.

After the sponsor, the analyst will need to talk to the relevant department managers about what happens in their departments. The information they will give relates to the functions their department performs, the reports that they need, the documents that are used and the volumes of transactions and records that are processed. Details will also be given about employees and permission to interview these employees should be sought and given.

The people who will give the most detailed information are those who perform the operational work of the department (raising invoices, taking course bookings, handling customer complaints etc.). They are the employees who can give the specific facts about actual procedures followed, tasks performed, problems with the way these tasks are performed and monitored, peak and trough times, and working relationships.

Where to interview them

Where possible the interview should take place at the interviewee's own workplace. There are a number of reasons why this is desirable.

▶ It avoids making interviewees feel that they are being 'summoned' to a meeting elsewhere.

▶ It is easier to establish a rapport with someone when they are in their own environment.

▶ They will have the relevant documentation to hand during the interview.

▶ It is easier to observe their working conditions, the nature of interruptions and how they handle these interruptions.

Before the interview

Detailed preparation must be undertaken before the interview.

▶ The objectives of the meeting must be clear. Is it to understand processes, identify problems and gather requirements or to confirm previous interviews? It will probably cover all of these but not to the same extent.

▶ Questions must be prepared. There is an optimum structure for an interview and this will be described later. However, the lines of enquiry need identifying and questions grouped accordingly.

▶ An agenda must be prepared. This is useful in a number of ways: it clarifies what the interview is trying to achieve and it makes clear to the interviewee what will be discussed. While it may seem self-evident that they know what is required, many interviewees only have a name and a time in the diary and are not clear as to what the meeting is about. Consequently, they will be unprepared. With an agenda, they can research any facts they are unsure of and gather any documentation they need to show and discuss. Having drawn up an agenda, it is important to send it to the interviewee about two days in advance so that they have time to assimilate it and prepare for the interview.

Figure 5.1 is a sample agenda showing a level of detail that will help Jerry Brand, the Administrative Supervisor at Woodland Transport, to prepare for the interview.

Controlling the interview

This is an aspect of the interview that can only partly be prepared for in advance. A successful model is shown in Figure 5.2.

Figure 5.1 Interview agenda.

**Agenda for interview with Jerry Brand
25 September, 9.30 a.m. – 10.30 a.m.
Venue: JB's Office**

SUBJECT: New Roadsheet System

1. Background
   - (a) Department objectives
   - (b) Roles and responsibilities
   - (c) Methods of report generation

2. Current system
   - (a) History
   - (b) Current procedures
   - (c) Number of users
   - (d) Documentation used/produced

3. Problems and issues
   - (a) Performance
   - (b) Availability
   - (c) Bottlenecks/delays
   - (d) Security
   - (e) Other

4. Requirements
   - (a) Additional facilities in new system
   - (b) New reporting facilities

The **context** allows the interviewee to describe their role and the main tasks involved in undertaking this role within the system under investigation. This can lead to more **detailed** questions which draw out detailed procedures, volumes, documents used and how these are completed. Once these have been uncovered it is reasonable to move on to the **problems** encountered in carrying out the tasks and whether these problems are to do with workflow, procedures, lack of access to information or human factors. Once the current situation and any shortcomings are identified it is time to ask about any **requirements** for

Figure 5.2 Interview control.

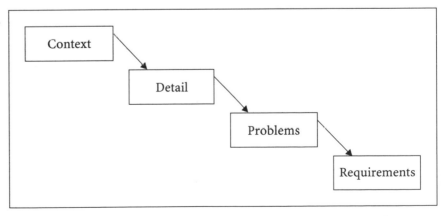

the new system. What does this particular interviewee wish for from the new system to make their job easier or more effective?

Another way of controlling the interview is by the judicious use of questioning techniques. There are a number of different types of question and the selection of which type to use depends largely upon the nature of the information required and the user who is answering the questions. The types of questions available include:

▶ *Closed questions*

These are question that invite simple answers with no embellishment. For example, 'Do you need authorisation to submit a claim?' – 'Yes'. 'Who from?' – 'The department manager'. Closed questions can also be used for eliciting information about volumes: 'How many of these do you handle in a day?' – 'Fifty'.

Closed questions are very useful with someone who is reluctant to stop talking and continually provides more information than is necessary or relevant. Throwing in a series of specific closed questions helps the analyst regain control of the interview. These are in contrast to open questions.

▶ *Open questions*

These are questions that do invite expansion and not a simple Yes/No response. 'Tell me about the authorisation procedures' allows a long and more detailed response. These questions are useful for encouraging anecdotes or 'war stories' about the current system (a rich source of problems with the current operations). They are also a good means of drawing out taciturn or timid interviewees. If an analyst gets a series of monosyllabic answers from somebody then they are unable to get a useful collection of facts about either the current system or new requirements. Consequently, they may ask a number of open questions that demand more than a one-word response. Open questions also allow an interviewee to explain procedures and issues to a level of detail that is useful to the analyst.

▶ *Probing questions*

This is a form of open question that follows up an earlier comment or answer. It can be a straightforward 'Oh?'; 'Tell me more about that'; or 'What exactly does that mean?'. Such questions allow both parties to reflect on a point that has been made and ensure that as much information as possible has been extracted from it.

▶ *Verification questions*

These are a particular form of probing question, confirming understanding and completeness. They could include such questions as: 'I understood you to say... Have I got that right?'; 'Would it be correct to say that the term Call-Off means...'; 'Have we left anything out of this part?'; or 'In these circumstances, you seem to do... are there any exceptions to this rule?'.

▶ *Sequencing questions*

These help to preserve a narrative in the description, so that the task has coherence. Examples might be: 'Could you talk me through a case step by step?'; 'What do you do first? Next?'; 'Why does this step follow that one?'; or 'Can these steps be reversed or taken in another sequence?'.

▶ *Anecdotal questions*

These are a form of open question, as noted above, to elicit illustrations to help understand the task or highlight problems. Anecdotal questions might be in the form: 'Can you think of a typical incident that illustrates what you do?'; 'If I were covering your job, what advice would you give me to get started?'; 'Have you ever had a situation where...? How did you proceed?'; 'What do you do if you get stuck?'; or 'What was the hardest case you ever solved?'.

Choosing the right question type and the right question at the right moment makes a significant difference to the quality of the facts that are obtained from the interview.

There are three further issues concerned with interviewing that should be borne in mind.

User sensitivity

Systems development usually leads to changes in working practice and can lead to job loss. As an agent of change, the analyst is often viewed with suspicion, and even hostility, by those not involved in the decision-making. It is important not to make users feel that they are being interrogated or criticised. Be careful to avoid phrases like 'improve efficiency', 'how could you do it better?' or 'we're here to investigate...'. Users see themselves as helping analysts in their work even though analysts tend to see themselves as providing systems to help users. It is important to be sensitive to uncertainties that may be detected and to be appreciative of help that has been given.

Avoid designing

It can be tempting to see immediately what solution is required to resolve a particular problem. Analysts must not give in to this temptation. The project is still at the investigation stage and there is insufficient information to think about solutions or designs yet. If a solution is suggested at this stage it is likely that trade unions, staff associations, the project sponsor and the project manager will be antagonised!

Note taking

While there is no standard format for recording the interview, it is important to take notes at the time and write them up as soon as possible after the interview. Controlling the interview is especially important, as there is a danger of failing to keep up with the interviewee or not hearing their response to a question as the previous answer is still being written down. It is important to ask interviewees to slow down or wait while that section of the notes is completed. Every so often it is useful to recapitulate the latest section of notes to ensure that the previous part of the interview has been understood and documented correctly. This also gives the interviewee a chance to remember anything else relevant to that topic.

When the interview is complete, the notes must be written up. This should be done immediately, as memory and hasty handwriting do not help accurate recording a day after the event. After they are written up, a copy should be sent to the interviewee and a copy filed with other project documents. The content of the interview record should be confirmed by the user, who must understand that these contents are the complete documentation of that interview. If it is not written down then it was never said! This is to deter 'I am sure I mentioned at a meeting that call-off date was a significant piece of information' discussions late in the project life. Hundreds of words are said in interviews, but it is the ones written down that count. Figure 5.3 shows a sample of an interview report.

Interviewing is one of the leading techniques for investigation and the rapport that can be established by a skilful and sensitive interviewer encourages user support for the project and a sense of ownership in the new system.

However, the interview, while a powerful tool, does have a number of shortcomings, including the issue that all that is said must be verified. The other techniques, shown below, can help to provide that verification and trap several facts and requirements that the interview may have missed.

5.3.2 Written questions

There are occasions when a user is unavailable for interview. At these times, the analyst could, with the user's prior agreement, put down the questions in writing and give a deadline by which answers should be returned. This is less effective than a face-to-face interview for eliciting information because there is little scope for immediate follow-up. However, unlike questionnaires (see below), the written questions do allow the analyst to target specific problems and allow scope for open questions as well as closed ones. For example, if Jerry Brand were unable to make a second interview and the pay issues needed further explanation, then the interviewer might submit the following.

> *Dear Jerry*
>
> *Thank you for your time yesterday. I am attaching a copy of the notes taken of the interview for your agreement. I understand that you are unavailable tomorrow, when I next visit Woodland Transport. I had hoped to visit you again, as I realised that I do not have all the information I need to understand the Drivers' Pay part of the system.*
>
> *Could I ask you to provide answers to the following three questions and return them to me by Monday 5th? Thank you.*
>
> *1. Could you explain how Contract Drivers' pay is calculated and how this differs from your own drivers' pay calculation?*
>
> *2. What procedures does your department have to follow in the event of an Agency Driver missing a shift? What impact, if any, does this have on the pay calculations?*
>
> *3. When are you required to prepare the Driver Absence Report?*

Figure 5.3 Meeting report – Stuart Talbot.

Meeting Report		Project Woodland Transport		Ref: MR01	
Author MPC	**Date** 29/08	**Time** 14:30	**Duration** 1 hour	**Agenda** MA01	**Page** 1
Participants: Stuart Talbot (ST) Woodland Mike Crawmore (MPC)			**Comments:** Initial meeting to identify Terms of Reference for Woodland Transport system		

Detail	X-Ref
1. ST provided some background to Woodland Transport's (WT) operation and the current position.	
2. WT is owned by the United Logistics Group and was created when United Logistics won the contract to operate Kronenhalle Brewery Ltd's (KBL) transport operation.	
3. WT office staff is divided into three departments: Logistics, Traffic and Administration. ST provided an organisation chart	Org chart
4. Logistics plan deliveries. The Traffic Office controls the drivers and Admin are responsible for general office administration and the production of management reports.	
5. WT employs 70 drivers who work on a two-shift pattern.	
6. The WT fleet currently comprises 80 tractors and 1 van and there are 170 trailers.	
7. WT's contract with KBL will shortly be under review by the new management at KBL.	
8. Negotiation for the new contract should start in three months' time.	
9. WT currently uses the CLASS system to control roadsheet production and confirmation. However, the system is old fashioned, the software house that built it has gone into receivership and new requirements have emerged since it was written. ST now wants this system replaced.	
10. MPC explained that his team would need to understand WT's current operation, problems and requirements in more detail before creating any specifications for a new system.	
11. ST agreed that MPC's team could talk to any WT staff as required to gain an understanding of the current system and to identify the requirements and scope for the new system.	
Action: ST to inform WT staff of requirements investigation	
Action: MPC to arrange meetings with WT staff asap	
12. ST and MPC agreed some initial terms of reference	PID
13. It was also agreed that MPC would report back to ST after the initial fact finding. Meeting date 06/09. Time to be agreed.	
Action: MPC to confirm meeting date/time with ST on 04/09	

Generally, as this example implies, this tactic is more appropriate following an introductory meeting. The user knows the analyst, a rapport has been established, much of the basic information has been gathered and so the questions have a meaningful context. It is far less suitable as an introduction to the project for the user. It would be harder for the analyst to frame meaningful questions if the analyst had not already met the user and was, to an extent, unfamiliar with the user's responsibilities.

5.3.3 Questionnaires

Questionnaires are employed in very particular circumstances and should be used with discretion. They may be considered in situations where the user population is too large to interview, or where the organisation is spread over several sites and the analyst needs information from representatives of all sites. The essence of the questionnaire is that it is a data-gathering mechanism for a large population of distributed users. In some circumstances it is impossible, because of time and cost constraints, to interview all the users concerned with a particular development project.

Questionnaires on detailed procedures are clearly inappropriate; two hundred separate questions on procedure cannot be usefully analysed or absorbed. However, questionnaires might be useful in finding out about satisfaction with the system's interface, information about volumes and frequencies of transactions or attitudes to aspects of the work and operation of the system. These questions can invite respondents to mark their responses on a scale from 1 to 5. These responses can then be analysed to identify where most people's attitudes, concerns or beliefs lie.

A difficulty with questionnaires is that there is no chance of interaction with the respondents if their answers should be unclear or if they should refer to something new to the analyst. Reading and responding to body language are impossible. For these reasons most questions will be closed and questions and responses need to be as unambiguous as possible. However, there are difficulties in framing questions in order to reach the unambiguous understanding sought by the analyst. The following two questions are intended to gain similar information but the second is much stronger.

1. Are you happy with the interface for this system?   Y/N
2. Please tick the box that fits your response most closely:

    'I find the function XXX simple to use'

Agree strongly	Agree	Neutral	Disagree	Disagree strongly
☐	☐	☐	☐	☐

This question can then be followed by a number of specific supplementary questions about usability issues such as ease of learning, helpfulness in correcting errors, satisfaction with on-line help and so on. This format gives more precise information than a simple 'Do you like...? Y/N'.

There are a number of other issues for the analyst to bear in mind when creating questions:

▶ Only ask one question at a time; do not inadvertently combine two questions in one sentence. For example, 'Are you happy with the interface and how easy it is to learn? Y/N' prevents the respondent from indicating that it was hard to learn but they are happy with it now.

▶ Avoid leading questions, which suggest to the respondent the answer they think you want to hear. 'Do you agree that management are supportive of new staff? Y/N' implies that a Yes answer is expected.

▶ Use the language and vocabulary that the respondents will recognise (Manager or Supervisor? Departments rather than functional areas etc.).

▶ Keep questions short and precise.

▶ Be sure that respondents know *how* to answer (by ticking a box, circling a number, deleting a non-applicable answer etc.).

▶ Keep the questionnaire as short as it can be to gain the information required. The respondents are usually busy people and if a questionnaire or survey is too long, it will end up in the waste paper bin, after an extended stay in the in-tray.

When the questions have been drafted, the analyst needs to pilot the questionnaire on selected people to ensure that the respondents correctly interpret all the questions. The analyst also has to check that the answers given on the pilot questionnaire can be successfully analysed. At this stage the questionnaire usually needs to be revisited with changes to the wording, some extra sections added or sections deleted or reorganised for a more logical question flow.

Only after successful piloting should the questionnaire be printed and despatched to the target respondents.

An appropriate deadline should be set for the return of all questionnaires. It may be possible to provide some form of incentive to complete the survey: 1 in 10 responses is a good response rate for a marketing survey, but it may feel too small a sample for the analyst's comfort. In some circumstances, questionnaires may be meant to be anonymous. In such situations, inviting respondents to send in their business card to be entered in a prize draw might be one way to persuade people to reply, as long as they can be reassured that the card will not be used to identify their responses.

Once questionnaires have been returned, they can be analysed. The advantage of a 5 or 7-point scale is that the results can be analysed using a commercially available software package such as MINITAB®.

It is important that questionnaires are not completely dismissed as a fact-gathering technique. They can be used to 'weed out' a large number of possible respondents so that fact-finding interviews can be better focused. Furthermore, they also have an important and significant role to play in evaluating competing software packages (see Chapter 14). Significant advantages, as well as cost and time savings, include:

▶ They are free of interviewer distortion and error.

▶ They give the respondent time to refer to documents and documentation. Questions which concern detailed factual data (e.g. 'How many customers live in the south west?') are suited to questionnaires.

Email questionnaires

Most organisations now have email or an Intranet, so it is possible to distribute questionnaires electronically. The principles of organising the questions and piloting the questionnaire are the same but the distribution and collection will be far quicker and cheaper. There are also commercial software packages that allow the creation of questionnaires that may be completed online. Responses may be fed directly into an analysis tool so the analyst only sees the results and not the actual responses. This is particularly possible where the questionnaire can be placed on a page on an Intranet server and respondents are directed to the relevant page by email. Alternatively, the analyst can distribute the survey by email for the respondents to reply electronically with the answers completed, or to print off and fill in by hand. This latter approach may seem unsatisfactory but it does reassure the respondents that their anonymity is protected. If the survey is looking at attitudes of staff and their response is negative, protecting their privacy is an important factor. Such anonymity is difficult to preserve in interviews.

5.3.4 Observation

Observation is another powerful method of understanding the context of the system. As the name implies, it simply involves watching the work to see how it is carried out, where it could be improved and what problems there are in undertaking the necessary tasks. To understand an environment, there is no substitute for being there in person and watching what happens. It makes the interviews much easier to prepare if the analyst has first-hand experience of the workplace.

Observation can be carried out on both a formal and an informal basis.

Informal observation can be used when visiting users for interviews. It is simply a matter of noticing the working environment, its physical layout, any bottlenecks or idle time that is apparent, any significant interactions between the staff and, more subtly, any 'atmosphere' or 'feel' in the workplace. Do employees seem keen and motivated, or sluggish and bored, or over-stretched? These can give important clues for the investigation.

Formal observation is carried out by agreement between the analyst, manager and person being observed. It is important to let the person know that it is not he or she who is the subject of observation, but the task that they perform. It is also important to remember that people behave and work differently when being observed from how they normally would. Simple self-consciousness is one reason for this, but another reason is mistrust of the analyst and the process. They may feel that if they do not follow the procedures manual precisely (and there are usually very good reasons why they may not) they may be disciplined. Consequently, they perform their work differently from how they usually do. Again, as with the interviewees, if the analyst can establish a good rapport with the user so that they realise that the analyst is not part of some unsubtle management plot, then this problem can be alleviated.

What is being observed?

There are a number of possible approaches to observation. One approach might be to follow an order from 'cradle to grave', to see exactly how it is initiated, handled, passed from one person to another and finally filed and archived. Such observation may also reveal delays in the process, places where there may be scope for error, as well as allowing an assessment of how successfully the document and process meets its specified targets.

Alternatively, the analyst may be observing a whole office, or just one user, rather than a transaction passing through the organisation. In this case, it is even more important that the people being observed have been forewarned and agreement gained. To find a stranger with a clipboard beside you, noting everything that you do during a day is disconcerting, to say the least.

As with the interviews, it is important to take notes and write them up as soon as possible after the session. Memory is notoriously unreliable and if left more than half a day key points can be either misremembered or completely forgotten.

Much of the investigation phase is like detective work, looking for threads, connections and corroboration. Close observation, both formal and informal, is a tool that can help in the detection of possible problems and desirable solutions.

An observation mnemonic, STROBE (STRuctured OBservation of the Environment; Kendall and Kendall, 1999), suggests deciding on a set of things that need to be observed and making special note of them. These may be: how are the desks placed? How many people work together? How near is the decision maker or manager's office to the work area? What storage and shelf space is there? What equipment is provided for staff? How much equipment is shared, how much equipment does each worker have sole access to? Are there trade journals or magazines in evidence? Once an analyst begins to look out for particular things on a visit to a user, it is much easier to notice the significant things – and significant exceptions. Before the study begins, it is useful to draw up a proforma listing of those things that should be looked out for. A suggested form is shown in Figure 5.4. This list will supplement the information gathered, for example, in an interview. The 5-point scale shown is one suggested way of documenting the informal observation but a textual description can be sufficient.

5.3.5 Protocol analysis

Protocol analysis combines aspects of interviewing and observation. One problem with an interview is that some jobs cannot be explained well in

Figure 5.4 Scales for observing the physical environment.

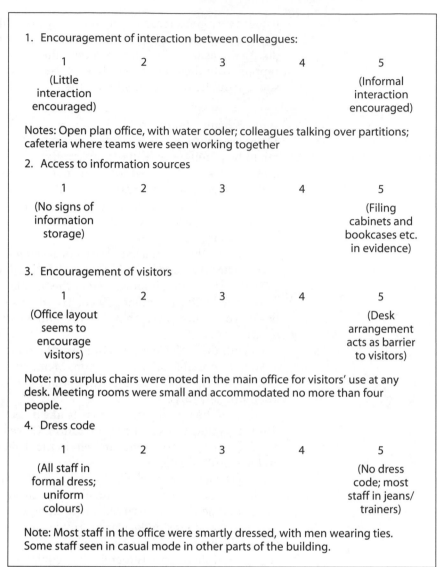

1. Encouragement of interaction between colleagues:

1	2	3	4	5
(Little interaction encouraged)				(Informal interaction encouraged)

Notes: Open plan office, with water cooler; colleagues talking over partitions; cafeteria where teams were seen working together

2. Access to information sources

1	2	3	4	5
(No signs of information storage)				(Filing cabinets and bookcases etc. in evidence)

3. Encouragement of visitors

1	2	3	4	5
(Office layout seems to encourage visitors)				(Desk arrangement acts as barrier to visitors)

Note: no surplus chairs were noted in the main office for visitors' use at any desk. Meeting rooms were small and accommodated no more than four people.

4. Dress code

1	2	3	4	5
(All staff in formal dress; uniform colours)				(No dress code; most staff in jeans/ trainers)

Note: Most staff in the office were smartly dressed, with men wearing ties. Some staff seen in casual mode in other parts of the building.

words. Try telling somebody how to tie a shoelace using words alone and a job that you perform easily suddenly becomes confusing and explained only with difficulty. Another issue that can cause problems is the 'taken-for-granted' information. It may be that the user does not mention a part of the job in an interview because they take it for granted that the analyst will know all about it from common sense. Because the analyst has in fact never heard of that aspect they will not know it has been omitted and so it is missed from the development.

For example, a programmer/analyst had worked only in IT since leaving school. He was asked to develop an accounting system and diligently interviewed the accountant to learn about the ledgers, Balance Sheet and the Profit and Loss Account. When he presented the system to the accountant, the question was asked: 'How do I calculate a trial balance?'. The developer had never heard of a trial balance and so did not know to ask about it: the accountant assumed that everybody knew that the ability to calculate a trial balance was a necessary part of any accounting package and did not bother even to mention it.

Protocol analysis is a technique that captures both the inexplicable and the taken-for-granted aspects of a job. Quite simply, the user performs a task in front of the analyst and describes each part of it – each action, each decision – at the same time as carrying it out. Anything that was taken for granted before is now brought out into the open and can be recorded. Any part of the job that could not be put into words can now be recognised and captured. Another technique for drawing out taken-for-granted details is prototyping, which will be examined in Section 5.3.8.

5.3.6 Document analysis

When examining the workings of a current system, it is important to get copies of all the documentation used in the current operation. Business documents are a rich source of both analysis and design material. Any future database, for example, will be populated and maintained through business transactions, which will be recorded on either paper-based or electronic documents. The analyst must know the formats of the data items on the documents so that they can become fields in database tables and input fields on computer screens.

The documents also represent the formal information flows of the current system. During the interviews the analyst should make a point of collecting samples of all forms, reports and documents.

Each document collected should then be analysed to identify the following information about it:

▶ What causes the document to be generated?
▶ Who generates it?
▶ Who checks it?
▶ How is it completed?
▶ How many people are responsible for completing it?
▶ Where does the data on the document come from?
▶ What is the purpose of the document?
▶ How is the document stored?
▶ How is it retrieved?
▶ How long is it kept for?
▶ How many of these documents are completed over what period of time?

These questions cover the whole document. The analyst also needs to answer the following questions about the data items themselves.

▶ When is each data item entered?

▶ Is the name for each item standard across the organisation?

▶ What is the source of each data item?

▶ What is the size and format of each item?

▶ Are any items optional, or should all be completed?

▶ What validation checks are required for each data item?

It is important to know how many of each document will be generated and used in a certain time frame (for example 70 invoices are raised each week). The system must also cope with expected peaks and variations in the number of transactions. It is not only the current usage that concerns us; if the business expects to grow by 12% per annum, the system must be able to cope with the volumes in three years' time, not just this year's predicted transactions.

As well as carrying out the detailed analysis of the document the analyst should also assess its usability, clarity and relevance. The analyst is particularly looking for ambiguity or obsolescence; for example, column headings that do not correctly indicate the data entered under that item.

Figure 5.5 shows a sample form for document analysis. An analyst may use this standard form to structure and frame questions about documents discovered in the system. This demonstrates how standard forms can be used to prompt as well as record facts about the system.

5.3.7 Workshops

The techniques described above are all traditional techniques for investigation and are suitable for analysing current operational systems. However, many projects are concerned with developing new systems, perhaps supporting new products or integrating a number of existing disparate systems.

There are a number of techniques available, and widely used, to help the analyst elicit requirements for circumstances where it may be more difficult to be specific about requirements.

There are times when one-to-one interviews are not the best way of obtaining requirements or understanding. There can be several reasons for this: there may be too many stakeholders to interview singly; the scope of the development may be very unclear or there may be too many conflicting viewpoints to resolve individually with stakeholders.

These problems may be resolved by holding a workshop to bring all stakeholders together. These are sometimes called Joint Application Development (JAD) or Joint Requirements Planning (JRP) workshops.

Why?
Some of the reasons for preferring workshops to interviews have already been given. However, there are also other advantages. If there is a disagreement between stakeholders it is easier to resolve these with everyone in the same forum with a skilled facilitator present to manage potential conflicts. At the end of the workshop all the participants should

Document description	System	Document	Name	Sheet
Stationery ref.	Size	No. of parts	Method of preparation	
Filing sequence	Medium		Prepared by/maintained by	
Frequency of preparation	Retention period		Location	
Volumes per	Minimum	Maximum	Average	Growth rate/ fluctuations
Users/recipients	Purpose		Frequency of use	

Ref.	Item	Picture	Occurrence	Value range	Source of data

Figure 5.5 Sample form for document analysis.

have reached a consensus and be in agreement about the development. This aspect of 'buy-in' is very significant when the final acceptance of the system is considered. Many systems have been sub-optimal and poorly used because the users and stakeholders felt that they had been railroaded into solutions that did not address their particular concerns. The workshop involves users and encourages their participation very early on in the development process, creating a greater sense of ownership of the new system. This reduces the danger of rejection at implementation.

A great strength of the workshop forum is the synergy that comes from so many people working together to solve a problem. The interactive nature of workshops encourages creativity and the generation of new ideas. Issues, problems and solutions will be explored in more depth than is possible for one person working alone or from relatively passive users taking part in analyst-led interviews.

Who?

Typically there will be a variety of participants at such a workshop: the analyst, users, management, sponsor and project manager. A facilitator, who will preferably have no direct interest in the system and so cannot be accused of partiality in case of disagreement, will run the workshop. There should also be a scribe who will take notes of all points made in the discussion and of conclusions, recommendations and post-meeting actions. It may be helpful to have a range of users present although the facilitator must ensure that more junior members of the organisation are not intimidated or overruled by senior staff.

If the project covers a large scope and there are potential disagreements over priorities it may be helpful to have a series of workshops starting with management levels. This first workshop will be to agree the high-level objectives and requirements, the broad scope and the priorities for development. Subsequent workshops will then look at more detailed requirements for the constituent parts of the system.

These later workshops will also require the analyst, the facilitator and the scribe. However, in these workshops the stakeholders will be end users rather than management. A programmer may also be in attendance with a prototyping tool to start constructing screens and dialogues to ensure that the requirements have been properly understood.

Where?

The workshop should take place in a specially prepared room. The participants should be seated in a way that precludes any suggestion of seniority or hierarchy, perhaps in a horseshoe or round table arrangement. The walls should have as much whiteboard space as possible with a number of flipcharts available for the scribe.

Ideally, the workshop should take place off-site so that the participants are not distracted – or tempted – by operational work issues. This is not always possible but at least the workshop should take place away from the work office. It should also be free from mobile phones and pagers!

How?

There are a number of techniques available to support the conduct of the workshop. If this is a preliminary workshop, with senior stakeholders establishing scope and priorities, the facilitator may ask the participants to focus on the issues we considered in Chapter 3. For example, participants may be asked to identify the mission that drives the development, its critical success factors and what data needs to be collected and analysed to monitor these critical success factors. From this analysis, the participants can agree on the dependencies between functions and the priority of functions, what is most urgent and what can wait a little longer. The data and functions identified in this initial workshop form the first set of user requirements.

Inviting everyone to write down what they see as the critical requirements for the new system on a sticky note can encourage active participation in the workshop. These are then stuck on to a wallchart (this is known as a 'talking wall') with the facilitator grouping them according to theme or function. Once these groupings are complete to the workshop's satisfaction, each can be discussed and amplified as required.

Whichever method is used, the facilitator must make sure that everybody present makes a contribution. At a workshop, all participants must be allowed to express their views and concerns. It is the facilitator's responsibility to provide a safe environment for everybody to make contributions, regardless of who else is present.

5.3.8 Prototyping

A prototype is a model or mock-up of the product being designed, in this case an information system. Prototyping can be used in the requirements gathering stage, during design and during build. In this section, prototyping is considered only within requirement definition.

Prototyping involves the analyst and the user working together. Using some form of quick-build software tool or Fourth Generation Language (see Chapter 10), the analyst prepares a mock-up of how the system could appear and work. At this stage, the focus is on what the system must do. Aspects of the HCI (Human–Computer Interface) such as layout and colour are not particularly considered as they detract from the functional requirements of the system. These usability issues will be considered later in the book.

The prototype will be built after an initial set of interviews and one could be prepared for each user. Using the prototype, the information from the interview can be quickly translated into a visual model that mimics their stated requirements although in a very limited form. The user can then test and explore the model and comment on its suitability and completeness. Most users are impressed by this rapid feedback of their stated requirements.

Prototyping is especially suitable for situations where the requirements are particularly unclear. Seeing the first visualisation often prompts the user to re-evaluate the functions they have already defined as well as prompting for more functions that they now realise they require from the system. However, their expectations do need to be carefully managed to prevent the requirements from getting out of control with the cost of the project escalating accordingly. In such circumstances it may also be useful to bring in a proprietary software package or explore web sites to help the users visualise possibilities. When proprietary software is being used to explore the problem situation, the analyst must ensure that the user is aware that the package is not being suggested or sold but is being used to explore an application area. It is often easier to say what is inadequate about, say, a production control package, than it is to define requirements in the abstract. Similarly, if an organisation does not have an e-trading capability it may be easier to explore other organisations' e-trading sites, rather than to identify requirements from scratch and in relative isolation.

Prototypes are also useful when the application is particularly complex and a more concrete expression of the application is needed before the options can be properly evaluated. Furthermore, if there is a history of difficulty between the user and analyst, prototyping is a valuable concrete tool to ensure that both sides understand the requirements. Demonstrating a prototype of a function with a user is a common way of uncovering any taken-for-granted requirements that were not mentioned in interviews.

There are drawbacks, not least that the prototype sometimes takes the place of documentation so that the system becomes harder to maintain. Project management standards and procedures need to ensure that this does not happen. Another danger is that if each prototype is treated as a standalone system issues of shared data and integration with other functions may be missed. It is important to remember that this is a tool in the investigation process and not a part of the system build or final system specification. Consequently, 'throwaway' prototypes constructed using simple presentation software may be particularly valuable at this stage.

5.4 Fact-finding in a computerised environment

Most organisations now have computers performing a significant proportion of their functions and activities. New systems may be installed to enhance those already in place, to update the technology and scope, or often to integrate discrete systems. Techniques for fact-finding may need to be adapted for these situations.

5.4.1 Interviewing

Most questions will relate to the use of the computer in performing the tasks and how it can be improved. Areas of discontent are likely to centre on the non-functional aspects of the system, i.e. the usability of the system, response times and reliability. Many documents that are used will be input screens. Transaction logs will help with identifying volumes of data and frequency of transactions.

5.4.2 Questionnaires

Again, these will be mostly concerned with user attitudes towards usability and reliability issues.

5.4.3 Observation

Observing a user at work on the computer can raise problems of interaction, in that the user is in effect demonstrating the system to the analyst who will need to sit very close to both user and terminal to follow what is happening. This may cause discomfort to some users.

The focus of observation will be on the ergonomics and workflow, assessing how easy it is for the user to access the data needed, whether or not they need to leave their desk to get information or to pass documents to colleagues.

5.4.4 Protocol analysis

The principles of this will not be affected by the computerised nature of the task; the user still needs to perform the task while providing a detailed commentary on each step.

5.4.5 Document analysis

The documents will largely be screens used for data capture. Storage information will now relate to database tables as well as individual transactions. The business user will not have that sort of information available so supplementary interviews with technical support or database administration may be appropriate.

5.4.6 Workshops

The focus and conduct of a workshop should not be affected by whether or not the work is currently computerised.

5.5 Mapping of techniques to user situations

Users usually wish to cooperate with the developers of their systems. However, there is always a danger that users will give misleading information or indeed fail to give important information at all. This is rarely because of a deliberate wish to sabotage a development, but more a matter of being focused on one aspect of the work and missing a broader perspective, or perhaps being inarticulate, finding it difficult to express what they intend. The types of problem that the analyst may encounter include the following. The words in square brackets represent a code for each situation.

▶ A user may be resistant to change and not be able to think of new ways of doing the job. In this case, the interview will identify current procedures and forms and perhaps problems with the execution but little in the way of fresh requirements. [Present-Oriented/PO]

▶ A user may not be clear as to numbers and volumes of information; this can result in misleading requirements if not verified. [Vague/V]

Table 5.1 Summary of fact-gathering techniques.

Techniques	PO	V	TFG	Tacit	New	Novice
Interview	Y	Y	Y	N	Y	Y
Observation	N	Y	YY	Y	N	YY
Protocol analysis	N	N	YY	YY	Y	YY
Document analysis	Y	N	Y	Y	N	YY
Workshop	YY	N	YY	N	YY	Y
Prototype	YY	N	YY	Y	YY	Y

Key: Y – Good fit; YY – Very good fit; N – Not a good fit

▶ The user may take some aspects of the job and its requirements for granted. These taken-for-granted parts of the job will not be mentioned in an interview. This leads to incomplete information and unrecognised gaps in the analysis. [TFG]

▶ Some jobs cannot be easily explained in words. This is especially true in application of manual skill and dexterity and in complex decision-making, such as diagnosis. These jobs possess *tacit*, rather than *explicit* knowledge. [Tacit]

▶ A greenfield (new) system may have no detailed requirements, because none of the stakeholders have experience in that domain. Users know in broad terms what they want, but not to any useful level of detail. [New]

▶ The analyst may have limited knowledge of the application domain and be trying to make sense of all that is said. This may lead to misunderstanding what is needed. [Novice]

Table 5.1 maps the fact-gathering techniques above onto these problems, to help the analyst develop a strategy for fact-finding in different circumstances.

5.5 Communication issues

Requirements capture and investigation are primary tasks of a systems analyst. While technical knowledge is a valuable asset, their interpersonal and interviewing skills will yield the information that is needed before technical knowledge is applicable.

The analyst may be dealing with users who are enthusiastic about a development or with users who are sceptical about management's motives. Users may be highly articulate or taciturn, but whatever the situation that confronts the analyst, the analyst needs to be able to respond appropriately to gain the users' confidence.

One way of gaining the users' confidence is to be familiar with the business domain and be able to demonstrate that familiarity early in the process. Often, this calls for a significant amount of research before the study begins. While it might be expected that an analyst will belong to the company and be familiar with the domain, that is frequently not the case. In Chapter 2 we saw that many companies outsource their IS/IT development; this includes the analysis phase, so the analysts may be external contractors. Even if they are employees of the company, they may not be familiar with all the workings of all departments and so will be learning about the issues for the first time as a part of the investigation.

One of the most important skills that an analyst needs is the ability to establish a rapport with clients at all levels, from sponsor down to end user. This includes winning the trust of potentially suspicious or hostile users. Interviews provide the natural setting for establishing an empathic relationship.

The analyst must also expect to gain the facts and requirements in a cumulative and iterative way rather than all at once. That means that they will have to conduct more than one interview with each user to clarify and expand information gained earlier. More importantly, they will have to select and employ other fact-finding techniques to suit the particular situation that faces them. Remember the statement at the beginning of this chapter: that a fact is a verified piece of data. The analyst must always assume that there is more verification to carry out and that there is more information available. This 'hidden' information more usually relates to requirements of the future system than to current processes. Management reporting requirements can be particularly vague and present an area where prototyping can shorten the exercise.

If the new system is to be package-based, the analysis will still be performed to this level of detail as the evaluation of competing packages needs to be carried out against elicited requirements.

5.6 Summary

This chapter has examined a number of techniques that can be employed during the analysis phase in order to understand the workings of the current system – if there is one – and the requirements for the new.

Some of the techniques are traditional systems analysis tools, such as interviewing, observation, document analysis and protocol analysis. Others – workshops and prototypes – have come into widespread use more recently and are valuable tools for those situations where the traditional methods are less useful.

In contrast to the early days of computing, most systems that are subject to a fact-finding and requirements gathering exercise are already computerised. This may affect how the exercise is performed, although the underlying objectives of the analysis remain the same.

EXERCISES

The CDD School of Motoring operates across the country, with branches (called schools) in 10 regions. Students sign up for a course of lessons at the end of which they are expected to take their driving test. Hitherto all regions have had their own computer systems networked to their own schools. This has led to problems of incompatible formats and data. The CEO, Charles Drover, has decided to commission a new computer system to give common processing across schools and across regions. He also wants the new system to make it easier for students to transfer to other schools or regions if it suits them. While this can be done now there is no formal mechanism and it is a cumbersome administrative process.

Required:

1   Define an agenda for the meeting with Charles Drover.

2   During subsequent fact requirements gathering at CDD, you collect a form that is used internally to record bookings. While analysing the form, you ask certain questions about it, such as:

  ▶ How many forms are produced in the system? (For example: 10–15 lessons per day)

  ▶ How long the forms need to be stored for; for example one year after the student's last lesson.

  ▶ The format of certain fields on the form; for example, the lesson number is a six-figure number.

  ▶ The sequence the forms are stored in; for example, the form might be kept in date, instructor, student order.

  Explain the relevance of each of these questions to systems development.

3   An analyst on the team has suggested issuing questionnaires, instead of holding one-to-one interviews. Describe what kind of information your team could get from questionnaires. Describe the strengths and pitfalls of using questionnaires for fact-finding, making appropriate references to the CDD scenario.

4   The following is a verbatim discussion between an analyst and an order clerk.

Analyst	Hello, Glenys, I want to concentrate today on looking at the procedures you undertake to process the orders that you receive directly from the customer, is that OK?
Order Clerk	Well, I suppose so, although I am pretty busy right now. How long will it take?
Analyst	About 20 minutes, can you tell me how you handle a typical order?
Order Clerk	What do you mean by a typical order?

Analyst	Well, one that goes through fairly normally, without problems.
Order Clerk	Well, I enter the customer account number into the computer system and it checks the credit worthiness of the customer. I can only proceed if the check is positive.
Analyst	And if it is negative?
Order Clerk	I thought you only wanted to talk about orders that went through without problems?
Analyst	Well, I've changed my mind.
Order Clerk (sighs)	Well, I pass them over to Jean Clerk, the supervisor.
Analyst	What does she do with them?
Order Clerk	I have no idea. Why don't you ask her? Eats them probably.
Analyst	Ha, ha! Anyway, where were we?
Order Clerk	<<phone rings>> Sorry, mate (what's your name?), I just got to take this. *Five minutes conversation while Order Clerk sorts out an order query.* Sorry about that... where were we?
Analyst	We were discussing order processing. So what happens when the system accepts the customer account number?
Order Clerk	I then enter all the products they want, together with quantities. The system checks that we have them in stock and, if they are, the order is priced up and an Order Confirmation is printed. If some goods are out of stock, then the products in stock are included on the Order Confirmation but those we cannot supply are retained in a part-order confirmation situation until we receive enough goods to provide the balance. We then send them on a separate Order Confirmation with a back order reference to the original Order. OK? <<phone rings>> Sorry, I have to deal with this. *Ten minutes conversation while Order Clerk discusses social arrangements* Everything OK?
Analyst	Yes, I think so. I will write this up. I think I can see how it all works. Well, I have used up my twenty minutes, but any last problems?
Order Clerk	Well, except for the system being slow, unreliable and lacking any usable features... no. See you round.

Analyst	Yes, thanks for the information, very useful meeting <<departs>>
Order Clerk	Idiot!

Identify the mistakes made by the analyst in this interview.

5   With reference to the verbatim record of the meeting between the analyst and the Order Clerk:

(i)   Produce a formal meeting report for this interview documenting the (few) points that emerged.

(ii) Prepare a list of questions (and their purpose) which you could ask at the next (better structured) meeting.

6   Another analyst has suggested holding a JAD (Joint Application Design) workshop, and inviting the key stakeholders to take part. He feels that this should save a lot of time in the requirements gathering phase.

(i)   Who should be invited to take part in such workshops?

(ii)   What would be the advantages of holding a workshop?

(iii) What would be the disadvantages of holding a workshop?

References

Hoffer, J. A., George, J. F. and Valacich, J. S. (1996). *Modern Systems Analysis and Design*. New York: Benjamin Cummings.

Kendall, K. E. and Kendall, J. E. (1999). *Systems Analysis and Design*, 4th edn. Upper Saddle River, NJ: Prentice Hall.

Fact modelling techniques

In this chapter you will learn:

▶ How to model the facts gathered during the investigation using:
  - Use cases
  - Process maps
  - Data flow diagrams (DFD)
▶ How prototyping can be used in requirements gathering
▶ How requirements are documented

6.1 Introduction

In many systems development projects there is already an operational business system which may be fully or partially computerised. Many projects are concerned with enhancing or replacing these current operational business systems. In such projects, the workings of the current system need to be modelled, supplemented by further requirements that users expect from the new system. This chapter illustrates three models that can be used to describe the fundamental behaviour of the system: use cases, which come from the work of Ivar Jacobsen, process maps (a simple type of flowchart) and data flow diagrams.

The three models stress different aspects of the system's requirements. Use cases model required behaviour of the system, stressing what the requirements of the user are, but not specifying how these requirements are (or will be) fulfilled. Process maps show how processes map on to the organisational structure and can be used to model the current system or design a solution. Finally, data flow diagrams are significant models for recording the detail of how a current operational system actually works.

There are two important reasons for modelling the current operations:

1. The current system may be carried out inefficiently and with considerable duplication of effort. It is important to understand how such inefficient procedures came into being and to improve them *where appropriate*. Such procedures will also reflect the culture of that part of the organisation and this can raise issues about how change is managed if these are not recognised early in the project.

2. The new system will not be designed in a vacuum but will build upon the functions that already exist. Requirements will include at least most of the current functionality as well as brand new features. Therefore some way of correctly capturing the *logical* as well as the *physical* function is required; that is, a way of identifying *what* is done, as well as *how* it is done.

Prototyping is an important activity in the development cycle. It has been used traditionally in the design and build phases, but it is now increasingly used in the requirements phase. This chapter will show how prototyping can help, both with eliciting requirements and also with the validation process.

The final aspect of fact modelling to capture is the recording of user requirements. At this stage, the focus moves towards the future. However, it is necessary to bear in mind that current functionality is still required, so it is important that such functionality is captured, at an appropriate level, in the requirements document.

6.2 Use cases

One of the features of a system that needs to be modelled is its *behaviour*, that is, how should it respond to inputs from different users outside the system? Inputs will trigger a number of functions that will in turn affect the data held within the system. Use cases are one way of showing, at a high level, what functions the system should perform. They can be subsequently elaborated to show a more detailed view of the interaction between the user and the system. A use case has been defined as (Constantine and Lockwood, 1999):

> ...a typical interaction between a user and a computer system... [that] captures some user visible functions... [and] achieves a discrete goal for the user.

The use case itself will contain a specification of the actions that the system must perform to achieve this discrete goal. It will also include variant and exceptional flows of actions within the use case.

UML speaks of 'Actors' in relation to use cases, an Actor being *any* agent who interacts with the system. Actors may be users, user roles or even a computer system that interacts with the system under consideration. A distinction can be made between *users* and *user roles*.

▶ A *user* is an individual who may have many different interactions with the system. For example, Ted Byers may be an employee who uses a course booking system.

▶ A *user role* is a person with a specific responsibility, which can be captured in a job description. Each relevant responsibility represents a possible interaction and it is that responsibility which is shown as the Actor. A role has been described (Wirfs-Brock *et al.*, 1990) as a relationship between a user and a system and is defined by a set of characteristics, needs, interests, expectations, behaviours and responsibilities. For example, Ted Byers may interact with the system as both a Course Administrator and an Invoice Clerk. What is important is what he expects from the system when he is playing the roles. This is more significant than the individuals who play those roles. We would prefer to develop a system for Invoice Clerks as a whole, not just Ted Byers.

In general, our Actors will be user roles rather than specific users.

6.2.1 Use case diagrams

The use case diagram is a simple model that identifies who requires which function in the system. Figure 6.1 illustrates two simple use cases for part of a training organisation's booking system. These main functions have been identified in early fact-finding interviews with users.
The elements in the use case diagram are:

▶ *Actor*. The matchstick figures represent the user role in the system. If the Actor is another system, it can be shown by a rectangle with an <<actor>> string before the name of the system. Actors are important because they help define the system boundary. They are external to the system and so are outside the system's control. Actors send inputs into the system and receive outputs from it. Time (for example, end of week) may also be considered as an Actor if it triggers certain functions to happen within the system.

▶ *The system boundary*. The rectangle represents the boundary of the system under consideration. It is important to explicitly model this boundary because many projects have been adversely affected by an

Figure 6.1 A simple use case.

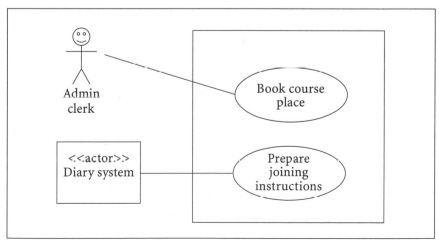

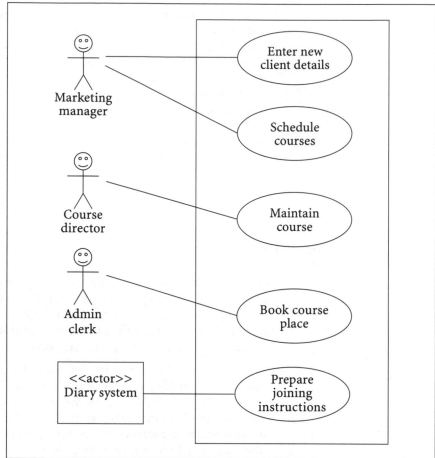

uncertain system boundary, leading to disagreement about the scope of the project.

▶ *Functions.* An oval represents a single function in the system that the Actor needs to perform. These are the *use cases* the system is going to support. The use case is a coherent and complete business function the Actor wants the system to do. The use case is named with a verb followed by a phrase; for example Raise invoice, Send order, Calculate discount, Amend product details.

▶ *Association lines.* These lines show which Actors use which use cases. These are the relationships between the Actors and the use cases.

The diagrams may be drawn as a global view of the entire system, as in Figure 6.2, or as individual diagrams for each business department or user role.

Use cases emerge from employing the fact-finding techniques considered in the previous chapter. In the use case diagram, the use cases are just shown with short descriptive names. The detail of what goes on inside each use case is documented in the use case descriptions or specifications that support each use case.

Figure 6.3 Use case specification.

Goal	The goal is what the use case is invoked to do.
Scope	The scope of the system under discussion.
Level	How high or low level the goal is for the primary actor. Defines whether the use case may be achieved at a single sitting or a multiple sitting. This reflects the difference between a task and a contributory activity.
Actor	Anyone or anything that exhibits behaviour that affects the system. Receivers of outputs from this use case could count as actors, although use case diagrams do not always show these.
Primary actor	The actor who (or which) initiates an interaction with the system to achieve the goal.
Stakeholder	Someone or something with a vested interest in the behaviour of the system.
Preconditions	What must be true before the use case runs; the state of the system before the task is invoked.
Trigger/event	The real world event that invokes this use case.
Success guarantees	What must be true after the use case runs; what has changed as a result of invoking the task.
Main success scenario	(Also known as a 'happy day' scenario) A step-by-step description of a use case scenario in which nothing goes wrong. This is the 'flow' element of the use case. This is a very important part of the use case specification.
Extensions	What can happen differently during the use case; these may be problems encountered (e.g. no customer record found), or non-standard situations (e.g. Delivery must be made only at a certain time, or if at another time, to a different address). Extensions represent the different scenarios that may be enacted within the use case.
Identification	These are numbers in the use case. Each step in the Main success scenario is numbered. Extensions are given extension letters (3a, 3b) and steps within each extension are numbered (3a1, 3a2, 3a3, 3b1, 3b2).
Cross-references	When a use case references another use case, the referenced use case is <u>underlined</u>.

6.2.2 Use case specification

In most instances, use cases are written in a stylised textual format, although they can be expressed using activity diagrams, flowcharts, Structured English or pseudocode. A well-written use case should be easy to read, consisting of sentences written in simple action steps. An extended notation (Cockburn, 2001) is described in Figure 6.3. This notation departs from Jacobsen's initial application of use cases, but makes it appropriate for the analyst modelling the results of a fact-finding exercise.

Figure 6.4 shows a completed example for the Admin Clerk needing to book a course place.

Cockburn suggests that the main scenario and extensions should be written with the structure:

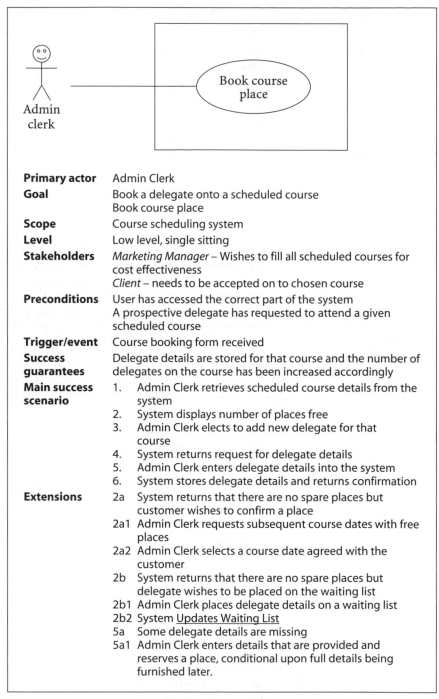

Figure 6.4 Use case specification
– book course place.

Primary actor	Admin Clerk
Goal	Book a delegate onto a scheduled course Book course place
Scope	Course scheduling system
Level	Low level, single sitting
Stakeholders	*Marketing Manager* – Wishes to fill all scheduled courses for cost effectiveness *Client* – needs to be accepted on to chosen course
Preconditions	User has accessed the correct part of the system A prospective delegate has requested to attend a given scheduled course
Trigger/event	Course booking form received
Success guarantees	Delegate details are stored for that course and the number of delegates on the course has been increased accordingly
Main success scenario	1. Admin Clerk retrieves scheduled course details from the system 2. System displays number of places free 3. Admin Clerk elects to add new delegate for that course 4. System returns request for delegate details 5. Admin Clerk enters delegate details into the system 6. System stores delegate details and returns confirmation
Extensions	2a System returns that there are no spare places but customer wishes to confirm a place 2a1 Admin Clerk requests subsequent course dates with free places 2a2 Admin Clerk selects a course date agreed with the customer 2b System returns that there are no spare places but delegate wishes to be placed on the waiting list 2b1 Admin Clerk places delegate details on a waiting list 2b2 System <u>Updates Waiting List</u> 5a Some delegate details are missing 5a1 Admin Clerk enters details that are provided and reserves a place, conditional upon full details being furnished later.

Subject... verb... direct object... prepositional phrase

For example:

Admin Clerk (subject) retrieves (verb) scheduled courses (direct object) from the system (prepositional phrase).

Figure 6.5 Use case diagram – Woodland Transport.

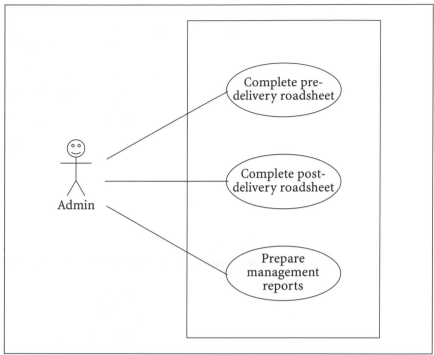

However, in analysis stages the prepositional phrase might be left out, as in certain parts of Figure 6.4. It can be added later when the use case is elaborated.

Figure 6.5 shows a use case diagram for the Admin role at Woodland Transport. Figure 6.6 is the use case specification for completing a roadsheet. This is at a greater level of detail than the previous example, but still has a manageable number of steps in the 'happy day' scenario.

When writing the use cases, it may become clear that certain parts are repeated. For example, the details of customer verification may be included in many different use cases. Instead of repeating the same details, the customer verification may be written in a separate use case and <<included>> in a number of others. For example, Figure 6.7 below shows that the use cases Raise invoice and Check credit both include the specification written for the use case Verify customer. Neither Raise invoice nor Check credit can stand on their own; they have to include Verify customer to run successfully. However, the included use case (Check credit) may stand on its own.

The <<include>> is shown by a broken line with an arrowhead pointing to the included use case.

Furthermore, in specification, it may be clear that one or more of the extensions is more detailed than first thought and hence is overwhelming the original use case specification. In such circumstances a new use case can be defined to <<extend>> the original use case. For example (Figure 6.8), Calculate discount may be required for trade customers. The specification for this may be split off to a separate use case, which is called when appropriate. In this instance the calling use case (Raise

Figure 6.6 Use case specification
– confirm post-delivery roadsheet.

Primary actor	Admin Clerk
Goal	To confirm the details of a post-delivery roadsheet
Scope	Roadsheet
Level	Low level, single sitting
Stakeholders	*Driver* – Their pay depends upon accurate capture of their week's work *Director* – needs accurate information for his reports to the client *Logistics* – needs the data to be correct, in order to plan efficient delivery schedules for client
Preconditions	User has accessed details of correct roadsheet and has driver's copy of roadsheet in front of him/her
Trigger/event	A driver has returned from the shift with a completed roadsheet
Success guarantees	System is updated with details of miles, delays and exceptions, fuel and oil drawn and time taken
Main success scenario	1. Admin Clerk enters start mileage and finish mileage from the driver's copy of the roadsheet 2. Admin Clerk enters fuel drawn from the driver's copy of the roadsheet 3. Admin Clerk enters finish time from the driver's copy of the roadsheet 4. Admin Clerk enters oil drawn from the driver's copy of the roadsheet 5. Admin Clerk enters the trailer number for each leg from the driver's copy of the roadsheet 6. Admin Clerk confirms that all legs completed/not delayed
Extensions	1a Finish mileage is lower than Start mileage 1a1 System rejects roadsheet details and returns to main menu 3a Finish time is earlier than Start time 3a1 System rejects roadsheet details and returns to main menu 6a Some legs were delayed/not completed 6a1 Admin Clerk enters delay information and action details

Figure 6.7

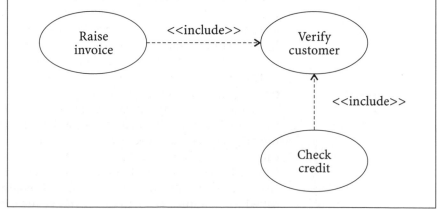

Figure 6.8

invoice) can exist on its own; it may run successfully without having to extend into `Calculate discount`. The <<extend>> is shown as a broken line with an arrowhead pointing to the base use case.

In both <<extend>> and <<include>>, the referenced use cases are underlined in the use case specification. Includes are usually in the main scenario, and extends (for example, `Updates Waiting List`, Figure 6.4) in the extensions.

Include and extend increase the richness of the use case diagram, but they need to be used with discretion, otherwise they complicate rather than simplify the situation. Use cases may only be connected through the <<extend>> and <<include>> constructs. They are not flowcharts.

6.2.2 Use of use cases

▶ *Goals, not processes*
The value of use cases is that they take the attention of both analyst and user away from pure procedure ('How do we do that?') and focus it more on the goal ('What are we trying to do?'). Early use cases might include some elements of current documentation, but as the project progresses, this documentation may be replaced by the generic word 'system', and later by specific references to parts of that system. The use case approach focuses more on the goals of the process, not the documentation that supports the current process.

▶ *First requirements*
Use cases are a powerful tool in capturing current functionality as a requirement of the system without being trapped in a framework that may be inefficient, long-winded and contain redundancy. For example, a use case might be *Create invoice*, without being derailed by the detail of how that process currently works, with coloured multi-copies filed in various places.

▶ *Exceptions and errors*
The extensions offer a means of capturing details about errors and exceptions and how they should be addressed. Many models fail to take these situations into account and hence they are not considered until a later stage in development, perhaps not until programming!

▶ The simplicity of the use case diagram and the narrative format of the specifications make use cases very accessible to business users.

6.3 Process mapping

Process mapping is a useful technique for both descriptive and diagnostic purposes. As with use cases, it can be used to model the current system and to design a solution. The technique derives from Business Process Re-engineering (Hammer and Champey, 1993) and was later expanded by Rummler and Brache (1995). It is similar to an activity diagram in UML, a model that has been called the 'OO flowchart' (Arlow and Neustadt, 2002)

As the name implies, it captures only details about the processes, not about the data that these processes use. However, it presents a rich depiction of component tasks within the process, the functions/user roles which perform those tasks and any relationships between the tasks. They show the number of 'handoffs' in the process; that is, the number of times the work is handed from one person or department to another. As each handoff can cause delay and possibly misunderstanding, it often follows that the more handoffs the less efficient the process. Re-engineering projects often include elements of reducing handoffs or indeed removing them altogether.

6.3.1 Notation

The basic notation for the map is similar to a flowchart, with tasks shown in sequential order. Each actor/department involved is given a segment to itself (a swim lane) with their part of the task shown in that segment.

A task in the process is shown as a simple rectangle, with a brief description of the task inside (Figure 6.9).

If a decision is to be made, it is shown as a diamond shape in the 'swim lane' allocated to the department that makes that decision. The flow between the tasks and from the various decisions, is shown by arrows, as in Figure 6.10.

Looking at our earlier example of booking a course, we might learn from our interview notes that the current procedures are as follows:

> The receptionist receives the delegate call and takes the request for the course booking. The receptionist passes the call to the Admin Clerk, who calls up the course details and booking function. The Admin Clerk interrogates the numbers of places left. If there are none, the delegate will be offered the choice of another course or to be put on a waiting list to be called should a vacancy arise. The Admin Clerk passes details of the delegate to the Marketing director, to be filed for later follow-up calls.

Figure 6.11 illustrates the process map for this narrative procedure.

Figure 6.9

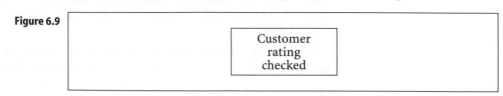

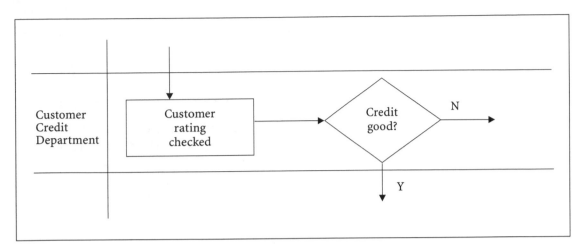

Figure 6.10 A department swim lane.

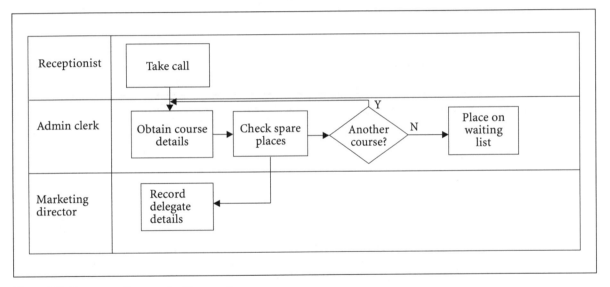

Figure 6.11 Process map for course booking narrative.

This simple example shows what happens in terms of procedure. Like most models, it can form a useful prompt for a follow-up set of questions. For example, one set of questions relates to performance measures for each stage: what are the success indicators? What monitoring is carried out to ensure that they are being met? Who are the customers (both internal and external) for each task?

Figure 6.12 illustrates a possible process map for Woodland Transport. The linking arrows do not show what is being passed between tasks, or what data is stored or accessed, only what tasks are performed, by whom and in what sequence.

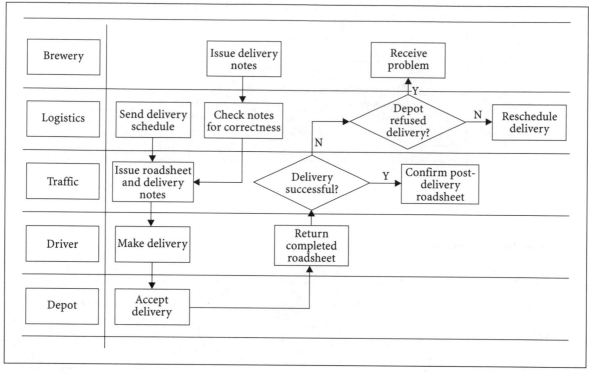

Figure 6.12 Process map – Woodland Transport.

6.3.2 Drawing the process map

The map itself can be constructed in a piecemeal fashion. It can be started with either a large piece of paper or a whiteboard, divided horizontally into appropriate swim lanes. Sticky notes can be used to map out an initial understanding of the tasks and the responsibilities. As the users talk through the task the map can be amended and added to as appropriate.

This talk through of the process map has the advantage of clarifying understanding of the processes and reducing the chance of missing information that the user takes for granted and so may forget to mention. Their participation in the mapping process, using such a large-scale chart with sticky notes, can also encourage user confidence and enthusiasm for the development process as a whole.

As with all of the models, it will take a number of iterations to get it right, but this repetitive aspect is a strength of the techniques, not a weakness, with each iteration enhancing familiarity and understanding.

6.3.3 The process map as a diagnostic tool

The diagnostic strength of the process map comes from:

▶ Acknowledging the handoffs
- What delays are caused?
- What is the scope for miscommunication?

▶ Exploring performance measures
- Where are the measurement points in the process?
- How accurate are the measurements?
- What corrective action is available?

▶ Recognising responsibilities and relationships
- By seeing how many people are involved in the tasks, it is possible to explore working relationships and identify opportunities for rationalisation.
- Roles and responsibilities can be clarified by mapping the processes across functions.

6.4 Data flow diagrams

A common top-down hierarchical approach is provided by data flow diagrams (DFD). This presents different levels of model, from the highest-level overview of the system and its interactions with the world outside, down to detailed description of each of the processes involved in performing the function.

Data flow modelling is used at different stages in the life cycle. The variants are:

▶ Current Physical Model: this describes the working of the current system, with any duplication of data and redundancy of effort.

▶ Current Logical Model: this is an intermediate step between modelling the current system and specifying the required system. The essence of logical modelling is to eliminate all references to physical activities – descriptions of how tasks are currently performed – and to leave a description of *what* the system is achieving, rather than *how* the actors perform their tasks.

▶ Required Model: this is similar to the Current Logical Model, but it is an enhancement. It models all the processes in the new system with the data that will be required to support the new requirements.

This section will describe the notation for the Current Physical Model, as this is the focus of this chapter.

All three models are hierarchic, as described above. All can begin at the highest level, with the Context Diagram, and be decomposed to lower levels as appropriate.

6.4.1 Context Diagram

A Context Diagram (Figure 6.13) is the highest level of DFD. It shows the system under discussion and its interfaces with any external actors.

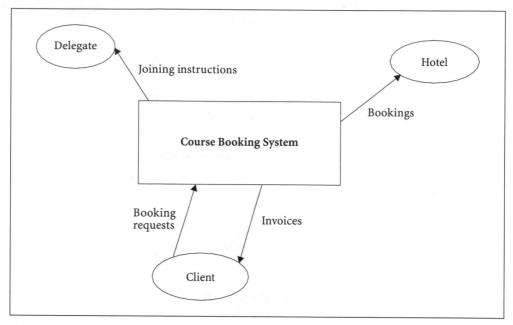

Figure 6.13 Context Diagram – course booking system.

The system under discussion is found in the large box in the centre of the diagram; the oval shapes around the box represent *external entities*, i.e. all those bodies, people, agencies etc. that communicate with it. The actual communication is shown by the arrows, or *data flows*.

The objective of the Context Diagram is to scope the required system. In some instances it adds nothing to the understanding of the requirements and, if that is the case, then the Context Diagram is unnecessary and can be dispensed with. If there is doubt or discussion about the scope then it is a useful tool to clarify just what is outside the scope and what is actually inside the system boundary. A context model could be constructed for the use case perspective, so the two models are very similar at this level.

6.4.2 Level 1 DFD

Whichever type of DFD is drawn (current physical, current logical, required) the notation is virtually the same. As this chapter is concerned with modelling the facts concerning the current system this will be the emphasis given to the notation, but any differences with the other types will be explained.

The notation for a DFD comprises four elements, two of which are to be found in the Context Diagram.

▶ External entity

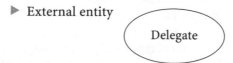

This represents anything that the system must interact with outside the boundary of the system. In the current physical system, it may be a person such as a delegate, a company such as a supplier, a government body such as the Inland Revenue, or a department inside the organisation but which is nevertheless outside the scope of the system.

In the required system, the external entities are the users of the system, who input data or receive the outputs of the system. External entities are analogous to the actors of the use case diagram. External entities may be duplicated on a DFD to improve the presentation of the diagram. Duplicated entities have a diagonal line across the top left-hand corner of the ellipse.

▶ Data store

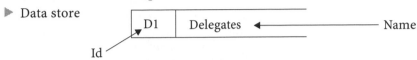

The data store represents anywhere that data comes to rest. In the required system that usually means a database record or a spreadsheet entry. The box at the left-hand end of the store is an identifier. The format for the Id is a letter followed by a number. The letter signifies:

- D – Digital (electronic data)
- M – Manual (e.g. filing cabinet, card index, whiteboard etc.)
- T – Temporary (e.g. in-tray, out-tray, transaction file)

The number is the unique identifier; the letter just describes the type of data store that it is. Data stores may be duplicated on a DFD to improve the presentation of the diagram. Drawing a double line on the left-hand side of the symbol represents this duplication.

Data stores are not explicitly shown on a use case diagram, so this is an important difference.

▶ Process

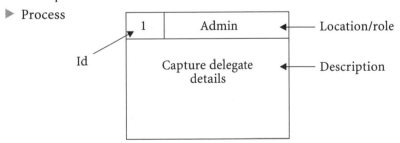

The process represents some form of manipulation or accessing of data. As the name implies, a process is an operation. The format is a rectangle, divided into three parts:

- The top left-hand box is a numeric identifier. It is purely for reference and does not imply sequence.
- The stripe adjacent to the identifier is *either* the location where the process is carried out *or* the role of the person who performs it. This is especially significant in modelling the current physical system. In

113

the required system model, the stripe will be left blank as it is the system itself that performs the tasks. The entry that would have been in the stripe is now the external entity that triggers the process.

- The description box is a terse and clear instruction of what the process is to do. The format is {imperative verb + object}. An essay or noun phrase is not sufficient.

Processes are similar to the use cases of the use case diagram.

▶ Data flow   Joining instructions ⟶

Data flows represent any information passed across the system boundary or between any two components of the diagram. It comprises an arrow, with (usually) the name of the data. It is *not* a process so the label will not be a verb. In the current physical system the flows may be documents being passed through the system. In the required system the data flows will be data inputs and outputs or reads and writes of data from data stores.

- A flow pointing *into* a data store represents some form of update, whether creation of a new record, modification of an existing record or deletion of a record.

- A flow pointing *away from* a data store represents a read-only operation, where data is referenced but not amended at all.

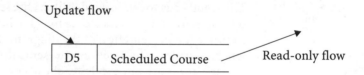

There are a number of rules concerning data flows:

- Data cannot flow between two data stores: it must go via a process.
- Data flows cannot link a data store with an external entity: they must go via a process.
- Every process must have *at least* one input flow as a trigger and *at least* one output flow. Processes may not generate data from nowhere, nor can they swallow data; all data that is output from a process must be related to the data that flows in.

These four components are all that make up a DFD. The art lies in combining them to form an accurate model of the system under discussion. Whereas many diagrams explore the system function by function the DFD takes in the whole of the system showing how all of the data is accessed and maintained. In this respect it is a more holistic approach, but is more complicated!

To illustrate the building up of a DFD, we shall look at the example of a music agency. There are three paragraphs that together describe a high-level overview of the system. After each paragraph the extract from the DFD that relates to it is drawn. The example is for a current physical system.

Figure 6.14 Initial DFD.

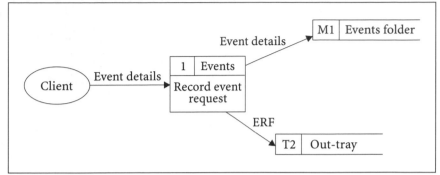

1. A Client sends a request for performers at an event to the Agency. The Events department open an Events Folder putting in the original details. They raise an Event Request Form and place it in the Out-tray to be collected and processed later.

   In this example (Figure 6.14), although the text implies that there are two processes it is acceptable, and more importantly, understandable, to combine them into one. The label in the process and the flows coming from it make it clear what is being done.

2. Someone from the Performers Department collects the ERFs from the Out-tray and looks through the Performers File for a suitable – and available – performer. They contact the performer with details of the event and a request to take part. When the performer accepts the event, the date and venue are put against their name in the file and the ERF updated with the performer's name. The ERF is put into another Out-tray to be collected later.

   Here the diagram (Figure 6.15) is expanded to show the new facts that have been discovered. The new information is built on the old rather than forming a new diagram. Again, it can be summarised in one process, but the number of flows in and out suggest that there is more happening in the process than can be easily understood from this diagram alone. This will be developed later in Chapter 8.

   Note the flow from process 2 to data store T2. This is because when the ERFs in the out-tray are processed the store itself, the out-tray, is being altered by the document's removal. That is why the update flow is shown. The process is also reading the document in order to carry out its task, so it also needs the read data flow.

3. A member of the Contracts Department collects the ERFs and prepares standard contracts using the Events Folder for the event details and sends blank contracts to both Client and Performer. The ERF is filed in the Events Folder.

   This final diagram (Figure 6.16) is a Level 1 DFD. It identifies the functionality that is required and also the data needed to support it.

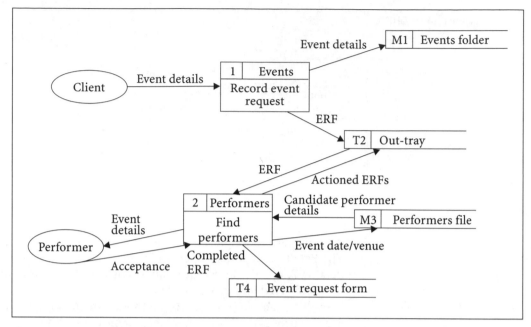

Figure 6.15 Enhanced DFD.

6.4.3 Level 2 DFD

Much of the Level 1 DFD may be self-explanatory. However, for the sake of ease of drawing some processes may be grouped together as was shown in process 2 in Figures 6.15 and 6.16. While the subject of the process is related the component tasks may be more complex as shown by the number of flows in and out of it. As a rule of thumb, if there are more than four or five input and output flows the process needs to be expanded. This is done by *decomposing to a lower level*.

Decomposition of a process simply means drawing another DFD, with the Level 1 process as the scope.

To illustrate this we will look more closely at what happens in process 2 of the Music Agency system. Again this represents a current physical description but the same principles apply to a required system.

On speaking again to the user from the Performers Department we learn the following facts:

> We keep the Performers' details in a filing cabinet, called the 'Performers File'. When we look for a performer, we search the file for the class of performer first, such as jazz band, tenor or pianist, and then look through the candidates for availability.

> When we find a candidate, we phone them. Often, we find we have to leave them a message – most of them tend to be busy or out when we call. If that does happen, then the ERF is put into a plastic folder with others that are waiting for a reply and left on top of the desk.

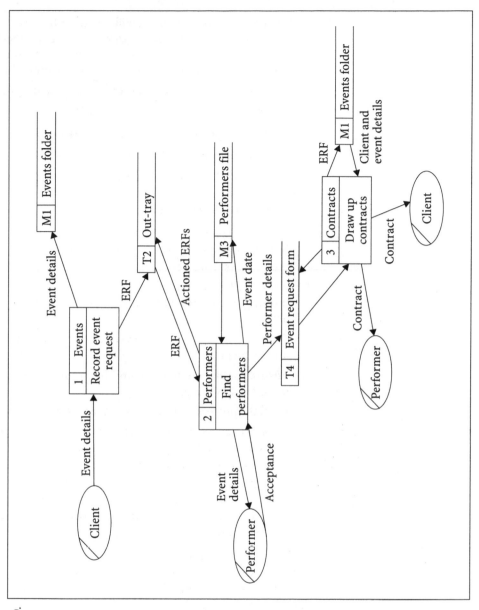

Figure 6.16 Finalised DFD.

117

When they get back to us, it will be either to agree or decline. If they agree, then we update their own file as we explained earlier and then amend the ERF. If they refuse, we have to go through the process over again with another prospective performer who fits the bill.

The important information that this gives us is that the process in fact has *two* triggers:

▶ When the Performers' Department clerk empties the tray T1

▶ When the performer returns the call to accept or refuse the work offer

Currently the DFD does not show that there are two triggers, so this needs to be shown more explicitly.

The steps for decomposing a DFD are as follows:

1. Draw the boundary of the Level 2 process. This comprises the process box from Level 1. In the location stripe at the top, write the name of the process from Level 1.

2. Draw the trigger that initiates the Level 1 process (in this case the purging of T1). Take the flow across the boundary and draw the lower level process that receives it.

3. Draw the DFD *inside* the new boundary that reflects all the tasks that are performed.

4. Ensure that all the flows to and from the Level 1 process are mapped on to the Level 2 process.

5. Label the process and data store Ids according to the following guidelines:

    - Each process should be referenced back to its 'parent' process. A decimal numbering system is used. Thus, process 2 is decomposed to process 2.1, 2.2 and so on.

    - Each data store should be referenced back to its 'parent' data store in a similar manner although the symbol '/' is used rather than the decimal notation. Thus, in process 2 there may be data stores D2/1, D2/2 etc.

Figure 6.17 illustrates the Level 2 diagram for process 2 in the Music Agency taking into account the extra information.

There is one difference between this Level 2 process and the original Level 1 process: the label on the flow from Performer into Process 2 (2.3). Originally, the interviewee led the analyst to believe that the flow was an *acceptance* of the offer. The subsequent interview modified that view to identifying it as a *reply* instead. The label on the Level 1 process should now be modified so that all levels are completely consistent.

It is theoretically possible to decompose DFDs to level 3 and level 4. It is rare to go this far down though and, if it happens, it is possible that too many processes at Level 1 have been combined. Rules of thumb to help decide whether or not to decompose further are:

▶ How precise is the verb in the process? Avoid woolly words like 'Process X' or 'Update y'. If a clear unambiguous verb cannot be found perhaps the process is still too complex.

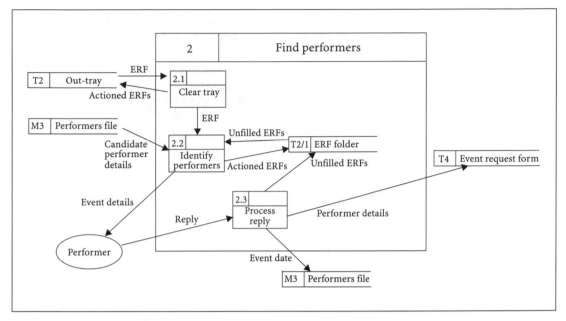

Figure 6.17 Example of a decomposed process.

▶ How many flows go into and out of the process? If more than four perhaps too much is happening inside the process.

When each process is decomposed to what seems its *elementary* level it is marked with a small asterisk in the bottom right corner to denote that it is an *elementary* process. This will not be decomposed further in any diagram.

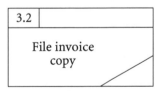

Data flow diagrams are important where a detailed understanding of the current system is essential. However, where there is no significant current system, or the probable solution is likely to be so different from the current operation, DFDs of the current system may be inappropriate and require a depth of analysis that cannot be justified.

6.5 Prototyping

As explained in Chapter 5, prototyping can be used as an aid to confirm or clarify requirements that cannot, for good reasons, always be made clear at an interview.

Prototyping can be achieved by the use of quick build software tools to simulate an interface or in a simpler, cheaper way with flipchart, pens and sticky notes.

A productive use of prototyping can be to follow activities such as use cases or process maps with suggestions as to how the business goals can be given information support. By providing the users with a mock-up of how their part of the system might look and work the analyst can trigger further discussion about what is needed and what alternative approaches could be used to meet the requirements. Such practice also frequently triggers additional requirements, which can be a double-edged sword. If the requirement is genuine, but was overlooked in the original conversations, it is a positive gain. However, some users experience an exhilarating burst of creativity when they first see a prototype model and begin to stipulate all manner of requirements that are inappropriate and not cost-effective to implement. This is a manifestation of the phenomenon known as 'requirements creep' and must be guarded against in order to preserve project deadlines and budgets.

Prototyping is by its nature an iterative task, and each time a demonstration is presented and discussed, a further refinement of the prototype is likely to be carried out. At this stage, however, we are looking at capturing and specifying requirements, not designing the system, so there should not be many iterations at this point in the process.

The main value of using prototyping at this stage is that it encourages the user to think through a related set of requirements and their implications. The agreed prototype should be documented, agreed requirements resulting from it should be recorded and the prototype kept until it is needed in later development stages.

6.6 Requirements catalogue

As well as modelling the goals and processes of the current system, it is important to capture the requirements as well. This section describes a template for user requirements. Together, all of the entries built up using this template comprise a *requirements catalogue*.

The template represents all of the information necessary to trace a requirement from initial request to final sign-off after testing. There are a number of software tools designed to support a requirements catalogue; for example, a relational database could be used with the fields representing the template entries. There are more specialised requirements tools to construct scenario models and help with the traceability of each requirement.

The information to be captured in the template will be:

▶ Requirement Id: this is a unique identifier for each requirement. Most systems have a larger number of detailed requirements than is initially expected. A unique Id will make them both easier to reference and easier to store on a requirements CASE tool.

▶ Requirement Name: this will be a simple statement, as concise as possible, about *what* the system is to do ('Record new customer').

▶ Source: the person who initially raises the requirement (or the source document that specifies it).

▶ Owner: the user who will take responsibility for the requirement and agree the acceptance criteria. This may be the source or it may be the department manager. With critical requirements it is common for the project sponsor to take the role of owner.

▶ Priority: not all requirements will be met. Some will be critical to the success of the project: these are *mandatory* and must be included. Others are important and add value to the system; others are wishes, which may help an individual user, but not necessarily add much value to the overall system. In many cases these would incur more time and cost to deliver than the project resources will allow. Some requirements will not be considered for inclusion. The acronym MoSCoW summarises these:

  – Must do

  – Should do

  – Could so

  – Won't do (at least, not this time)

▶ Functional requirements: this is a straightforward description of what the requirement will achieve. This could be a simple 'The system will capture customer details from the input form'.

▶ Non-functional requirements: the usability requirements, response times, constraints on privacy, security, availability etc. These may not be completed at the beginning of the requirements gathering process but must be captured by the end of the elaboration phase. If there are special security and privacy restrictions on a requirement these may be captured, but response times, availability and so on will be negotiated later. Usability requirements are discussed more fully in Chapter 11. Non-functional requirements such as response times should be given a target performance measure (e.g. 'system must return data within 3 seconds'), but an acceptable tolerance should be noted as well. There is a danger that without such leeway the design is so constrained by unreasonable targets that it becomes too expensive.

▶ Rationale: the requirement must have a business rationale. It may be that it is a core business activity, or it may increase throughput of transactions or allow management timely access to data.

▶ Related requirements: few requirements will be standalone, neither affecting nor being affected by any other requirements. Relationships between all requirements must be captured here so that if changes are proposed it is easier to analyse the impact on the whole system of these changes. This entry will be built up slowly as requirements are analysed during the process.

▶ Suggested solution: this is not likely to be completed until the later stages of the elaboration or indeed until the construction phase when the development team propose options for solutions. A requirement may be met in a number of different ways. This entry is to record the *possible* solutions that are being considered. Again, this will not be completed during the fact-modelling stage.

▶ Resolution: the agreed solution to the delivery of this requirement. If the requirement has been classified as 'W' the Resolution entry will read: 'Not to be met'.

▶ Change history: the requirement will be subject to a number of changes, rewording, reprioritising and decisions before it is finally signed off. This entry allows a version control mechanism to ensure that what is finally implemented can be traced back to the original requirement and that any changes can be similarly traced and audited.

Figure 6.18 shows a suggested requirements catalogue form for Woodland Transport.

Figure 6.18 Requirements catalogue

Requirements Catalogue		**Date:** *01 June 2003*
Req. Id: 15 **Priority:** M	**Name:** *Confirm Roadsheet*	
Source: *Kim Watson (Head of Traffic)*	**Owner:** *Kim Watson (Head of Traffic)*	

Functional description:

The system must record details of the Roadsheet once it has been returned by the Driver. The Traffic Clerk will enter details of the completed Roadsheet for the system to maintain data on deliveries, driver hours, tractor, mileage, fuel drawn and trailers used.

Non-functional description:

Description	Target value	Acceptable range
Time to confirm successful entry	*3 seconds*	*5 seconds*
Access	*Traffic office staff*	*N/A*

Rationale

This is a key part of the activity. Capturing this data enables management to monitor tractor usage, staff hours, fuel consumption of the tractors, trailer location.

Related requirements

None

Suggested solutions

Resolution

Change history

Amended 15 June 2003, as result of Change Request 0004

6.7 Conclusion

This chapter has described four approaches to documenting the findings of the fact-finding phase of the development. Three approaches to modelling the processes and goals have been described: use cases, process maps and data flow diagrams. All three models are useful in different circumstances and it is a matter of choosing the right tool for the job. Although data flow diagrams are currently out of favour (they are not in the UML), their emphasis on document flow and data stores in the wider perspective of the system may be useful in certain applications. The place of prototyping has been reiterated and the last element, documenting the requirements that have been elicited, has also been considered. A software package may be used for storing these requirements.

EXERCISES

The Inter-Regional Athletics Association

The Inter-Regional Athletics Association (IRAA) is a body that organises athletics meetings across the country. The following details come from preliminary interviews with representatives of Competitions, Registration and Venues departments.

Every season the Registrations department of IRAA receives requests for registration forms from athletes who wish to join. The athletes are sent blank forms which they complete and return. Once the forms have been sent back the athlete's details are kept in the Members File, kept by Registrations.

The Competitions department is responsible for compiling the season's calendar of meetings. For this they need to have details of which venues are available and what facilities they offer for (for example) pole vaults or steeplechase tracks. The Venues department has details of these facilities on file but the venues themselves have to notify the Competitions department of their availability on particular dates. Before the calendars are completed the venues send in confirmation that they can host a meeting on the dates selected for them. The calendar is then sent out to the venues, athletics clubs and the members.

The Venues department is responsible for maintaining information about each venue and its facilities on their Stadiums File.

When they have received the calendars athletes send in entry forms for the particular events they wish to take part in at specific meetings. (An Event consists of a code (e.g. M100m) and a title (Men's 100 metres)). When this entry form is received details are checked against the calendar and against the member file. The athlete is then added to a competitor's list which is kept for each meeting. Each Meeting will comprise a number of Events, while each Event will be competed for at a number of Meetings. A Timekeeper is appointed for each Meeting. Competitions maintain a list of all timekeepers and officials around the country who can officiate at meetings.

When all of the entries for the meetings are completed the Competitions department prepares a programme for each meeting; this lists which events are to be competed for, who is taking part in each event, and who is officiating as Timekeeper. The Timekeeper may not be identified until it is time to prepare the programmes. When the programmes are complete they are sent to a printer for publication.

One of the Timekeeper's responsibilities is to send back a report on the meeting. If any of the athletes are accused of disreputable behaviour, or cheating, the Competitions department will consider suspending their membership.

1 Draw a use case diagram representing the following use cases: Create New Member, Prepare Calendar, Schedule Meeting, Prepare Programme.

2 Draw a Level 1 data flow diagram to show IRAA's procedures.

3 Draw a process map to show how a meeting programme is compiled. The process begins with the publication of the calendar, includes the applications by athletes to compete and the appointment of the timekeeper.

Woodland Transport

The requirement to pay drivers and to produce certain pay reports at Woodland Transport has been recognised in the case study introduction (Chapter 1). The Administration Department is responsible for producing the Driver Pay Hours Report and the Driver Hours Worked Report. Two further functions are required to complete the information required to output the correct information. These are **Maintain Pay Rules** and **Enter Absence Details**.

Required:

4 Draw a use case diagram for the requirements of the Administration Department.

5 Produce a use case specification for the information required for the Administration Department to Maintain Pay Rules.

Change Request workflow system

The Information Technology department requires a Change Request workflow system that monitors a request for work from initial request through to implementation. Requests for system changes have to be made by a designated Sponsor. The type of change requested might be a Defect Notification, Functional Change or Perfective Maintenance. The system maintains a list of authorised Sponsors.

When requesting a system change the Sponsor has to enter the following information into the system:

Data item	Relevant type of change
Date of request	All change requests. The system automatically allocates the system date in this field. This can be overtyped by the sponsor.
Time of the request	All change requests. The system automatically allocates the system time in this field. This cannot be overtyped by the sponsor.
Sponsor name	All change requests. This is a pull-down list of authorised sponsors.
System name	All change requests.
Error message	Defect Notification only
Date of error	Defect Notification only
Time of error	Defect Notification only
User Id	Defect Notification only
Severity of error	Defect Notification only. Defects are classified on a scale of 1–5, where 1 is the most urgent.
Specification of requirement	Functional Change only
Business justification	Functional Change only
Priority	Functional Change only. Functional Changes are classified on a scale of 1–5, where 1 is the most urgent.
Aspect of the system	Perfective maintenance only
Perfective suggestion	Perfective maintenance only

Once the Sponsor has entered the change request into the system, the status of the change request is set to Notified and a unique Job Number is generated by the system and displayed on the screen.

All notified change requests are allocated by the system to a Project Manager who is responsible for investigating the request and estimating how long it will take to implement. The system maintains a list of project managers authorised to deal with change requests and one of the project managers enters the estimate into the system. If the change request is for a defect and the project manager agrees this defect, then the change is immediately authorised for development. However, if the request is for Functional Changes or Perfective Maintenance, then the Sponsor is responsible for authorising the change on the system once the Sponsor has seen and agreed the estimate for the work. All unauthorised change requests remain on the system for one year until they are deleted. The date of estimate and date of authorisation/unauthorisation are recorded against the change request. The status of the change is also updated to estimated, authorised or unauthorised, as appropriate. It is not possible for a change to be authorised for development until it has been estimated.

Authorised changes are assigned by a project manager to a programmer or programmer team for development. The system maintains a list of programmers and programming teams authorised to undertake changes to systems. The status of the change is defined as 'In progress' until the programmer has completed the programming and unit tested the change. The programmer then notifies the system that the change is complete. The change request is then defined as completed and is available for system and regression testing. Changes cannot be tested until their status is completed. Once system testing has been completed, the system tester indicates that the change is tested and this information is entered into the system. This change is now available for implementation in the next release. Once the system is tested it is released into the live environment by the Implementation Team, who notify the system that the change is now implemented. Only tested changes are available for implementation.

During the process, the amount of time spent on the change is recorded on the system. The number of hours estimating, developing, testing and implementing the change are recorded and compared with the original estimate.

6   Develop a use case diagram for the change request workflow system.

7   Develop a use case specification diagram for the use case(s) concerned with the initial notification of the change request into the system.

References

Arlow, J. and Neustadt, I. (2002). *UML and the Unified Process*. Reading, MA: Addison-Wesley.

Cockburn, A. (2001). *Writing Effective Use Cases*. Reading, MA: Addison-Wesley.

Constantine, L. and Lockwood, L. (1999). *Software for Use*. Reading, MA: Addison-Wesley.

Hammer, M. and Champey, J. (1994). *Reengineering the Corporation*. London: Nicholas Brealey.

Jacobson, I., Christerson, M. Jonsson, P. and Övergaard, G. (1992). *Object-Oriented Software Engineering: A Use Case driven Approach*. Reading, MA: Addison-Wesley.

Rummler, G. A. and Brache, A. P. (1995). *Improving Performance: How to Manage the White Space on the Organizational Chart*, 2nd edn. San Francisco: Jossey Bass.

Wirfs-Brock, R., Wilkerson, B. and Weiner, L. (1990). *Designing Object-Oriented Software*. Englewood Cliffs, NJ: Prentice Hall.

Class and data models

In this chapter you will learn:

▶ What is meant by a class model

▶ The component symbols of a class model

▶ UML notation for a class model

▶ How to draw a class model for the system under investigation

▶ An alternative notation for modelling static data

▶ The universal relation approach to normalisation

7.1 Introduction

Most systems are commissioned to handle objects or things. For example,

▶ Land flight 001 safely at Birmingham Airport

▶ Pay employee Stan Jackson at the end of the month

▶ Print off the report I have just written for the Managing Director

This chapter looks at a model for describing the underlying structure of these objects or things. It is called the class model. The chapter concludes with an alternative, but more restrictive, model for data rather than objects: the Entity Relationship Model.

7.2 Class models

A class model is a graphical description of the *object classes* in a system and how they are associated with each other. In a business system, the class model will capture details about the particular things that the business needs to operate, such as Customers, Invoices and Payments. In a real-time system, such as a process control system, the model will show the components of that system, such as Monitors, Switches and Signals. Interface design is well suited to object modelling; Windows, Boxes,

Lines, Buttons, Keys and Pointers could all be represented as object classes in an appropriate model.

The scope of this text is confined to business information systems so that is what the rest of this chapter will address. However, object and class modelling can be applied to a wide range of applications and this is one of its attractions.

7.2.1 Object

An object is a 'thing' that has a place inside the boundary under consideration. It is something that is the subject of data and which performs or undergoes some form of operation. It is also something that can be interacted with, either by a user of the system or by another object or device in the system. A printer, for example, could be an object.

The following might be typical objects in a business system:

▶ Order number 1257
▶ The Assist Partnership
▶ Martin Pearson
▶ Larry the Lamb

To interact with an object means that it can be sent a *message* and it responds in a particular way, depending upon its *state*. For example, a message might be sent to *fulfil* order number 1257.

Examples of objects in Woodland Transport might be:

▶ Tractor No. 123
▶ Roadsheet No. 900
▶ Stan Billford

A message might be sent to *service* tractor number 123.

Some issues of identifying objects are illustrated in the following example. The items Registration Number, Colour, Number of Doors, Car, Engine Size, Driver and Mileage, may need to be recorded in a system. Which of these items represent objects and which represent the states of an object?

Of these, only Car probably represents a thing that can be interacted with. It is described by the items Engine Size, Number of Doors etc., but these cannot themselves be interacted with. Some of these items will have persistent values, such as Colour or Number of Doors, while others will have dynamic values, such as Mileage and Driver. Dynamic elements indicate the state of the object.

It helps if every object can be uniquely identified, so Registration Number would probably provide that for a Car.

Here is how the FordFocus object might be represented.

FordFocus:
Registration Number = T456 ARC
Engine Size = 1600 cc
Number of doors = 5
Colour = silver
Mileage = 23,012
Driver = Susan Slack

7.2.2 Class

Although we might be interested in particular objects and messages sent to those objects, the technique becomes more powerful when we consider classes. Every object is an instance of a class. A class (or object class) is a description of all the objects that belong to it. Thus, tractor no. 123 is an object that fits the class Tractor. Tractor will contain **attributes** such as registration number, date of last service, horsepower, date last fuelled and miles driven. The class definition will also include **operations** that the tractor is subject to. These might include refuel, increment mileage and record service. All tractors in the system will be expected to contain these attributes and be subject to the same operations. A class, therefore, is a template for objects of the same type; objects are individual instances of a class. It is important to recognise this distinction.

Object	Class
Order Number 1257	Order
The Assist Partnership	Company
Martin Pearson	Employee
Larry the Lamb	FictionalCharacter
Tractor No. 123	Tractor
Roadsheet No. 900	RoadSheet
Stan Billford	Driver

A class can represent objects that are tangible, such as Car, Person or StockItem, or conceptual, such as an InsuranceClass or RiskCategory. Alternatively, it could represent an event such as an Accident or a Claim. Finally, it might be a role, such as Customer and Claimant. What marks instances of these classes out as objects is that they contain identity, state and behaviour. If something does not contain these three elements, it is probably not an object.

An object is said to 'hide data', by encapsulating it with the operations that act upon it (Figure 7.1). Only the object itself knows what data it

Figure 7.1 An object.

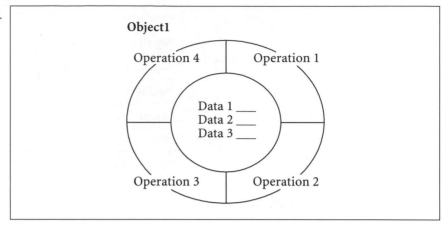

holds and how. Any other part of the system that needs to access or modify the data has no need to understand how it is structured; it just sends a message and the receiving object responds appropriately.

When Object1 is required to respond to an event or an enquiry entered into the system it may need to send a message to Object2 asking for information to help fulfil that event or enquiry, as in Figure 7.2.

The message might be to amend the value of a customer's account, or to return the quantity in stock of a part. The message will not dictate *how* the object is to perform the operation, only requesting that it does. In the example given above, Object1 asks Object2 the stock level of widgets. It does not need to know how Object2 finds out or calculates this information, it only needs to know that Object2 provides this service. This shows objects *collaborating* to perform a service required by the system. This will be further demonstrated in the next chapter when interaction diagrams are discussed.

As we have already mentioned, objects that share the structure or template are collected together and classified into *classes*.

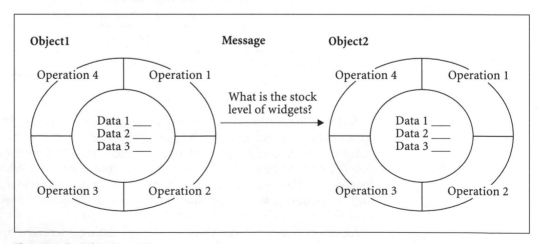

Figure 7.2 Two objects interacting.

Identifying classes is not a trivial task and is best performed iteratively. However, classes might be suggested by:

▶ Identifying all the data items in the system and grouping them into potential classes. Data items may be identified from the documents used and the reports generated by the current operational system. Such documents may suggest related groups of data (for example, Invoice, Credit Note, Statements), although care must be taken to concentrate on the logical grouping of data rather than their physical manifestation. This will certainly take a number of trial and error passes but will yield a good first selection of classes with potential attributes.

▶ Identifying the organisational functions and breaking them down into classes. This involves looking at individual functions, such as Sales, HR and Procurement and studying what they do. For each of their activities, we ask, 'What do they need to perform this? What are they using, creating, referencing?'. This may again suggest a first set of classes.

▶ Noun searching. This is a common way of finding classes, but it is important to realise that not all nouns will end up as classes because some nouns are vague or ambiguous. Imprecise nouns must be investigated further to see if they really are classes. A library, for example, may talk about Titles (identified by the ISBN and recorded in the catalogue), Copies of the titles (the physical copy which is placed on the shelves and loaned out to members) and also Books. Intuitively, Book might be expected to be a class, but does Book refer to Copy or to Title? Out of the three terms one will *not* be a class as it just duplicates one of the others.

If the noun is actually an attribute (such as colour in the car example), clearly it will not also be a class. The way to test this is to further ask if the noun in question has any behaviour of its own which needs to be modelled. If the answer is no, then the noun represents just an attribute and the next task is to identify which class it belongs to.

Another point to remember when identifying the classes is that all of the classes together represent the system (what will eventually become the computer system). There will not be a class called Woodland Transport System, because the Woodland Transport System itself comprises all of the classes that are being discovered and modelled.

What distinguishes objects and classes from other traditional modelling techniques is that the object combines the data it contains and the functions that act upon it (the operations), as shown in Figure 7.1. Traditional and structured approaches model data and function separately, in discrete models, and this will be illustrated in Chapters 8 and 9.

In UML classes are represented simply as rectangular boxes with three partitions, as in Figure 7.3. The name of the class is given in the top partition and is usually a noun. The first letter is capitalised, for example; Driver, Order, Tractor and Trailer. If the name has more than one

Figure 7.3 An example class.

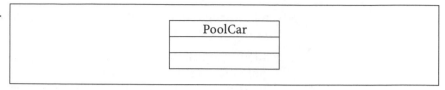

word then each word is joined and capitalised in the class name, for example: OrderLine, PoolCar and PartQuestionAnswer.

Once the classes are initially identified they may be elaborated by capturing the attributes and operations of the class.

7.2.3 Attributes

An attribute is the name given to the data items that are contained within the class. In Woodland Transport the class Driver might be expected to include name, address, telephone number, National Insurance number and type. These represent the first set of attributes that need to be recorded.

To find the attributes for Driver the analyst must study the documents used in the current system to find out what Woodland Transport already knows about its drivers. This will be supplemented with interviews with the users concerned with this aspect of the system. Enacting scenarios with the users (Chapter 8) helps identify other attributes that were missed on the first passes. As these are uncovered, they can be added to the model.

The attributes for PoolCar are shown in Figure 7.4. These are usually shown in lower case with constituent parts shown with a capital letter. The first letter of the attribute name is not capitalised; for example: driver, dateLastServiced and regNo.

The minus sign (-) next to the attributes shows that they are *private* to the class. They are hidden from other classes in the system. Classes sending messages to the class PoolCar do not know what attributes it contains. This is the principle of encapsulation or data hiding. Classes do not know what private data items are held by other classes in the system under consideration.

Figure 7.4 Class and attributes.

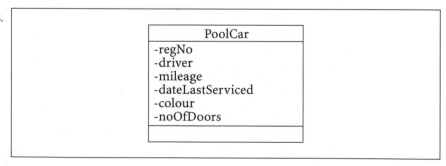

7.2.4 Operations

When classes are first identified the analyst will be more concerned with the persistent data (attributes) associated with that class, not with the functionality that acts upon it. However, should the functionality change over time the class should still remain valid – and easily maintained to reflect any changes in requirements. A convenient way of doing this is to hold details of these functions or *operations* within the class itself. Rather than naming high-level functions that access and maintain data across the system, operations are identified for which the class itself is responsible. These operations are invoked by *messages* being sent to the class by other classes. It is convenient to name the operation in the class with the same name as the message. The detailed content of the operation (that is, what the class will do when that operation is invoked) will be defined in the *method* associated with the operation and is usually left to the later stages of the development process.

Thus, in the class PoolCar it may be possible to identify a number of operations that will be invoked during the car's lifetime. These will mostly relate to dynamic attributes, such as mileage and driver. For example, when the car returns from a journey the class Trip (where journey details are stored) may send the message amendMileage() to PoolCar. PoolCar has a specified operation amendMileage() which has an associated method for updating the mileage attribute for the PoolCar in question. This method may be very simple; for example, 'replace mileage with new mileage'. Messages and operations are named using the same conventions as attributes.

Further exploration may reveal that the system needs to keep a service history for the car, so an operation updateService() may be identified. Operation names are drawn with paired brackets – () – to show that they may receive parameters.

These two operations, amendMileage() and updateService() are required to maintain the data attributes in the class. Further operations will become clear when the interaction diagrams are constructed (Chapter 9). At the earlier stages of analysis it is unlikely that the class model will include many operations. Figure 7.5 shows a create operation (which all classes must possess) together with the two examples already considered.

The plus signs (+) shows that these operations are *public* and so accessible to the rest of the system. This is essential for most operations, as other classes must know what services each class provides.

7.2.5 Associations

The class model can now be extended to show how classes are related to each other. This relationship, or *association*, indicates that there is a necessary connection between two classes to provide some requirement. For instance, a Customer class must have an association with an Order class to allow orders for specific customers to be listed. The association is shown in Figure 7.6.

Figure 7.5 Class, attributes and operations.

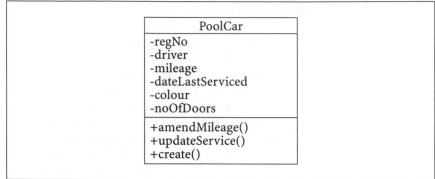

Figure 7.6 Customer–Order association.

Figure 7.7 Trip–PoolCar association.

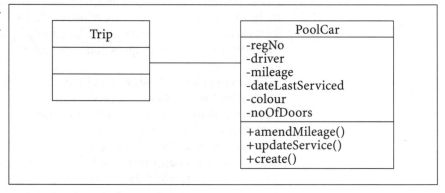

It has already been noted that classes communicate through *messages*. In the example given in the previous section, Trip sent a message to PoolCar. These messages move along the association lines defined in the class model. If there is no association between the classes then the two classes cannot communicate directly.

The association line can be named in order to clarify the nature of the business relationship but if it is self-evident (as in this example), there is no value added by doing this. Whereas the class is characterised by a noun, the association is characterised by a verb. Thus, a Customer places an Order. A Trip is made by a PoolCar (Figure 7.7).

Further elaboration of the model may be made by representing the business rule that a customer may place more than one order, but each order can only be placed by a single customer. This introduces the concept of *multiplicity*.

The 1 at the Customer end shows that there will only ever be a single occurrence of a Customer object associated with any given Order object. The asterisk at the other end shows that there is no limit to the number of Order objects associated with any given Customer.

The notion of multiplicity can be extended to show the minimum and maximum values in the association.

The following examples show the range and notation of multiplicities available:

▶ Exactly one (1..1)

The 1..1 association below shows that DeliveryNote must be associated with Leg. It is a mandatory association. If an instance of DeliveryNote is created it must be linked to exactly one instance of Leg.

▶ Many (0 or more)

The 0..* association below shows that a Driver may be associated with 0, 1 or many RoadSheets. The zero implies that the association is optional. An instance of Driver may exist without any associated RoadSheets.

▶ Optional (0 or more)

The Leg to Delivery Note association shown above has now been elaborated to show that a Leg instance has an optional association with DeliveryNote.

▶ One or more (1..*)

In the next example, the class RoadSheet is in a mandatory association with Leg. There must be at least one instance of Leg for each instance of RoadSheet.

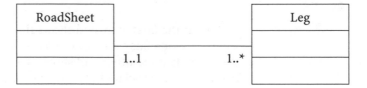

▶ Number specified

In some circumstances the actual minimum and maximum values may be defined, as in this example where a Leg has a minimum of 1 Location (the start point) and a maximum of 2 (the start point and the destination).

The multiplicity symbol needs to be shown at each end of the association. The first pass at the Woodland Class Model, including the multiplicity symbols, is shown in Figure 7.8.

The associations between RoadSheet and Tractor, Tractor and Driver, and Trailer and Leg raise questions about the nature of the

Figure 7.8 Woodland Transport – initial class model.

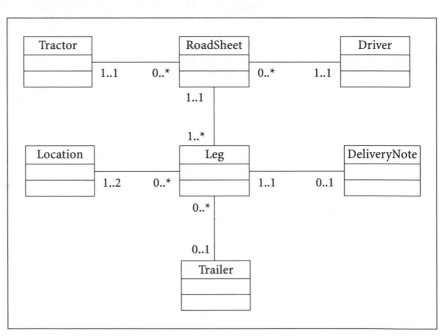

recorded system. If the system is to capture details of business operations over a period of time, the class model will allow the users to identify every roadsheet that a driver has complete and every roadsheet that a tractor has been allocated to. The model supports this business requirement.

Where a class needs to collaborate with any other class to meet the system requirements, that collaboration takes place along an association. As the collaborations become clearer during the analysis the model will build up. As with all the models their development is an iterative process, capturing the requirements as they are revealed during the study.

7.2.6 Many-to-many relationships

The class model also supports a many-to-many relationship. For example, it may be possible for certain Tractors to be driven by more than one Driver and a Driver may be able to drive many Tractors owned by the company. This is shown below.

This suggests that each Driver is qualified to drive one or more tractors owned by the company and that each Tractor may be driven by one or more drivers. The presence of this relationship is significant. In the original formulation of the class model (Figure 7.8) there is no direct association between Driver and Tractor and this implies that there are no restrictions in the business; any driver can drive any tractor and any tractor can be driven by any driver. However, the presence of a relationship suggests that there are real business restrictions; for example, tractor 321 can only be driven by drivers Knowles and Watson, whilst Watson can only drive tractors 321, 345 and 346. The many-to-many relationship models this situation.

In some circumstances, the association between the classes also holds information. For example, in the following example, the data item order quantity is associated with combinations of Product and Order. Data items must be stored in classes, so in this instance a new association class is created to hold this information.

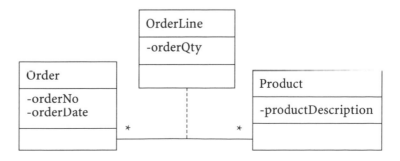

There is only one class instance of OrderLine for each combination of Order and Product. If there were more, then it would be necessary to convert this association class into an object class in its own right.

7.2.7 Generalisation

It has already been noted that a company may own a number of pool cars, which are allocated to drivers. The same company may have lorries to deliver their products to customers. Examination of the class Lorry suggests attributes such as registration number, maximum load, load status, no of wheels, mileage and date last serviced.

Examination of the operations might yield changeDriver(), recordLoadStatus(), amendMileage() and updateService(). At this stage, the analyst needs to consider whether the overlap in details between PoolCar and Lorry means that they are the same class or whether they should remain as discrete classes. Object-oriented modelling allows a third decision: perhaps they are part of a more general class called Vehicle. A Lorry and a PoolCar could be defined as specialist instances (or specialisations) of vehicle. Attributes and operations shared by the specialisations would be held in the generalist (generalisation) class, while those specific to each would be held by each subclass. Figure 7.9 illustrates how this is captured in the model.

Figure 7.9 Generalisation.

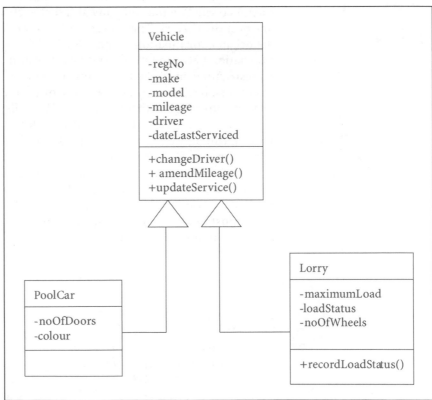

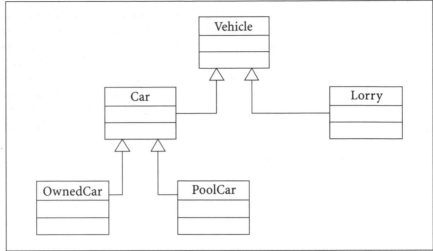

Figure 7.10 Two levels of generalisation.

Both specialisations are said to *inherit* the attributes and operations of the generalisation. So in this case each instance of Lorry has the attributes regNo, make, model, mileage, driver, dateLastServiced, maximumLoad, loadStatus and noOfWheels, together with the operations changeDriver(), amendMileage(), updateService() and recordLoadStatus(). Similarly, each instance of PoolCar has the attributes regNo, make, model, mileage, driver, dateLastServiced, noOfDoors and colour together with the operations changeDriver(), amendMileage() and updateService().

It is possible to have more than one layer of inheritance. For example, a company may own some cars and lease others from a pool. Beneath Vehicle will be the specialisations of Lorry and Car, while below Car will be OwnedCar and PoolCar. These two specialisations will inherit all attributes and operations from Vehicle and also those from Car. This is shown in Figure 7.10.

7.3 Data modelling

Class modelling allows the analyst to model the requirements of the system in terms of objects responsible both for their data structure and their functionality. The facility to communicate instructions and requests by passing messages from object to object means that there is no need to define a separate functional specification showing how the system's requirements are to be achieved.

However, a more restricted modelling option exists. This is to use a traditional way of modelling the structure of the system to just show the persistent data (attributes), taking little explicit account of its functionality. The technique for doing this is *Logical Data Modelling*, or *Entity Relationship Modelling (ERM)*. In this section we look to combine some elements of Entity Relationship Modelling with relational modelling.

An ERM is, superficially, very similar to a class model. It too identifies those 'things' in the system about which the organisation wishes to hold data. It also shows which of them are related to each other. The similarity does have limits, though, and while many aspects of the diagram could be read as a class model, it prefers to show some information in separate complementary models (data flow diagrams and entity life histories).

A key objective of the ERM model is to show the underpinning logic of the system's data. The end result is that data items are not duplicated in the structure but are to be found once and once only, in the place where it makes most sense for them to be found. This precision is optional within the class model, where such issues as primary keys, foreign keys, derived data items and repeated data items are often deferred until later in the development process.

The principle behind ERM is that the structure of data in a system is relatively static. While the processes using the data will change over time the underlying structure will change very little. Thus, if the designers can capture the structure correctly at the outset, changes to the system can be relatively easy to implement. All functionality will have shared access to the data no matter which user role is responsible. This means that changes to the functions such as responses to new products, changes in the competitive climate, reactions to economic fluctuations and so on, can be handled by creating or modifying functional programs without having to make significant changes to the data structures.

There are a number of different notations for ERMs, most of the variations relating to expressions of cardinality. The notation shown in this chapter has been used as a standard in the UK since the early 1990s.

7.3.1 Entities

The basic unit of the model is the entity or more precisely, entity type. For the purposes of modelling a business organisation, an entity has close similarities with objects in that both represent a *thing* that is of interest to the system under discussion and which holds data. As with an object, it can represent something tangible (such as an Employee), something conceptual (e.g. Department) or an event (e.g. Appraisal), as long as it contains persistent data.

The entity is represented as a box with round corners, as shown below.

Order

The precise shape of corners (round, square) is not important. The shape suggested is a convention but has no bearing on the logic.

An entity can usually only be classed as an entity if there is the possibility for more than one instance of it to exist. As with the class model, if the analyst is modelling a system for company Woodland

Transport, they may identify entities representing staff, customers, units of production etc., but not one that represents Woodland Transport itself, because there can only be one of these.

In order to identify any occurrence of an entity, it has to have an *Identifier* or *Primary Key,* such as Part No. (for Product), Customer No (for Customer), etc. In addition to these primary keys each entity will have a series of *attributes*, just as the class possesses attributes.

7.3.2 Relationships

The entity is described as having *relationships* with other entities, rather than associations. A relationship defines a logical business connection between just two entities. Thus, a Customer may place many Orders, but an Order can only be placed by one Customer. This is an example of a 1:*m* relationship and is shown in Figure 7.11. The 'crow's foot' signifies the entity in the relationship that can have many occurrences.

Although logically any one order can be for multiple products and any one product can be the subject of many orders (a many to many relationship), in some methodologies ERM recognises only 1:*m* relationships. The reason for this is that many-to-many (*m:m*) relationships may be 'hiding' data that needs to be explicitly considered. Figure 7.12 shows an *m:m* relationship between Order and Product.

A further attribute that has to be stored is Quantity Ordered: how much of a particular Product is requested on a particular Order. This information cannot be stored on Order (unless it is a business rule that all Products on that Order must be ordered in the same quantity) or on Product (unless the business rule is that the Product can only be ordered in a certain quantity). Both of these suggested business rules are unlikely, so the solution is to create another entity to fit between Order and Product (see Figure 7.13)

It was stated above that only 1:*m* relationships are permitted. However, there are occasions when 1:1 relationships can occur. Thus, if an invoice

Figure 7.11 Customer–Order relationship.

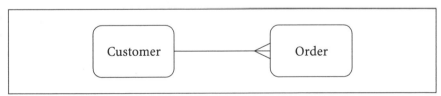

Figure 7.12 Many-to-many relationship between Order and Product.

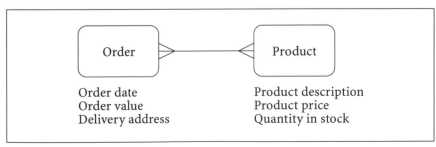

Figure 7.13 Resolution of many-to-many relationship.

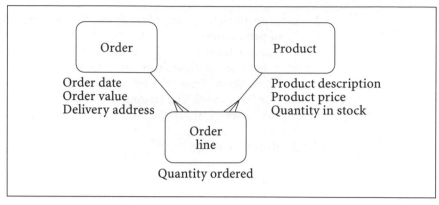

Figure 7.14 One-to-one relationship.

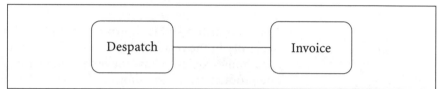

is sent after acknowledgement of each despatch, there may be a relationship as in Figure 7.14.

However, in most cases 1:1 relationships are in fact describing the same thing. An examination of the attributes in Despatch and Invoice would show that most of them were the same. The differences are that Invoice has its own primary key and contains monetary values, while Despatch will have a Delivery Address. In such a case, the two entities are aspects of the one set of data and should therefore be merged to make just one entity.

Returning to the Customer and Order relationship, there is another consideration to take into account. Many companies only recognise a customer when they place their first order. Others, however, will invest money and effort recruiting specific customers and create their records for marketing purposes before they place the order. Figure 7.15 shows

Figure 7.15 Optionality in an ERM.

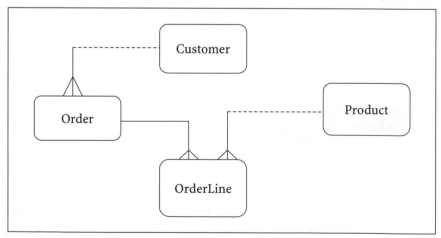

how this *optionality* of the relationship between Customer and Order is recorded.

The dotted and solid lines indicate that, in this case, a Customer *may* place 0,1 or more Orders, while each Order *must* be placed by one and only one Customer. A Product *may* be ordered on 0,1 or more Order Lines, while each Order Line *must* be for one and only one Product.

A specific entity occurrence should be uniquely identifiable by the value of an attribute or combination of attributes. For example, a Member may be identified by the attribute member-name or a specific Book recognised from the combination of the two attributes author and title. This identifying attribute or combination of attributes is termed the entity identifier.

7.3.3 Attributes

We have allocated identifying attributes to entities already. An intuitive approach has been adopted and this can be demonstrated with an order-processing example where the following attributes have been initially allocated to entities.

Attributes

Customer-name	Product-description
Product-price	Bin-location
Amount-stored-in-bin	Order-date
Order-qty	Invoice-date
Customer-address	Customer-tel-no
Customer-type	Customer-credit-limit
Customer-credit-line	

These data items may be intuitively allocated to entities. The attribute or attributes forming the *identifier* of each entity is underlined.

Customer
Customer-code,   customer-name, customer-address, customer-type, customer-credit-limit, customer-credit-line, customer-tel-no

Product
Product-code,   product-description

Product Location
Product-code, Bin-location,   amount-stored-in-bin

Order
Order-no,   order-date

Invoice
Invoice-no,   invoice-date

Order Line
Order-no, Product-code,   order-qty, product-price

Determinant

A determinant is defined to be any attribute, or group of attributes, on which some other attribute is fully dependent. The concept of a determinant is useful in recognising possible identifiers of an entity.

In the allocation of attributes to entity descriptions we wish to ensure that all attributes not in the identifier are fully dependent upon the whole of the identifier of that entity. So, for example, given a value for customer-code (the identifier of Customer) there is only one value for customer-address, customer-name and customer-tel-no. Where there is more than one attribute in the identifier, it is necessary to ensure that all attributes not in the identifier are dependent upon the whole of the identifier not part of it.

For example, the following description has been developed for the entity Order Line.

Order Line

Order-no, Product-code,   order-qty, product-price

Order-qty depends upon both attributes in the identifier because it represents the number of products requested on a particular order. However, product-price depends only upon product-code. The price does not change with every order that requests it. In this case product-price is reallocated to an entity in which it is fully dependent on the identifier.

If one does not exist then a new entity must be created with the part-identifier becoming the whole of the identifier of the new entity. The decomposition for Order Line is given below.

Order Line   Order-no, Product-code, order-qty
Product   Product-code, product-price

This ensures that attributes not in the key are determined by the whole of the key, not just part of the key.

Furthermore, we would also wish to guard against hidden relationships between data items not in the identifier. For example, consider the entity description developed for Customer.

Customer

Customer-code,   customer-name, customer-address, customer-type, customer-credit-limit, customer-credit-line, customer-tel-no

On further investigation it emerges that customer-type determines customer-credit-limit. In these circumstances customer-type must be examined to see if it is a possible identifier for the whole entity. Obviously in this case it is not (a value of customer- type clearly does not return one value of customer-address). In this circumstance the dependent attribute must be taken out of the entity and inserted in a new entity (which might have to be created) where it is fully dependent upon the identifier.

Customer
Customer-code,   customer-name, customer-address,
                             customer-type, customer-credit-
                             line, customer-tel-no

Customer Type
Customer-type,   customer-credit-limit

However, the attribute customer-tel-no in Customer also seems to
create some unwanted data dependencies. A value of customer-tel-no is
likely to be a possible or candidate identifier for the whole data set. If this
is so (and in this case it is) then this is acceptable. Customer-code has
been selected as an alternative to telephone number because it is shorter
and more stable. Customer-tel-no and customer-code are both
candidate identifiers for the whole entity, but in this case the latter has
been selected as the primary identifier.

The discovery of a new entity, Customer Type, raises the issue of how
it is related to other entities on the ERM. It is fairly intuitive to realise that
Customer Type will have a 1:*m* relationship with Customer. However, it
should also be noted that the identifier of Customer Type is repeated in
Customer. In fact, relationships are represented through data in this way
in the relational model. The 'many' end of the entity must have the
identifier of the '1' end in its own data attribute set. In some cases this
identifier also appears in the identifier of the other entity (for example,
the identifier of Product, product-code, is also part of the identifier of
one of its detail entities (Order Line). In other cases the identifier of the
master entity is a non-identifier attribute of the entities it is related to.

For example, the identifier of Customer Type is a non-identifier
attribute of Customer. This existence of this so-called posted identifier (or
foreign key) in the detail entities leads to a further reconsideration of the
data sets created above. In the example below, the foreign keys are shown
with an asterisk (*).

The relationships between Customer and Order and Order and
Invoice must be reflected in the entity descriptions.

Final allocation of attributes to entities

Customer
Customer-code,   customer-name, customer-address,
                             *customer-type, customer-credit-
                             line, customer-tel-no

Customer Type
Customer-type,   customer-credit-limit

Product
Product-code,   product-description, product-price

Product Location
*Product-code, Bin-location, amount-stored-in-bin

Order
Order-no,   order-date, *customer-code

Invoice
Invoice-no,   invoice-date, *order-no

Order Line
*Order-no, *Product-code,   order-qty

Hence it is recommended that attributes are added to the entities where their values depend upon the identifier, the whole of the identifier and nothing but the identifier. The aim is to produce a set of entities in which every determinant is a candidate identifier of the whole entity. Entity descriptions arranged in this way are said to be in Boyce–Codd Normal Form (BCNF).

Normalisation effectively produces a set of data groupings, which are known to be free of problems as well as providing a flexible and robust basis for data design. It can be approached in a number of ways. In this section we have adopted a 'top-down' analysis in which attributes are progressively added to the entity descriptions as they are uncovered. This addition is performed under the auspices of BCNF. This has been called the universal relation approach to normalisation (Benyon, 1990).

Figure 7.16 shows the entity relationship model for the normalised entities defined in this section.

In the Woodland Transport example the class model and ERM are very similar. However, there are three important differences:

Figure 7.16 ERM: normalised entities.

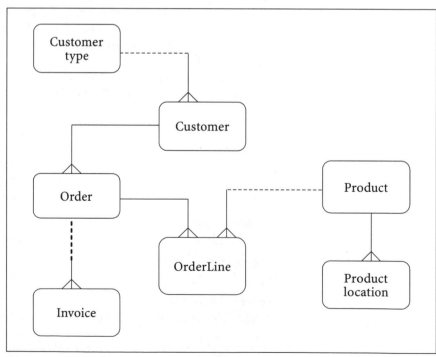

Figure 7.17 ERM: Woodland Transport.

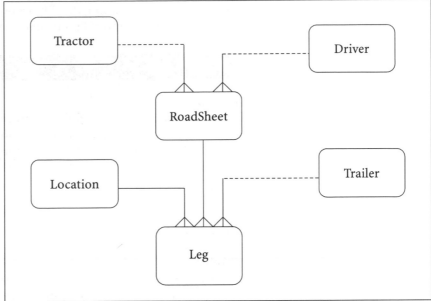

▶ The classes include the functionality that they can perform or experience (responsibilities) whereas the entities contain only data.

▶ The associations show connections to help perform the functionality or obtain necessary data to perform it (collaborations), whereas the relationships reflect a logical connection. In Chapter 9 it will be shown as well how relationships are used for navigation from entity to entity to support the system functionality.

▶ The information held on the class Delivery Note is to be found in the entities Leg, Trailer and Location (in Figure 7.17). Logically, there is no need for an additional entity. However, the class model is not trying to capture the logical structure, avoiding duplication. Instead, it models the system as it is perceived to operate, with the inclusion of concepts such as Delivery Note and possible duplication of data.

Chapter 9 will explore further how the ERM is supported by and supports the system's functionality.

7.4 Summary

This chapter has demonstrated two approaches to modelling the persistent structure of the system. The first approach is based on the OO paradigm of modelling the system in terms of discrete objects which combine data and operations to be performed by those objects including the updating and reporting of the state of the data. These objects will communicate (or collaborate) with each other by means of message passing.

The other approach comes from the database philosophy of modelling the structure of the data independently of the system functionality and avoiding, through normalisation, the duplication of data items that is to be found in most administrative and business systems.

EXERCISES

NENEWELL Ltd

NENEWELL Ltd has been awarded the contract to run passenger trains over part of a railway network. It requires an automated information system, based at its central office, to assist with the scheduling of trains.

Within NENEWELL's area are a number of depots at which drivers and locomotives are based. Each depot is responsible for providing drivers and locomotives for trains which start their journey in its area. Each train is hauled by only one locomotive. Locomotives are divided into classes. Although a train on the timetable normally runs each journey with the same class of locomotive, there is a requirement to keep details of possible substitute classes in case of unavailability.

Drivers are allocated to trains within the system. A record is to be maintained of which drivers are suitably trained and qualified to drive which class of locomotive.

1   Draw an Entity Relationship Model of the NENEWELL system.

Change Request workflow system (see Chapter 6)
2   Develop a class model for the Change Request workflow system.

Inter-Regional Athletics Association (see Chapter 6)
3   Draw a class model for IRAA.

GDL Timber Distribution System (see Chapter 3)
4   Draw a class model for GDL Timber Distribution.

5   Draw an Entity Relationship Model for GDL Timber Distribution.

6   Comment on the difference between the class model for GDL Timber Distribution and the Entity Relationship Model constructed for the company.

References

Benyon, D. (1990). *Information and Data Modelling.* Oxford: Blackwell Scientific.
Howe, D. (2001). *Data Analysis for Database Design.* Oxford: Butterworth Heinemann.
Lano, K., Fiadeiro, J. L. and Andrade, L. (2002). *Software Design Using Java 2.*
    Basingstoke: Palgrave Macmillan.

Logical function models

CHAPTER OVERVIEW

In this chapter you will learn:

▶ What is meant by an Interaction Diagram

▶ How to construct Collaboration and Sequence Diagrams

▶ About the role of the Required Data Flow Diagram

▶ How to construct process specifications with Structured English and Decision Tables

8.1 Introduction

This chapter looks at models that may be used to define the functional logic of the required system.

Chapter 7 illustrated two paradigms for persistent features of the system:

▶ The class model, from the object-oriented (OO) approach to development. This encapsulates both persistent data and all the operations needed to maintain and access that data.

▶ Entity Relationship Modelling (ERM), from the structured approach to development. This models just persistent data with no indication of the functionality required to maintain it.

This chapter develops the specification further by modelling how the processing will be specified for each of these paradigms.

▶ OO supports the functional requirements of the system by passing messages between the object classes required by the use case. In most cases a number of classes have to participate in realising the use case. This chapter describes two models showing this realisation:

   – Collaboration diagrams, which show the interactions between all objects that need to collaborate in the function.

   – Sequence diagrams, which show the sequence of interactions required in the collaboration.

▶ Entities in an E–R diagram are altogether more passive; the function that is triggered by the user has to know what each entity contains, and is responsible for each access and update. The functions, therefore, need to be specified in algorithmic detail.

To make the functionality easy to verify and to follow, a hierarchic (top-down) model is used: the data flow diagram (DFD) as described in Chapter 6. This presents a high-level overview of the functional scope of the required system under discussion. This view can then be decomposed to atomic levels where each part of the functionality is described in an algorithm.

Models used for the structured approach are:

▶ DFD set: a hierarchy of diagrams, decomposed from overview to a more detailed level.

▶ Structured English: an algorithmic expression of the operations that take place for given parts of the system; these describe the atomic elements of the DFD set.

▶ Decision tables: an expression of how complex decisions could be executed in the atomic level of the DFD set. Simple decisions can be explained through the Structured English but where a number of interrelated and nested decisions are involved the decision table provides a clearer, graphical description.

8.2 Interaction diagrams

The class model, as described in Chapter 7, presents the system in terms of its persistent data, encapsulated with the operations for its creation, maintenance, retrieval and deletion. The functional requirements that trigger activity upon the data are represented in use case diagrams and their supporting descriptions (Chapter 6). In order to achieve the objective of a use case collaboration is needed between all objects affected. The collaboration is performed via the concept of *messages*.

8.2.1 Message passing

A message is a request made by one object (*sender*) to another (*receiver*). The message does not stipulate how the operation should be performed (only the object receiving the message knows this), just that it should be done. The message will include any parameters needed to define the values required in that specific instance of the message.

For example, `getCustDetails()` is a generic message and this will be the signature of the operation in the class that receives the message. If this is the class `Customer`, then `getCustDetails()` will be added (if it is not already there) to the operations section of that class, as conventionally the name of the operation is the same as the name of the message it handles. The brackets show that parameters (values) will be passed in the message.

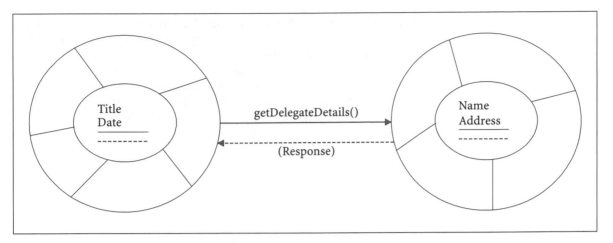

Figure 8.1 Message passing.

An instance of the message would be getCustDetails(A123), which asks the Customer class to retrieve details of customer with the account number A123.

As a further example, when producing joining instructions for a course, an object ScheduledCourse needs to retrieve the details of all the delegates booked onto it. To enact this, ScheduledCourse sends a message to the Delegate class asking for the name and address of all delegates booked on that course. This message is called getDelegateDetails() and it invokes the operation getDelegateDetails() in Delegate. This is shown in Figure 8.1.

When the receiver receives this message it triggers the operation and produces the required response or an acknowledgement that the operation has been performed. In this instance the operation getDelegateDetails() is defined as the retrieval of name and address details from the Delegate class. Messages that contain parameters will retrieve the relevant delegate details.

So, in this example, getDelegateDetails() will be defined as an operation of Delegate. The detail of what getDelegateDetails() actually does (retrieve name and address) will also be documented here.

The direction of the message is shown as an arrowhead at the end of a solid line. The response is an arrowhead on the end of a broken line. In many instances this line is not shown but is implied.

It is convention to use the name of the message as the name of the operation in the class that receives that message. The development of interaction diagrams allows the gradual population of the third section of the class box.

Furthermore, messages can only travel down associations. If required associations do not exist in the class model, then they must be created.

8.2.2 Collaboration diagrams

Collaboration diagrams represent the actors and all the objects that need to interact in order to achieve the use case objective. Collaboration diagrams represent the behaviour specified in the use case irrespective of time sequence. Collaboration diagrams may be drawn for each use case or for each scenario through the use case.

In the course booking system there is a use case for the booking of a delegate on to a course. As the course is residential, held in a hotel, a bedroom must be booked for the delegate. The Actor is the Admin Clerk who uses the system to perform the task. The 'happy day' scenario (Section 6.2.2) steps to be followed are:

1. Clerk accesses scheduled course details from the system
2. Clerk enters delegate details into the system
3. System creates a new delegate object and stores it
4. System subtracts 1 from number of free places on that course
5. System adds 1 to number of required hotel rooms on the hotel object belonging to the scheduled course

The first pass of the class model for the required system is shown in Figure 8.2.

The collaboration diagram is shown in Figure 8.3. The arrows represent messages passing from one object to another. Usually the responses are not shown on the diagram. The receiving object is activated by receipt of the message, so for the receiver the message represents an *event*. The numbering on the arrows represents a dependency between the calls. The collaboration diagram (and sequence diagram) are written for object instances (rather than classes). Hence the boxes on both diagrams are objects. This is shown by underlining the class name and prefixing by a colon, which denotes that it is an anonymous object used to demonstrate the required interaction.

One possible extension to the use case is that there may not be room on the scheduled course so the delegate is put on a waiting list.

At the moment, the class model does not support this, so first of all it must be enhanced by the addition of two more classes: CourseTitle (as

Figure 8.2 Partial class model for course booking system.

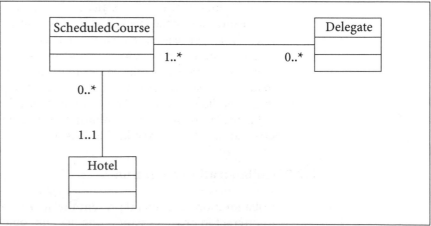

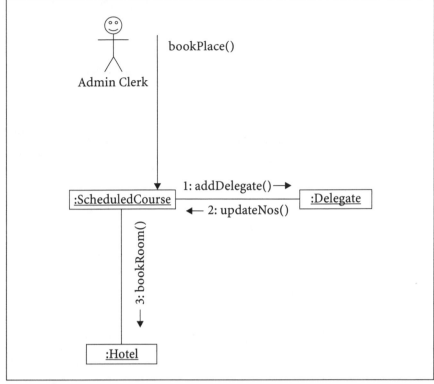

Figure 8.3 Collaboration diagram: delegate booking.

distinct from ScheduledCourse) and WaitingList. The new model is shown in Figure 8.4.

A complication for the collaboration diagram is that in this scenario there is a test to carry out: are there enough places on the ScheduledCourse? This is shown by letting the ScheduledCourse pass a message to itself. The numbering changes to allow both the happy day and this extension. The first message is to carry out this test. If the test fails and the extension is modelled, the numbering is decomposed as

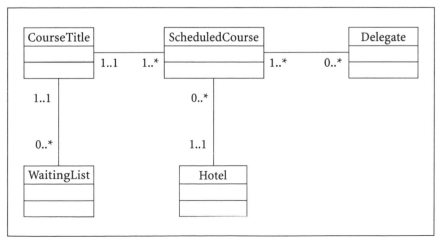

Figure 8.4 Extended class model for course booking system.

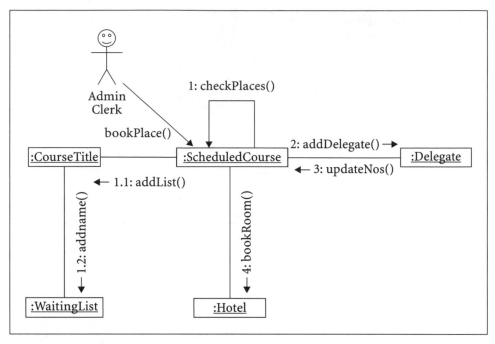

Figure 8.5 Extended collaboration diagram: make booking.

shown in Figure 8.5. If the test is successful, the numbering continues as normal.

During the fact-modelling phase of the requirements gathering, the class model for Woodland Transport was built. As always, this is an initial pass at the model. Modelling the logical processing may cause it to be enhanced in the same way as the Course Booking model.

Some of the requirements that the model must support are:

▶ Produce pre-delivery roadsheets
▶ Complete post-delivery roadsheets
▶ Produce reports on:
  – Delays by Delay Type
  – Last known trailer Location
  – Tractor Utilisation
  – Movements by Movement Type
  – Driver absence, by absence type and by driver
▶ Distinguish between driver types
▶ Produce Pay Data

Each of these will be captured in a use case, as described in Chapter 6, and then each use case is modelled in a collaboration diagram. Figure 8.6 shows the initial class model and Figure 8.7 shows a use case diagram for some of the functions of the Admin Supervisor and Traffic Clerk.

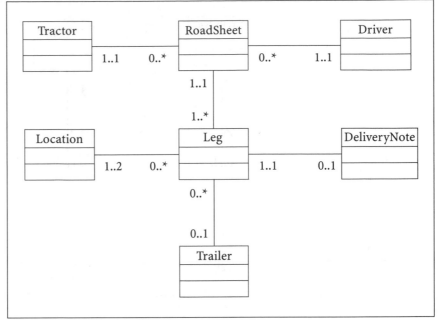

Figure 8.6 Woodland Transport class model.

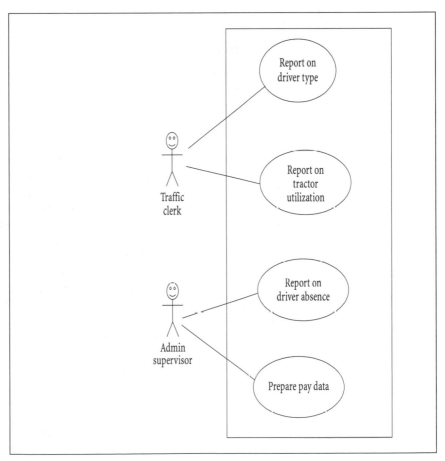

Figure 8.7 Use case diagram – selected functions.

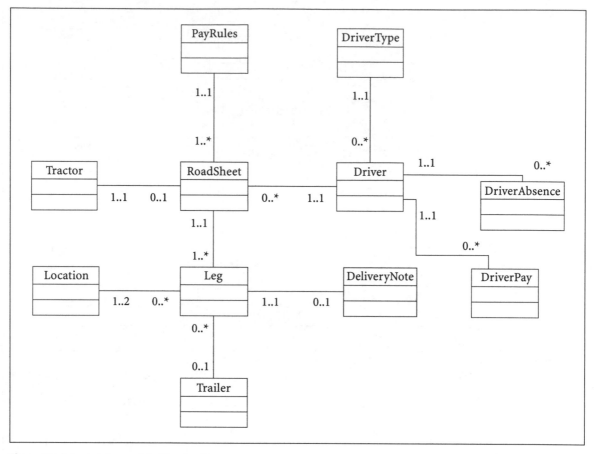

Figure 8.8 Extended class model – Woodland Transport.

The Admin Supervisor needs to prepare pay data. In order to do this extra information is needed that is not held at the moment. This information includes the driver type, pay rules and each driver's absence record. More classes are needed to maintain this data: Driver Type, Driver Absence and Pay Rules. The changes to the class model will accommodate these requirements (Figure 8.8).

The use case for Prepare Pay Data needs to look at the Driver, the Roadsheets for that driver, any Absences for the driver during the week, and the DriverType. The users have informed the analysts that it is necessary to keep data on each week's pay for the driver, rather than simply calculate and print; so a new object, DriverPay, is also needed. It is the users who, as always, specify the requirement.

The collaboration diagram supports the class model associations, demonstrating that only those classes that have an association may collaborate directly. The collaboration diagram to support the function Prepare Pay Data is shown in Figure 8.9.

In this instance, the objects are read, with the exception of the creation of DriverPay. Therefore, DriverPay must have a Write message, to show that it is created, while the other objects are only asked to return values

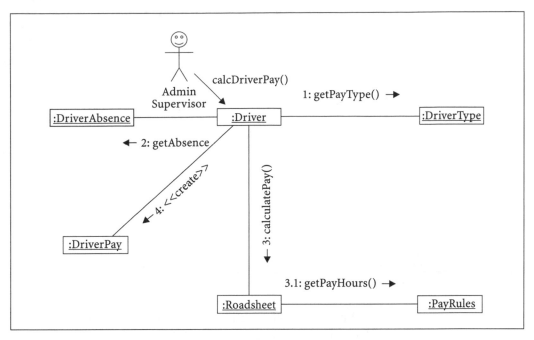

Figure 8.9 Collaboration diagram – Prepare Pay Data.

(Read/Calculate). The Write message is denoted by surrounding the write verb with 'guillemets' (<<create>>).

8.2.3 Sequence diagrams

The collaboration diagram is one Interaction Diagram; the specification needs another one to flesh out the sequence of the collaboration. This is supplied by another Interaction Diagram: the *sequence diagram*, which makes the sequencing of messages explicit. Sequence diagrams present the *lifeline* of each object through the collaboration. The lifeline is represented by a vertical (dotted) line drawn down from the object, which is at the top of the diagram. The Actor responsible for initiating the function is also shown at the top. Figure 8.10 shows the layout of a sequence diagram.

The sequence moves from top to bottom. It is not necessary to put the objects across the top in any particular order, although readability can be improved by placing the objects that are called early towards the left of the diagram. The actor will normally be shown at the left, as it is the actor that invokes the function being performed.

When an object receives a message, acts upon it and responds, it is said to be *activated*. The period of activation (or focus) is shown on the diagram by a narrow rectangle on the lifeline. If the diagram does not explicitly show the response being given by the called object it is implicitly recognised by closing the activation (the rectangle). Alternatively, the return of control to the calling object can be shown by a dotted line with an arrowhead pointing towards the calling object.

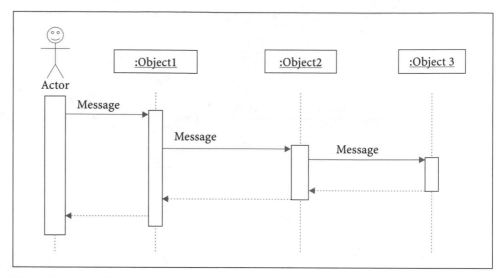

Figure 8.10 Layout of a sequence diagram.

Just as the collaboration diagram supports the class model, so it itself is supported by the sequence diagram, which shows messages passing only between classes that collaborate, i.e. those that are in association.

As with the collaboration diagrams there is one sequence diagram for each function or each use case.

Figure 8.11 shows the sequence diagram to support the function 'Make Booking'. For the sake of simplicity and clarity, in this example only the 'happy day' scenario is shown.

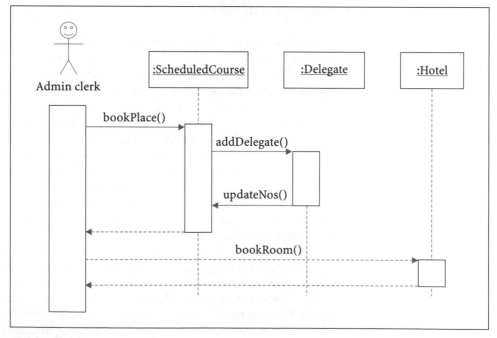

Figure 8.11 Sequence diagram – make booking.

Alternative paths and exceptions can be shown in a sequence diagram but they considerably increase the complexity of the model. For the purposes of this text and this stage in the life cycle, the level of complexity shown here is sufficient.

A second example of sequence diagrams, Figure 8.12, shows the model for the Woodland Transport scenario shown in the collaboration diagram for Prepare Pay Data.

Sequence diagrams are part of modelling an object's *behaviour*. This theme of object behaviour will be expanded in Chapter 9.

The Interaction Diagrams shown so far, collaboration diagrams and sequence diagrams, expand the class models in four ways:

▶ They verify the associations between classes; if a message is passed between two objects then their classes must have an association on the class model.

▶ They show how many of the operations are triggered.

▶ By exploring the collaborations needed for the functions, the analyst can validate the class model; this frequently entails enhancing the model with new classes, new associations, new attributes and new operations.

▶ The messages passed in the collaboration and sequence diagrams represent operations in the classes. This allows us to populate the third section of the class description. For example, from Figure 8.12:

+getPayType() becomes an operation in the DriverType class
+getAbsence() becomes an operation in the DriverAbsence class
+calculatePay() becomes an operation in the Roadsheet class
+getPayHours() becomes an operation in the PayRules class

8.3 Structured function models

In an Entity Relationship Model (ERM) the data structures in the entities are not hidden from the rest of the system in the same way that data is hidden inside objects. Therefore, when a function is invoked the data needed is accessed by a central set of instructions rather than by message passing. This central set of instructions has knowledge of how each entity stores its data and so issues precise instructions rather than a simple command like a message. In a structured methodology this central set of instructions is usually documented in a Data Flow Model.

8.4 Required system data flow modelling

Chapter 6 explained the purpose and construction of data flow diagrams with particular reference to the Current Physical Model.

This chapter is concerned with the logical specification of the new system and so will focus on the Required DFD.

This version of the DFD presents the logic of the new system in terms of the data that it stores and what functions are required to maintain that

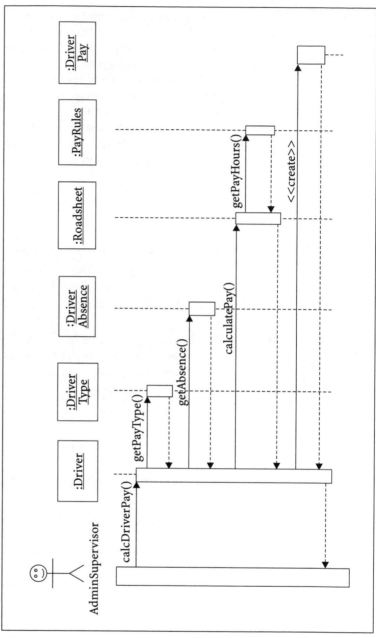

Figure 8.12 Sequence diagram: Prepare Pay Data.

Figure 8.13 ERM: course booking.

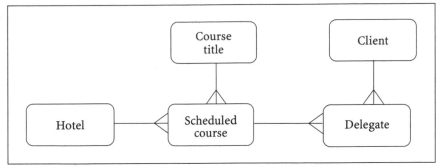

data. The boundary of the system is no longer that with the outside world, but between the functions and the actors who invoke them. An explanation of the differences in notation between Current Physical and Required models will clarify this.

▶ *Data stores*

In the required system the stores will be electronic (D) because when specifying the new system we are looking at how the computer system will handle the data. This is in contrast to the current physical where many data stores will be manual (M) with paper versions of the stored data.

In the required system the data stores map onto the entities in the ERM. Consider the Course Booking ERM shown in Figure 8.13.

The data in the data stores must correspond with the data on the ERM – they are different views, but views of the same system, nonetheless. Thus, the new system must have Course information, Client information (for billing purposes), Delegate information for Joining Instructions and sending pre-course reading material, and Hotel information for booking the courses and delegates into the hotel. The DFD, therefore, must have at least the following data stores:

D1	Delegate

D2	Course

D3	Client

D4	Hotel

The question remains whether Course covers both Scheduled Course and Course Title. It is legitimate in a DFD to allow a single data store to encapsulate two related entities. There is no hard and fast rule to this, but a rule of thumb would be to look at the functions accessing the data in the different entities and whether or not they have to coexist. For example, in an order-processing system Order and Order Line coexist in that they are logically aspects of the same thing and are created and deleted together. It is reasonable to have a single data store, called Order, in which both entities are stored.

In our course-booking example a Course Title can exist before and after any Scheduled Courses for it have been created, run and archived. Different people have interests in each. The Course Administrator needs to access the Course Title to prepare materials and facilities, as well as Scheduled Course to issue details of joining instructions to delegates and hotels. As the Course Title is likely to be maintained independently of Scheduled Course there is a case for making them separate data stores, so we now have a fifth:

D5	Scheduled Course

▶ *Processes*
Processes are similar to those drawn for the current system with one important difference: the box along the top of the process box, which held the location or user role responsible for that process, is now blank. The entry that was recorded there in the current physical model is now transferred to the external entity that initiates the process.

Processes may no longer be connected by a data flow; all processes now are linked only to external entities and data stores.

▶ *Data flows*
The flows are labelled with the logical name of the data being transported, rather than the name of a physical document. Thus, a driver might return a 'confirmed delivery' on a flow rather than 'signed copy 3'.

▶ *External entities*
As indicated above the external entities are now the actors and user roles within the system who interact with the system. An order is no longer sent in by a Customer but now entered by the Sales Clerk. Whoever interacts with the system directly is now represented as an external entity. Recipients of outputs from the system, such as reports, will be shown as external entities.

Figure 8.14 shows the required system DFD for Woodland Transport.

8.5 Elementary process descriptions

Chapter 6 explained how DFDs are decomposed from Level 1 to the lowest level of detail applicable. This is as true for the required model as for the Current Physical model. When the elementary level has been reached there is still more detail to include. The lowest elementary processes of the DFD must be documented. English text is not especially suitable for these process descriptions as such text is notoriously

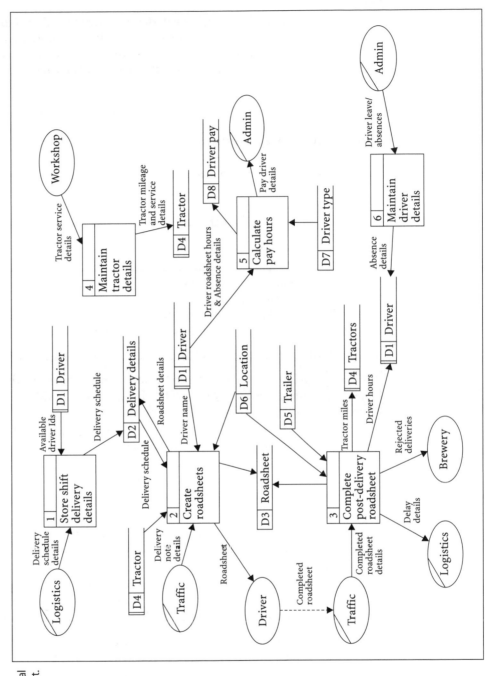

Figure 8.14 Required logical system – Woodland Transport.

ambiguous. This chapter will describe two techniques that can be used to define the content of the process descriptions more precisely: Structured English and Decision Tables. Both of these techniques can be used independently of the DFD and indeed may also be used as a use case specification.

8.5.1 Structured English

Structured English is a form of English that is made less ambiguous by removing any adjectives and adverbs and defining one discrete statement on each line.

Structured English recognises four basic constructs:

▶ Sequence: Each command is listed, one per line, one under the other as in:

```
Accept application
Store Applicant data
Add to list of Applicants
Write letter of Acknowledgement
```

All of these actions will be performed, in the sequence that is shown.

▶ Selection: If there is a condition which influences which action to take, this is marked by the syntax IF...ELSE...ENDIF.

```
Assess application
  IF Applicant's qualifications do not meet criteria
    Write letter of Rejection
  ELSE Store Applicant Data
    Add to list of Applicants
    Write letter of Acknowledgement
  ENDIF
```

Only those actions which meet the IF or ELSE conditions respectively shall be performed. Any action which does not depend on either condition will be written before the IF statement or after the ENDIF statement. Indenting the IF entries makes it easier to read and to see which ENDIF belongs with which IF statement. Selections can be nested inside each other, as the example below will demonstrate.

▶ Iteration: If an action needs to be carried out a number of times, this can be shown by using the construct DOWHILE...ENDDO.

```
DOWHILE still forms on pile
  Read first application form
  Read application details
    IF application is for overseas student
      Request proof of financial support
    ENDIF
    IF course has vacancies
      Check qualifications
```

```
            IF Applicant's qualifications do not meet criteria
               Write letter of Rejection
            ELSE Store Applicant Data
               Add to list of Applicants
               Write letter of Acknowledgement
            ENDIF
         ENDIF
      Read next application form
   ENDDO
```

▶ CASE: If there are a number of alternative courses for a selection, CASE provides a good shorthand, to save a series of IF...ENDIFs.

```
   DOWHILE still forms on pile
      Read first application form
      Read application details
         IF application is for overseas student
            Request proof of financial support
         ENDIF
         IF course has vacancies
            Check qualifications
            DOCASE
            CASE exam results meet requirements
               Make final offer to applicant
            CASE results not known
               Make a provisional offer
            CASE results not good enough
               Reject application
            ENDCASE
         ELSE (course full)
         ENDIF
      Read next application form
   ENDDO
```

Structured English is a simple means of building up a description of a task using these basic constructs. It removes most ambiguity and should improve clarity.

Structured English definitions can be extended to create Data Action Diagrams. This enforces a review of the process definitions and improves the readability of the process. Data Action Diagrams use brackets to connect the decision points in the Structured English constructs and to emphasise the dependencies shown by the indentation. They can also be extended to show explicit access to data stores (entities), so reinforcing the point made earlier in the chapter that the function that is triggered by the user has to know what each entity contains, and is responsible for each access and update. The functions, therefore, need to be specified in algorithmic detail.

The following standards enhance the functional detail of the Structured English.

Data entry fields	Enter
Default values that may not be overwritten	Allocate
Default values that may be overwritten	Confirm
The source of any default value	(Default value)
Mandatory fields	Underlined value
Loops (test at the top)	DOWHILE...ENDWHILE
Loops (test at the bottom)	DOUNTIL....ENDUNTIL
Selection	IF...(ELSE)...ENDIF
Multiple Selection	DOCASE..CASE..ENDCASE
Sequence	DO...ENDDO
Display field values and their source	Display field [ENTITY NAME]
Calculate field values	Calculate
Store entity values	Store [ENTITY NAME]
Update stored field values	Update fieldname [ENTITY NAME]

These standards can be applied to both conventional processes and object classes. For example, For the process ALLOCATE STOCK in an order processing system:

```
┌DO Allocate Stock
│   Allocate order-no
│   Confirm order-date (system date)
│ ┌DO customer details entry
│ │   Enter customer-no
│ │   Display customer-name, customer-address [CUSTOMER]
│ │ ┌IF customer details correct
│ │ │ ┌DOUNTIL
│ │ │ │   Enter product-no
│ │ │ │   Display product description [PRODUCT]
│ │ │ │   Display discount-price [PRODUCT PRICE]
│ │ │ │ ┌IF product details confirmed
│ │ │ │ │   Enter order-qty
│ │ │ │ │   Calculate line value (order-qty * discount-price)
│ │ │ │ │   Store [ORDERLINE]
│ │ │ │ │   Update allocated-stock-level [PRODUCT]
│ │ │ │ ├ELSE
│ │ │ │ │   Re-enter product code
│ │ │ │ └ENDIF
│ │ │ └ENDUNTIL no more products
│ │ ├ELSE
│ │ │   Re-enter customer number
│ │ └ENDIF
│ └ENDDO
│   Calculate order total (sum of line values)
│   Store ORDER
│   Update orders-year-to-date [CUSTOMER]
│   Update orders-year-to-date [REGION]
└ENDDO
```

For the object class CUSTOMER:

```
CUSTOMER
IF customer does not exist
    Enter customer number, customer name, customer address
    Enter orders year to date = 0
    Allocate discount code
ELSE customer is live
    DOWHILE customer is live
        DOCASE
            CASE credit checked order received
                Update orders year to date with orders year to
                date+1
            CASE name and address change notification
                Enter customer name
                Enter customer address
            CASE discount code re-allocated
                Enter discount code
            CASE End of Year
                Store orders year to date = 0
        ENDCASE
    ENDWHILE
    IF customer notifies removal OR three years since
        last order
        DO mark customer as dormant
            Allocate dormant date (system date)
            IF customer notifies removal
                Store reason for removal = customer notification
            ELSE three years since last order
                Store reason for removal = no orders
            ENDIF
        ENDDO
    ENDIF
ENDIF
```

These detailed definitions will provide the basis for detailed program design and programming.

However, there are some sets of decisions and actions that are too complex to be captured clearly, even in Structured English. Another tool is needed to unpick such situations as interpreting rules in legislation, loan-making, insurance claims and so on. This is to be found in the Decision Table.

8.5.2 Decision table

The following narrative summarises an interview with an accounts clerk in a mail order book club.

Priority treatment is given to members who order more than £100 value of books in a year, and have a good payment record, or who have been members for over ten years.

This statement is ambiguous, as it is not clear if poor paying members of over ten years standing will receive priority treatment. Drawing a decision table will highlight this ambiguity and the analyst will be able to express the logic precisely.

A decision table is useful for representing the conditional logic of processes where different actions are taken depending upon the occurrence of a particular combination of circumstances. This represents a typical discussion where staff explain that 'when x and y happen then we will do this and that, on the other hand, y might not happen and, in this case, we will do something else...'. In such situations, the analyst will often feel confused and unsure that the rules of the enterprise have been completely understood. Expressing the logic in the form of a decision table should clarify the rules governing the options.

A decision table is divided into four parts, as shown in Figure 8.15. The conditions, that determine which actions will result are listed in the *condition stub*. Combinations of these conditions are then identified and expressed as *condition entries*. The possible actions that can occur as result of different condition combinations are listed in the *action stub*. The decision table is completed by entering an X to show which actions apply in each column.

Limited entry decision table

The simplest type of decision table is a limited entry decision table, in which conditions are expressed as questions, which may be answered by a simple Yes (Y) or No (N) (Figure 18.15). The condition entries, or rules, are then specified as combinations of these answers. This type of table is self-checking to the extent that there is one rule for each possible combination of conditions.

The relevant action for each combination of conditions is recorded by an X in the action entries.

The construction of a limited entry decision table can be illustrated from the example book club narrative.

Figure 8.15 Decision table structure.

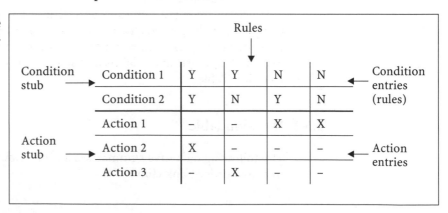

		Rules			
Condition stub →	Condition 1	Y	Y	N	N	← Condition entries (rules)
	Condition 2	Y	N	Y	N	
Action stub →	Action 1	–	–	X	X	← Action entries
	Action 2	X	–	–	–	
	Action 3	–	X	–	–	

1. Identify all conditions, being careful not to include mutually exclusive conditions such as Good Payment Record and Bad Payment Record. The conditions are binary, so the inclusion of one entails the exclusion of the other. Write the conditions down in the Condition Stub, with the most significant or critical one first. If more than four conditions apply, then divide the table in two.

    C1: Good payment record?
    C2: Order value > £100 p.a.?
    C3: Member > 10 years?

2. Identify all actions possible, and record them in the Action Stub in the sequence in which they occur.

    A1: Priority treatment
    A2: Normal treatment

3. In the case of a limited entry table, the number of rules can be calculated by using the formula (2^c), where c is the number of conditions. Ensure that all the condition entries or rules have been expressed. In this example, three conditions generate $2^3 = 8$ rules, since each condition entry can be Y or N. This explains why the division of a table at four conditions was suggested above: 2^5 gives 32 rules, which may be rather unwieldy. A suggested format for allocating the Ys and Ns is given below, known as the halving rule. For z rules, the first row will have $z/2$ Ys and $z/2$ Ns, reducing until the last row, which is always YNYNYN etc. In this way, every possible combination of Ys and Ns is given; see Table 8.1.

Table 8.1 Initial decision table.

Good payment record?	Y	Y	Y	Y	N	N	N	N
Order value > 100 p.a.?	Y	Y	N	N	Y	Y	N	N
Member > 10 years?	Y	N	Y	N	Y	N	Y	N
Priority treatment								
Normal treatment								

4. Action entries are now made. These are derived by applying each combination of conditions to the actions described in the narrative. This produces the table in Table 8.2.

5. In limited entry tables there should be 2^c rules in total, where c is the number of conditions expressed in the Condition Stub. Check the table completeness by counting the rules.

Extended entry decision table
The concise nature of the decision table has prompted its extension to include circumstances where the condition entries are expressed as values of some kind. An extended entry decision table may also include symbols

Table 8.2 Final decision table.

Good payment record?	Y	Y	Y	Y	N	N	N	N
Order value > 100 p.a.?	Y	Y	N	N	Y	Y	N	N
Member > 10 years?	Y	N	Y	N	Y	N	Y	N
Priority treatment	X	X	X		X			
Normal treatment				X		X	X	X

Table 8.3 Limited entry decision table.

Member < 1 year	Y	N	N	N
Member 1–5 years	–	Y	N	N
Member 6–10 years	–	–	Y	N
No Discount	X			
Discount 10%		X		
Discount 25%			X	
Discount 50%				X

or codes in the action entry section of the table. Consider the limited entry decision table of Table 8.3.

Using a Limited Entry Decision Table for this example appears unsatisfactory since the conditions are all related to each other. Only one action can take place and the table looks unnecessarily complex. Table 8.4 describes the same logical procedure in a simpler way by using an extended entry decision table.

Table 8.4 Extended entry decision table.

Length of membership	<1	1–5	6–10	>10 years
Discount %	0	10	25	50

Hybrid decision tables can also be constructed where the conditions are a mixture of Y and N and other values, as shown in Table 8.5.

Whether by Decision Tables or Structured English, every bottom-level process on the DFD set must be documented clearly and unambiguously for the required system.

Table 8.5 Hybrid decision table.

Good payment record	Y	N	Y	N	etc.
Length of membership	<1	<1	1<5	1<5	
Accept	X		X		
Reject		X		X	
Discount %	0		10		etc.

8.6 Conclusion

The Logical Function Specification is a key part of the requirements specification. If the OO approach is being followed, the logical functionality will be concerned with the collaboration between the objects involved in the function. The Interaction Diagrams (collaboration diagrams and sequence diagrams) each relate to just one use case.

The section on DFDs looked at differences in notation between the Current Physical (caught at fact-modelling time for a structured environment) and the Logical Required version. Many proponents of DFDs (e.g. Yourdon, 1989) recommend that little, if any, time be spent on the current physical system and most effort be put into modelling the required system. There are no firm rules to help guide the analyst here, but rather the constraints and environment in which they are working on any given project.

The processes on the lowest level DFD are documented by Structured English, Data Action Diagrams or Decision Tables. All these are also candidate models for an elaboration of a use case specification.

EXERCISES

It's a Frame-Up

'It's a Frame-Up' is a picture framing shop divided into two parts: the shop front, which deals with customers and their orders and the workshop, which cuts and assembles the frames. The owners have decided to computerise their operations as much as possible. Below is a description of the operations as they have been specified. The users of the system will be the Shopfront, Framer and Manager[Buyer].

The customer brings in an item to frame (a picture, certificate, tapestry etc.) to the shop front. The assistant measures the item and helps the customer choose appropriate moulding and card mount to set it off. The assistant completes an order record with a description of the picture, customer name, address and telephone number, details and sizes of the mount and moulding chosen. A copy of this is given to the customer. The order is transferred to a set of 'jobs', one job for each picture to be framed. Copies of the jobs are printed off as 'job sheets' and sent to the workshop for framing.

The jobs are batched up until the framers have time to read them. The framers read all the batched job sheets and assess the amount of moulding, mount card, glass etc. required, and compare that with what is in stock. Most moulding and mount is bought in to cater for specific jobs, so there is rarely spare stock. The framers complete a skeleton purchase order based on their assessment. This skeleton is then completed by the manager of the business who then places the order with the appropriate supplier. He completes and places the orders every afternoon.

When the manager collects the deliveries he puts them into store and notifies the framers that they can start work on that batch. The framers carry out the work specified on the job sheets and annotate the job sheets to show that it is finished. They pass the completed pictures etc. to the shop front complete with the job sheets. The shop assistant subjects every frame to a quality inspection to make sure that it meets the specification in the order book and that the quality of the work is of the acceptable standard. If the shop assistant thinks that it is not acceptable it will be returned to the framers, with reasons, and with the job sheets still attached.

If the work passes the test the assistant will annotate the job and call the customer to let them know the picture is ready to collect. The manager is given a report of all of the completed jobs at the end of each working day. The manager is also given a report of all the materials purchased during each week.

Below is a partial class model.

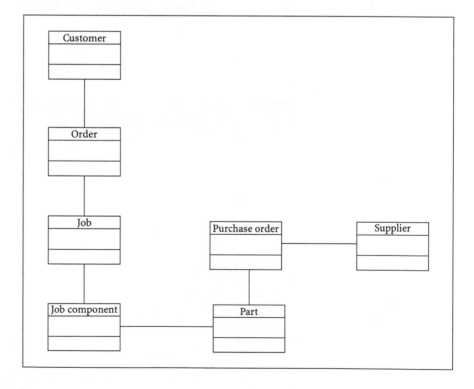

The manager of the shop has commissioned a study to automate many of the processes involved in the administration of the business. The proposal that the consultants have put forward allows the shop assistant to enter the order details by computer, creating order and customer records. The system can calculate the stock needed to carry out the task and raise a purchase order as appropriate. The manager, in his role as Purchasing Manager, receives this. When the stock is received the Purchasing Manager enters the details into the system. This updates the stock files, the Purchase Order, and also the Customer Order to flag that it can now be met. The workshop will be able to notify the system when an order has been met and amend the stock records accordingly.

When the shop assistant has inspected and approved the work, he or she updates the order on the computer to show that it is finally complete. At the same time, they will be able to access the customer details to contact them with news that their order is ready. The Manager will be able to produce whatever reports he needs from his own terminal.

1. Complete the multiplicities on the class diagram.

2. Draw a collaboration diagram for each of the two use cases:
   ▶ Assess Materials for Order
   ▶ Raise Purchase Order

3. Draw a sequence diagram for each of the same two use cases.
   ▶ Assess Materials for Order
   ▶ Raise Purchase Order

4. Draw a Level 1 Required DFD to reflect the proposed IT system that will be used in 'It's A Frame-Up'.

Change Request workflow system (see Chapter 6)

5. Develop a sequence diagram for the realisation of the use case(s) concerned with the initial notification of the change request into the system. Assume that there is an extra attribute on Sponsor called numberOfChangesToDate which increases by one when a change is notified. Only model the 'happy day' scenario.

6. Develop a collaboration diagram for the realisation of the use case(s) concerned with the initial notification of the change request into the system. Assume that there is an extra attribute on Sponsor called numberOfChangesToDate which increases by one when a change is notified. Only model the 'happy day' scenario.

GDL Timber Distribution System (see Chapter 3)

7. Draw a Level 1 Required DFD to reflect the operational system described in the GDL Timber Distribution System (the operational procedure of the text).

Woodland Transport Pay system

8. Express the rules for applying the Pay Rules using Structured English and/or an appropriate decision table.

References

Benyon, D. (1990). *Information and Data Modelling*. Oxford: Blackwell Scientific.

Howe, D. (2001). *Data Analysis for Database Design*. Oxford: Butterworth Heinemann.

Lano, K., Fiadeiro, J. L. and Andrade, L. (2002). *Software Design Using Java 2*. Basingstoke: Palgrave Macmillan.

Yourdon, E. (1989). *Modern Structured Analysis*. Englewood Cliffs, NJ: Prentice Hall.

Logical event models

In this chapter you will learn:

▶ About the significance of events and effects

▶ How to construct extended Entity Life Histories

▶ How to construct Statechart Diagrams

9.1 Introduction

So far, our specification has produced two perspectives of the system:

▶ The static/persistent view represented by Class Models on the one hand (Object-Oriented) and Entity Relationship Models on the other (Structured). Both of these models represent the underlying information structure of the system environment.

▶ The processing view represented by Interaction Diagrams for the Class Model and Data Flow Diagrams for the Entity Relationship Model. The Interaction Diagrams (collaboration and sequence diagrams) show how objects collaborate in order to perform a function. Data Flow Diagrams describe the way that data is transformed and stored as it passes through the system.

There is a third perspective, which unites these two: events. Events cause changes to the state of the system's data, so whether the development approach is Structured or Object-Oriented the effects of events on the system need to be modelled.

Event models record how events affect each entity or class and model time and business constraints. The models that achieve this are:

▶ Statechart Diagrams: these are used mostly with Class Models.

▶ Entity Life Histories: these are used mostly with Entity Relationship Models.

▶ Update Process Models: these are mostly used with Entity Relationship Models. They have certain similarities with collaboration diagrams.

In many respects, the two perspectives (Object-Oriented and Structured) can be brought together in the event model. Although it was developed as a structured technique, ELHs can be applied to class models as they focus on how an instance of an entity or object passes from creation to destruction.

9.2 Events and effects

An *event* is something that happens in the real world causing stored data to be updated. An event could be the arrival of a new customer, the cancellation of an order, the payment of an invoice or the booking of a course. Although the data is updated because of the event it is important to separate the process from the event, which is the trigger for the process to happen.

As a result of the above events, the system invokes processes to:

▶ Create a Customer entity (or object)

▶ Delete an Order with its Order Lines

▶ Update the quantity available field on the Parts entity (or object)

▶ Mark an Invoice as having been paid, with the amount paid and the date of payment

▶ Create a Booking record or object.

These changes to the data are *effects*. Again, the effect is distinct from the process that brings it about. An event represents a trigger or *precondition*; an effect represents a *postcondition*.

Whatever diagram is used to model the events and their effects the labels used in the diagrams should always be for the event, not the process. 'Receipt of Order' is an event; 'Create Order' is a process. One important reason for keeping the two distinct is that more than one event can be responsible for triggering a process. For example, a Customer can be created because a new Customer has placed their first Order, or because the Marketing Department has identified a Customer who we will probably do business with in the future but who has not yet placed an Order.

Three types of event can be distinguished:

▶ External event – a transaction arriving from the outside world, for example, 'Receipt of Order'. These events can be found on the input flows on a Data Flow Diagram.

▶ Internal process event – this occurs when a predefined condition within the stored data has been met. For example, a Purchase Order Request event takes place when stock levels in a warehouse reach predetermined reorder levels.

▶ Time-based events – this refers to the occasions when data is automatically updated at a predetermined time of day, or week or month. Typical examples are the levying of interest on an account on the last day of the month or the archiving of files two years after the last transaction on them.

The effects that any of these events can have are:

▶ Creation of a new record or object: Receipt of Order causes the creation of an Order and a set of Order Line records.

▶ Modification of fields on a record or object: Payment of an instalment will cause an amendment of the amount-owed field on a Customer record or object.

▶ Deletion of a record or an object: Removal of an Item from the catalogue will lead to the deletion of the Item record or object.

Modification can also take place when data items in a created entity occurrence are inserted for the first time. For example, the despatch-date of a particular order will not be known on the creation of the Order. It will only be inserted later in the Order's life and is thus a modification of the Order entity. Such data items are called *optional attributes*. When looking for events to maintain the data the analyst should look at what causes these optional attributes to be completed or to change value.

Effects on relationships in an ERM can also be regarded as modifications: if a fleet car is allocated to a new driver the New Driver Notification event is a modification of Car, not a deletion followed by creation.

There are occasions when a single instance of an event may affect an entity or object in one of several mutually exclusive ways. For example, the event Transaction acting on the entity Account might have different effects when the transaction is a payment to when the transaction is a withdrawal. A withdrawal transaction might require a check on the balance first with the possibility of rejecting the transaction; in contrast, a payment transaction may only update the account balance and record transaction details. In these circumstances, the event name should be qualified by a description of which of the exclusive events apply, such as Transaction (payment) or Transaction (withdrawal). The processing required will be determined at the time of the event either by the stored data or by the data accompanying the event.

In carrying out this part of the specification there are a number of places to look for possible events:

▶ The Data Flow Diagram: every flow that enters the system from an external entity represents an event *as long as it results in the update of a data store*. If it is an enquiry only then it does not count as an event.

▶ If an update process is triggered by time (often shown as a flow from a data store into a process and a flow from the process back to the store), this is an event. Archive events and periodic purges of data are examples of this.

▶ An examination of the entities and their attributes. Are there any optional attribute values that need to be completed after the entity is created? What are the events responsible for this? They may be evident on the DFD but this should not be taken for granted.

▶ The entities themselves should be checked – have creation and deletion events been identified for them all? If not, there may be events missing.

9.3 Entity Life Histories

An Entity Life History is a graphical way of representing the effects of all the events on an entity – and every occurrence of that entity, from its creation to its removal from the system.

One of its advantages is that it helps to enforce the business rules, in that some events may only affect an entity at certain points in its life. For example, a Loan account will record all of the payment instalments made against it. However, no payments can be made until the Loan has been approved. The Entity Life History will be structured in such a way that no payments can be accepted until approval has been given. Should a payment be entered before the approval has been granted the transaction will be rejected. In this way the Entity Life History (ELH) provides the designers with guidelines for maintaining the business integrity of the data and anticipates the controls discussed in Chapter 12.

9.3.1 Notation

The notation for ELHs is based on Michael Jackson's notation for JSP program design. This revolves around three constructs: Sequence, Selection and Iteration.

The ELH is a tree structure with the root being the entity at the top of the tree.

▶ The bottom leaves of the tree represent the events. The diagram is read from left to right, so the Birth event (Creation) is the leftmost event and the Death event (Deletion) is at the right.

▶ If at one point in the life of the entity more than one event *could* happen and it is not possible to predict which this is represented by a selection.

▶ If one or more events can happen several times over, such as instalment payments, this is shown as an iteration. An iteration symbol means that, during the life of the entity, the event can happen 0, once or many times.

Figure 9.1 illustrates the notation for an ELH.

These basic constructs can be combined and built up to model the most complex of life histories. There are one or two extra features that can be built into the diagram for particular circumstances and these will be introduced later in the chapter. However, the basis for all ELHs lies just in these three constructs.

9.3.2 Building the Entity Life History

At first, one ELH is drawn for each entity on the ERM. However, some entities are very simple, being created, deleted and nothing else. In such cases no purpose is served by drawing the ELH. However, if there seem to be more than three events affecting an entity then it is a candidate for modelling with an ELH.

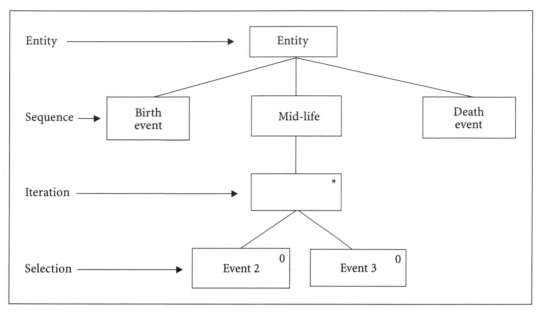

Figure 9.1 Notation for Entity Life Histories.

The first step in building the ELHs is to develop an *entity–event matrix*. This involves both the ERM and DFD.

To show how an ELH is built up, we shall revisit the music agency from Chapter 6. The ELH will be of the entity Booking.

First, we show a subset of the ERM (Figure 9.2).

Figure 9.2 Subset of the music agency entity relationship model.

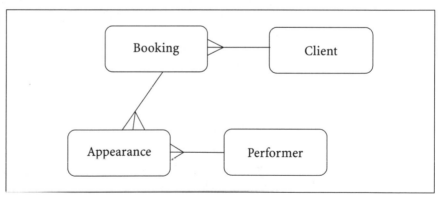

The attributes of Booking are:

Booking No (key)
Date Booking received
Type of Booking
Date of Booking
Address of Booking
Client No

Fee
Deposit amount
Date Deposit paid
Number of performers required
Type of performers required
Date performers booked
Comments

In parallel with the ERM, we need to see the required Data Flow Diagram. Figure 9.3 presents the view of the agency concerned with maintaining the Bookings and Performers data. The Client data has been omitted for the purposes of brevity in the example. The data store Booking includes the entities Booking and Appearance.

The DFD identifies the following events:

▶ Notification of new Booking

▶ Changes to Booking

▶ Cancellation of Booking

▶ Archiving of Booking

▶ Deposit received

▶ Performer accepts Booking

▶ Notification of new Performer

▶ Notification of changes to Performer details

▶ Performer leaves list

An event that might be expected – the day of the Booking – does not make any difference to the data held about it, so for our purposes it is not an event. Once the events have been identified like this, the analyst needs to return to the users to find out precisely what effect the events have on the entities and what constraints there are on the sequence in which the events are allowed to happen.

For each event it is necessary to analyse its effect on the entities: the effect is classified as a Create, Modify or Deletion.

▶ Create an occurrence (C)

▶ Modify an occurrence (M)

▶ Delete an occurrence (D)

This is achieved by drawing a matrix with one axis listing the entities from the ERM and the other the events from the DFD (see Figure 9.4).

There are two checks that should be made at this point:

1. Every entity must have at least one creation event and at least one deletion event.

2. Every event must affect at least one entity.

When the matrix is completed an ELH is drawn for each entity that is perceived to be complex. In this instance, the entity Booking is complex, with three modification events affecting it.

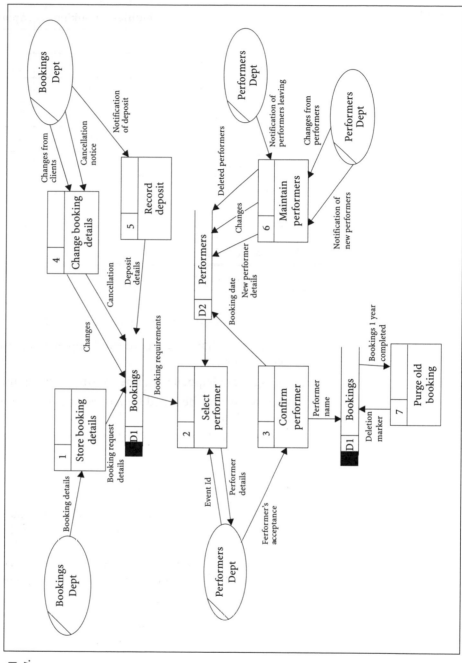

Figure 9.3 Required logical
DFD – music agency.

Figure 9.4 Event–entity matrix.

Entities	Booking	Appearance	Performer
Events			
Notification of Booking	C		
Changes to Booking	M		
Booking cancelled	D	D	
Booking plus 1 year	D	D	
Deposit received	M		
Performer accepts Booking	M	C	M
Notification of new Performer			C
Notification of changes to Performer details			M
Performer leaves list		D	D

On further questioning, the users explain the following business rules:

▶ Changes to a Booking record can happen at any time between creation and deletion.

▶ Changes can happen a number of times during the life of the entity.

▶ Clients will only be asked for a deposit after a Performer has accepted the Booking.

▶ When the Booking is archived, the Appearance record is archived as well.

▶ If a Performer leaves the system altogether, any outstanding Appearance records will be deleted.

With these rules in mind, it is time to begin building the model. Construction begins by drawing the entity and the birth and death events (Figure 9.5).

Next, the modifications may be added. A check has to first be made with the user to determine whether there are any rules concerning

Figure 9.5

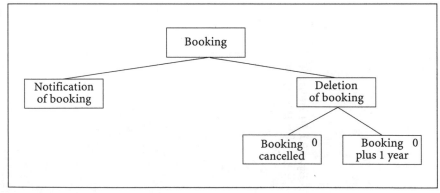

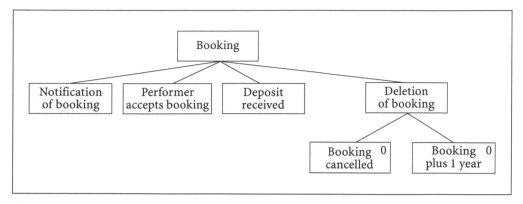

Figure 9.6

sequence. In this case, there is a constraint: that the deposit can only be accepted after the performer has accepted the booking. So this is added to the diagram as shown in Figure 9.6.

The one remaining event poses a problem: it can happen at any time or possibly never, but if it does happen, it could be at any time between creation and deletion. There is an extra construct to show this possibility: the parallel life. The parallel life means that an event can take place at an unpredictable time simultaneously with others in the life cycle. A change to reference details is a common occurrence of this. Parallelism is demonstrated in Figure 9.7.

Parallelism indicates that all of the branches that hang from the parallel bars can happen at any time in relation to the other branches. In this example, in the 'Life' box, the `Deposit Received` must still follow `Performer Accepts Booking`, but a change can happen before, between or after these two events.

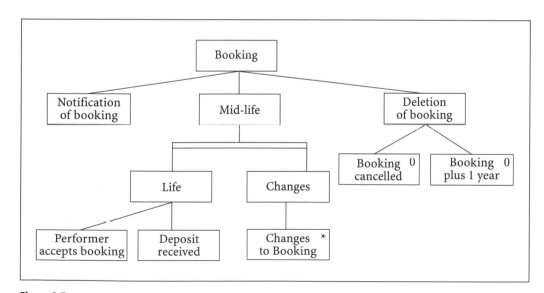

Figure 9.7

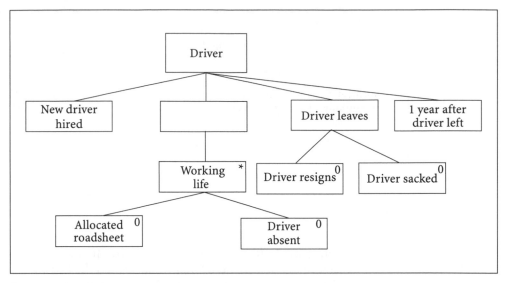

Figure 9.8 ELH – Driver.

If every event's place in the sequence can be predicted parallelism will not be appropriate.

In the case of Woodland Transport, the entity Driver can be subject to the following events:

▶ New driver joined

▶ Driver allocated to Roadsheet (many times)

▶ Driver can be absent (many times)

▶ Driver leaves (sacked or resigns)

▶ 1 year after driver leaves (archive event)

Although there is no forecasting when a driver may be absent a parallel structure is not required here because it is not possible to allocate a Roadsheet to a Driver who is absent. The suggested ELH for Driver is shown in Figure 9.8.

9.3.3 State indicators

State indicators are a method of controlling the sequencing of events. They may be thought of as an additional numerical attribute within each entity. Each time an event affects an entity the state indicator is updated to indicate that the particular effect has occurred. Holding a state indicator in each entity means that it is possible to detect the state a particular entity occurrence has reached within its life. Without a state indicator complex logic may be needed referencing many attribute values in different entities.

Knowing the current state of an entity occurrence makes it possible to determine whether it is valid to apply the effect of a particular event to an

Figure 9.9

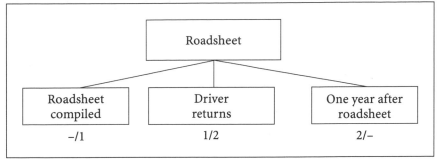

entity occurrence or whether an error condition exists. This implicit validation logic will be carried forward from the specification into logical design and built into the processing logic.

Given that state indicators reflect the structure of the ELH diagrams it is a mechanistic task to add them to the diagrams.

The notation for recording state indicators is to record, under each event, the *prior value* followed by the *set-to value*.

▶ A valid prior value gives the value of the state indicator that must exist for the effect of an event to take place.

▶ A set-to value is the value given to the state indicator once the effect of the event has been completed.

It is important to note that:

▶ There may be more than one valid prior value of the state indicator for an event.

▶ There will be only one set-to value for each event within each ELH.

The prior value for the birth event and the set-to value for the death event will both be null (–). At birth, the state indicator will be set-to 1 and so on through the life of the entity. A sequence will be straightforward, as in Figure 9.9 for Roadsheet.

Alternatives within a selection will have the same prior values. The event following the selection will have as prior valid values all the set-to values within the selection structure (Figure 9.10).

Iterative events will include the set-to state indicator value set by the last effect of the iteration, as in Figure 9.11. The event following the iterated effect must include the set-to value of the effect preceding the iteration as iteration events need not actually occur.

9.3.4 Operations

The last feature of Entity Life Histories is the detailed specification of the effects of each event. This is done by attaching *operations* to each leaf on the diagram.

The following operations can be performed. The precise format of these operations is flexible but they all follow the principle of the three effects: Create, Modify and Delete.

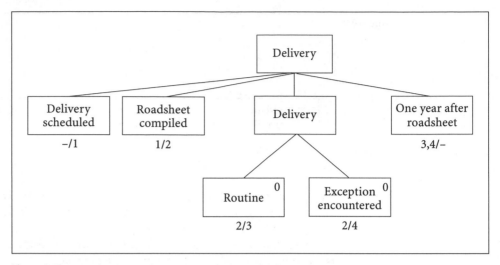

Figure 9.10

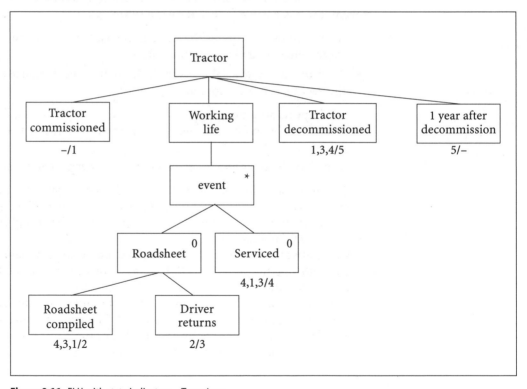

Figure 9.11 ELH with state indicators – Tractor.

▶ Store all attributes {Create}

▶ Store [attribute] (= First value of optional attribute) {Modify}

▶ Replace [attribute *n*] by input {Modify}

▶ Replace [attribute *n*] by [calculation] {Modify}

▶ Set State Indicator to [n] {Create/Modify}

▶ Remove {Delete}

There are some standards that include operations for forming and breaking relationships with other entities. These can be left to detailed design; the purpose of the operations at this stage is to specify what happens to an entity and any of its attributes when an event occurs. As stated above, the format of the operations can be adapted to suit specific circumstances or to local standards.

The annotation of the diagram with the operations is done by:

▶ Listing all of the operations that will affect the entity, with a number.

▶ Writing the number of the operation under the event.

In order to identify the operations, we should first establish the attributes.

▶ Tractor No

▶ Date of Commissioning

▶ Date of Decommissioning

▶ Engine Size

▶ Miles

▶ Date Last Fuelled

▶ Fuel Drawn

▶ Date Oiled

▶ Oil Drawn

▶ MPG

▶ Status (Free/Allocated)

▶ Date Last Serviced

▶ Miles Last Serviced

Operations
1. Store attributes
2. Set Status Free
3. Set Status Allocated
4. Replace Date Last Fuelled with input Date
5. Replace Fuel Drawn with input
6. Replace Date Oiled with input Date
7. Replace Oil Drawn with input
8. Replace Date Last Serviced with input Date
9. Replace Miles Last Serviced with input Miles
10. Store Date of Decommissioning
11. Remove Tractor

Figure 9.12 shows the operations attached to their respective places on the ELH.

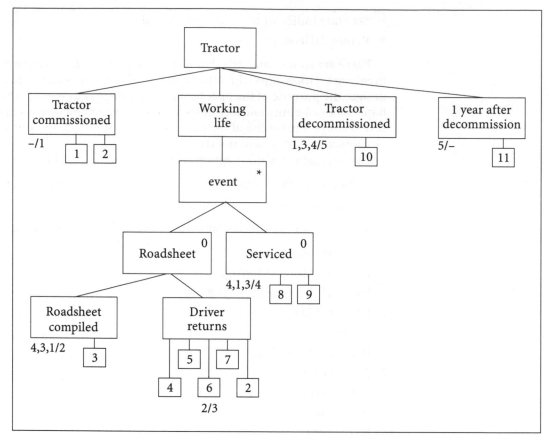

Figure 9.12 ELH with operations added – Tractor.

By attaching the operations to the Entity Life History, the technique helps to align the Structured ERM with the OO Class Model; now the entity can be seen in terms of both data and operations.

9.4 Update Process Models

So far the event–entity matrix has only been read from the entity end. However, to specify the handling of the event itself the other axis has to be considered (Table 9.1). This leads to the specification of processing by means of the Update Process Models.

If the event 'Performer Accepts Booking' is considered, we see three entities are affected. This may be modelled by drawing each of the entities affected and linking them with arrows, as shown in Figure 9.13.

When this event happens, only one occurrence of each entity is affected. However, many events are more complicated and it may be that more than one occurrence of an entity is created or deleted in response to an event. In this case, the construct of iteration is drawn. The construct

Table 9.1

Events	Booking	Appearance	Performer
Notification of Booking	C		
Changes to Booking	M		
Booking cancelled	D	D	
Booking plus 1 year	D	D	
Deposit received	M		
Performer accepts Booking	M	C	M
Notification of new Performer			C
Notification of changes to Performer details			M

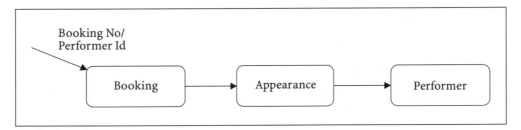

Figure 9.13

comprises a box labelled 'Set of X', with an iteration of X drawn underneath. This is illustrated in Figure 9.14, for the scenario of a Customer placing an Order, with associated Order Lines, each Order Line being for an Item.

It may be that items that are in stock are treated differently from items that are out of stock. This involves a selection, with similar notation to the selection in ELHs. This is illustrated in Figure 9.15.

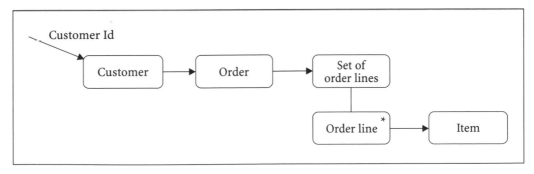

Figure 9.14

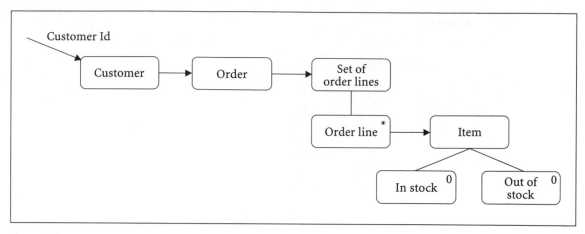

Figure 9.15

A rule of thumb for the notation is to show the arrows that travel from entity type to entity type horizontally, towards either the left or the right.

The last thing to add is the set of operations. These are taken directly from the ELHs for each of the entities shown. This will be illustrated using the event Order Received; see Figure 9.16.

Operations
1. Store attributes
2. Replace Customer-Balance with (Customer-Balance + calculated order-value)
3. Replace Quantity-in-Stock with (Quantity-in-Stock – Order Line value)
4. Replace Quantity-Reserved with (Quantity-Reserved + input quantity)

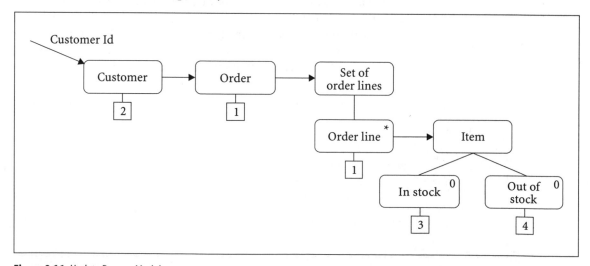

Figure 9.16 Update Process Model.

These operations are all taken from the corresponding event boxes on the respective ELHs. Together, they provide a specification for the handling of each event. At the construction phase, the access paths will be expanded and decisions made as to how they will be physically implemented.

9.5 Statechart diagrams

Statechart Diagrams or State Transition Diagrams are particularly defined within the Object-Oriented approach to systems development.

9.5.1 States

The state of an object refers to a condition that an object finds itself in at a particular time.

▶ A television can be in one of three states: on, off or standby.

▶ A video recorder can be in one of five states: on, recording, waiting to record, playback, off.

▶ A car park barrier can be in one of two states: raised or lowered.

The state will change in response to a message or signal. One instruction will set a video recorder on 'Waiting to Record' and a further signal, time-initiated, will change that state to 'Recording'. Note that if the state is 'Off' or 'Playback' the time signal will not be able to produce the state 'Recording'.

In real-time control systems, such as the above examples, these states are obvious and easy to model. The scope of this text, however, is business information systems, and although the same underlying principle applies it is not always so intuitively easy to recognise the different states of an object. However, there are significant examples where a business object changes state as it passes through its life, for example; an order may progress from unfilled to filled to shipped to accepted. Each of these states would be represented by a value of an attribute, perhaps a status value that is changed from U(nfilled) to F(illed) to S(hipped) to A(ccepted) as the appropriate messages are sent to the object.

The state of an object refers to its ability to respond to a message invoking one of its operations. If, for example, the Woodland Transport Roadsheet has not been completed pre-delivery, it is not in a state to respond to the event post-delivery. When that event occurs, it is expected that the roadsheet will be in a state to receive and process the data that accompanies it.

States are shown graphically for each class as a series of boxes, as in Figure 9.17.

9.5.2 Transitions

The transition from one state to another occurs when an event happens that results in a message being sent to the object. The message must be

Figure 9.17 Statechart diagram –
Roadsheet.

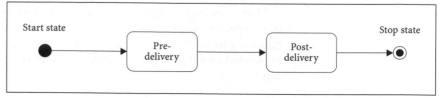

one that invokes an update operation, rather than just a read data message. The transition is shown on the diagram as a labelled message between the two states.

There are aspects of the transition that need to be noted, although they are not always shown on the diagram. These are *guards* and *actions*.

▶ The guard is a pre-condition for the transition to take place. For example, in Woodland Transport the objects in the class `Tractor` must be serviced when a certain mileage has been driven since the last service. The guard could be expressed as [Mileage = Miles Last Serviced + 6,000] / Book Service on the message arrow.

▶ Action – this is the behaviour that takes place as a result of the transition. In the example above, the action is 'Book Service'

An event action can happen whereby an object may or may not undergo a transition to a different state. Let us look at the course booking scenario for an example.

If a scheduled course has a maximum number of places, every time a delegate books onto the course, it may or may not become full. How this is handled is illustrated in Figure 9.18.

The scheduled course has two states here: *full* and *not full*. There are two events that can cause a transition from one state to another: a booking being made and a booking being cancelled. However, the only event that can cause a change from *full* to *not full* is a cancellation, so that is shown as a message in that direction, with no conditions. If the cancellation occurs while the course is *not full*, the message does not result in a transition to a new state, so we show it leading back to the same state.

Figure 9.18 Statechart diagram –
Course.

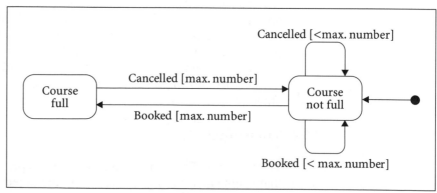

The event Booking can cause a change of state under certain conditions (when it leads to the maximum number of bookings for that Course), so a guard may be placed on its transition. If it does not breach that guard then again the message travels back to the same state. If it does breach the guard then we show the transition to the other state with the terms of the guard written on the message.

9.5.3 Nested states

As most systems are extremely complex, there needs to be some way of simplifying the representation of the statechart diagram. Nesting allows this simplification. Figure 9.19 demonstrates nesting in the class Order. The events to do with the fulfilling of the order are nested in their own separate box, while the two possible outcomes, *Cancellation* and *Despatch*, are shown outside the nested portion of the diagram. As the transition to the state Despatched can only derive from the state Picked, the message comes from that state. However, the state Cancelled can occur at any time before Despatch, so the message comes from the super-state Fulfilling, indicating this possible global event.

Statechart diagrams are very popular in real-time and telecommunications systems but may be more limited when modelling business information objects. However, there are often situations where objects pass through states and these are represented in the class by some sort of 'flag' field. Table 9.2 shows some examples.

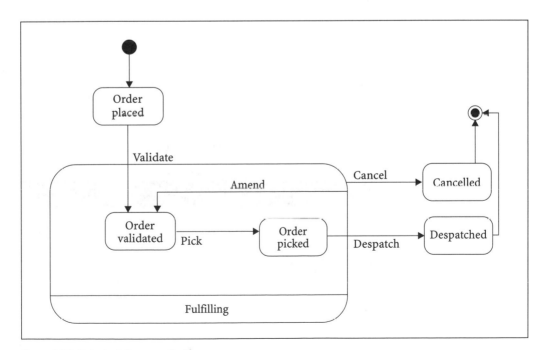

Figure 9.19 Statechart diagram – Order.

Table 9.2 States in business information systems.

Object class	Possible states
Invoice	Received – Authorised – Unauthorised – Part paid – Fully paid
Order	Received – Picked – Delivered – Accepted – Rejected – Amended – Cancelled
Job	Received – Authorised – Allocated – Completed – Tested – Released – Withdrawn
Claim	Received – Authorised – Unauthorised – Paid – Rejected

9.6 Summary

This chapter has discussed the third perspective of specification: that of the event. It has looked at how the two approaches under discussion, the Structured and the Object-Oriented, handle events. In doing so, it has revealed a certain symmetry between the two approaches to systems development.

The Structured approach contained two models in its approach to the subject: the Entity Life History and Update Process Model, both derived from the entity–event matrix. The ELH is a diagram that shows the effect of every event between creation and deletion. The ELH is a very valuable tool for capturing business rules and, by means of the State Indicators, enforcing them. Update Access Paths show the navigation needed through the data model to process an event. They form the basis of the processing specification.

The OO approach includes the Statechart diagram. This is a model which, like the Entity Life History, charts the effects of events on the object, showing what is responsible for the transition from one state to another. Adorning the model with rules in the form of guards allows such transitions only to take place under correct conditions. Statechart diagrams are especially useful for real-time systems but can also be useful in modelling certain business objects.

EXERCISES

A notebook computer is purchased by a company IT department. A record is created when it is purchased. After it is purchased it may be allocated to a department. During its period of allocation it may be transferred to another department and it may also be given a 12-monthly service. These events may happen many times, or never. After the department no longer needs it it will be put back into store from where it may be allocated to another department if required.

At the end of its life it will be either sold or scrapped. It can only be disposed of when it is in store, never when it is allocated to a department.

1   Complete an entity–event matrix for the following entities: Notebook, Service, Allocation.

2   Draw an Entity Life History for the entity Notebook.

3   Draw a statechart diagram for the class Notebook.

Change Request Workflow system (see Chapter 6)

4   Develop a statechart diagram for the class Job Request.

5   Develop an Entity Life History for the entity Defect Notification. As well as taking into account changes in status (as above), recall that hours worked on the defect also have to be recorded. However, there is no need to distinguish between the different types of hours worked (between estimating, coding, testing etc.).

6   A government department handles payments to building contractors. Each payment normally goes through the following stages:

   1.   Receipt of Invoice from contractor
   2.   Matching of Invoice against Order
   3.   Authorisation of Payment of Invoice
   4.   Raising Cheque
   5.   Despatch of Cheque to Contractor

   Other stages (alternatives to above)

   2a   Unmatched Invoices. These are held until an Order is located to match them against. An unmatched Order is held for 30 days.
   3a   Rejected Invoice

   During this process, many contractors phone up asking about the progress of their Invoice and its subsequent Payment. Bought Ledger Clerks respond to these queries by accessing their accounts system, which identifies the current status of all Invoices and Payments. The department is now considering putting this information online so that contractors can access this information via the Internet.

   Draw a statechart diagram for the class Invoice, stating any assumptions that you make.

Reference

Bennett, S., McRobb, S. and Farmer, R. (1999). *Object-Oriented Systems Analysis and Design using UML*. New York: McGraw-Hill.

Rapid Application Development (RAD)

CHAPTER OVERVIEW

In this chapter you will learn about:

▶ Problems of meeting business deadlines

▶ Elements of RAD

▶ Prototyping – throwaway and evolutionary

▶ Requirements-gathering techniques for RAD projects

▶ Suitable candidates for RAD

10.1 Introduction

A difficulty that many developers and project managers face is how to develop information systems quickly enough to meet business needs and opportunities. In a rapidly changing business world there is an overwhelming need to get new systems to market as quickly as possible.

For example, FC plc, a finance company, plans to launch a new product in the market-place, prompted by a government initiative on tax-free saving. At least three competitors are known to be launching an equivalent product within the next five months. If the company is to gain a business advantage from this initiative it must launch before the competitors. However, it has to produce a computer system to support and maintain the product before launch date. The hardware and networks are in place but specific data records need to be generated and the software has to be written. A feasibility study conducted last month shows that a staged development to support this product will take nine months to roll out. This is unacceptable to the business sponsors who have insisted that the system should be tested and implemented within four months, otherwise the business opportunity will be lost.

This chapter describes an approach to systems development that attempts to preserve software quality whilst pursuing the speedy software production needed to meet FC's business needs. The approach is called Rapid Application Development (RAD) and follows work originally carried out by James Martin (Martin, 1991). RAD is applicable to a specific range of situations, which will be described later in the chapter. The approach also depends for its success on certain principles and these will also be described later in the chapter. However, the key to a RAD implementation is the incremental handover of functionality rather than developing and handing over the entire working system.

10.2 Systems development life cycle for RAD projects

The essence of RAD is the agreed early delivery of the most critical parts of the project. However, if the project is to deliver with the appropriate quality it must still follow the same overall development process. That is, the system cannot be built until it is designed and it cannot be designed until the requirements are properly analysed. Hence the techniques described in the previous chapters still remain valid. However, to achieve the incremental delivery of the system the developers must build and deliver working prototypes.

Unfortunately, RAD has been confused with an approach that tempts some managers and could best be described as 'Just Do It' (JDI). This means attempting to code with little previous design effort and no analysis beyond the initial high-level statement of requirements. But be warned: JDI is not RAD! Neither approach will be rapid unless certain principles are adhered to. Express trains are not fast just because they are called expresses!

In order to stage the delivery of the new system the application life cycle must comprise iterations of development and implementation. This chapter describes a typical life cycle for RAD assuming that the initiation and feasibility stages of the project have already been completed.

▶ Stage (i): Requirements gathering

This stage is concerned with gathering the high-level requirements of stakeholders and prioritising the development of those requirements. This is usually carried out in what James Martin called a Joint Requirements Planning (JRP) workshop. Participants will be senior managers of the departments affected by the system together with an analyst and a facilitator.

The objective of this workshop is twofold. Firstly, it must identify the business objectives and their information requirements for all the business functions in the agreed scope. Secondly (and this is usually the most contentious part), it must prioritise and partition the delivery of the agreed functionality.

Thus, in the FC plc application, the users may be Customers, Marketing, XProduct (the new department set up to handle the product) and Accounts. Each will have a set of requirements that the new system must satisfy and each will feel that their own requirements are the most urgent and should be the first to be put in place.

Eliciting the high-level requirements for each department will be relatively straightforward using techniques such as critical success factor analysis and scenario building. However, having documented these requirements, the next stage is to partition and prioritise the development. This calls for keen negotiation and conflict resolution skills on the part of the facilitator. However, consensus can usually be reached with the active participation of the project sponsor. It is important to remember that, in a workshop like this, corporate politics can be as big an issue as IT considerations.

In our example, the workshop agreed that Marketing has the greatest priority, followed narrowly by XProduct. The rationale for this is that the marketing systems need to be in place before the product launch to attract customers as quickly as possible. The systems to support the product itself need to be completed and tested before launch but can follow the development of the marketing system. It was agreed that the other stakeholders' systems could wait until after these two sub-systems – but not by much!

▶ Stage (ii): Functional prototyping

After prioritisation is complete the function to be developed first (in this case Marketing) is subjected to functional prototyping. This is concerned with eliciting finer grained requirements and identifying any non-functional requirements that can be established at this stage.

The team working on this will include an analyst, a programmer with a CASE or prototyping tool, a member of the Marketing department who will be working on XProduct and a team leader who will probably be from the IT department. The key point is that the member of the user department is not a token user, to be consulted from time to time, but an equal full-time member of the team.

The outputs from this stage will be a detailed set of prototyped requirements for Marketing (or whichever department's phase is being worked on), a set of non-functional requirements, review documents and development plans for the next stage.

▶ Stage (iii): Design and build

This stage takes the requirements, earlier prototypes and CASE documentation and turns them into a detailed design. This design is preferably built on an advanced CASE tool that automatically converts the design into database tables and program code. The team undertaking this stage is the same as the one that undertook the functional prototyping.

Because this design and build stage uses the same tools, rather than paper designs and conventional programming languages, the elapsed delivery time is considerably shortened. Testing the design and build will be an integral part of development, not just a stage in its own right. At this point, therefore, testing to the users' satisfaction should require little additional effort.

At the end of this stage the Marketing department's requirements should be completely met. All that is needed now is the final stage.

▶ Stage (iv): Implementation

This covers the usual implementation activities including training the new users, data conversion/creation and cutover.

Documentation for the implementation should also be handed over at this stage.

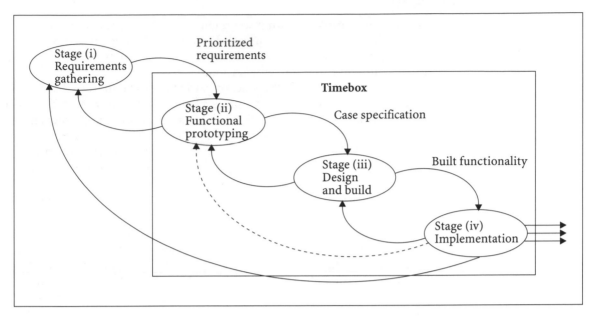

Figure 10.1 Incremental development process.

One of the keys to RAD is that this life cycle is followed for each department or set of functions that have been prioritised. Once the Marketing system (or, strictly speaking, sub-system), has gone live, the XProduct functions can be developed in the same way, following Stages (ii), (iii) and (iv). Figure 10.1 illustrates the development process.

The arrows backtracking from Stage (ii) to (i), (iii) to (ii) and so on reflect the testing of each product against the objectives stated in the earlier stages. The arrow backtracking from (iv) to (i) reflects the testing of the coded system against the original requirements before release. The dotted arrow from (iv) to (ii) shows the iteration of the cycle until all phases are implemented within a timebox structure.

Timebox

The business imperative in the XProduct scenario is to have the system ready to support an immoveable launch date so the delivery date of the system must be guaranteed. The project management mechanism to achieve this is called a timebox. A timebox is simply an agreed period of time in which the task (stage) is to be completed. If cost or functionality has to be compromised to meet that date, then so be it; the deadline for each timebox is fixed and cannot be moved. By breaking the project down into a series of timeboxes, each of which results in the delivery of working functionality, the users can receive their portion of the new system when it is promised and, most importantly, when it is required. Timeboxing leads to the frequent phased delivery of products to the end users.

The whole project will begin with a timebox to complete the Business Study, Feasibility Study and Requirements Gathering. Thereafter, the system will be broken down into timeboxes with each functional area (Marketing, XProduct, Accounts and so on) occupying a timebox of its own. These comprise the stages described earlier: functional prototyping, design and build, and implementation.

For a project such as FC the timeboxes will have to be short so that the crucial releases are in time for the project launch. It may have been decided at the JRP workshop that only the first two phases are critical to the launch as long as the rest of the system is in place not later than one month after the launch. In this case a timebox of seven weeks will allow these two critical phases to be implemented within fourteen weeks; just two weeks short of launch date, with the third phase also in progress. The length of the timeboxes will be dictated by what is feasible for the team to achieve and what the business imperatives demand. However, timeboxes are typically between three and eight weeks in length, with elapsed duration beyond these likely to be adversely affected by changing user and business requirements.

If, as the deadline for a timebox draws closer, some functionality is clearly not going to be ready the release will still go ahead without the missing element. The functional prototyping stage will therefore also include its own prioritisation to recognise what is critical and what can safely be deferred to a later delivery of the software. The one factor that does not change is the timebox deadline. The MoSCoW principles described in Chapter 5 will assist in the prioritisation of requirements.

The timebox can only work satisfactorily if two conditions are met. Firstly, the development team includes a user representative who is on hand to make and criticise design decisions and test the development as it proceeds. The timebox assumes that time is fixed and functionality is variable. This is a culture change for most users who expect functionality to be fixed and time (within reason) to be variable. Hence the development team must include a user who recognises this and can explain the concept to other users. Secondly, the development is conducted using a prototyping tool, which will support models and, as much as possible, convert these models to full working systems. The key element here is that developers must have powerful software development tools to rapidly develop the systems to a sufficient software quality.

10.3 Prototyping

Prototyping was briefly described in Section 5.3.5, during the description of requirement-gathering techniques. As explained above, RAD requires the prototyping of agreed sections of the development.

There are two commonly used forms of prototyping: 'Throwaway' or 'Rapid', and 'Evolutionary' or 'Incremental'. They each have a life cycle model, discussed below.

10.3.1 Throwaway prototyping

This is used mostly as an analysis or design tool, using a software tool or simple flipchart paper to map out screen designs, functionality and processing. The program code behind the screens may be very restricted; sufficient to show how the system should behave in response to an agreed input. Thus data values may be coded into the program (rather than retrieved from a database) and the software is relatively untested and hence is seldom robust. To an unsuspecting user this prototype might resemble the required system but in fact it is more like a film set. A film suggests a real street with natural lighting, weather and solid buildings, whereas in reality it is built of flimsy façades and lit by artificial spot- and floodlights. The software prototype may also provide such an illusion and in doing so assists users in defining their requirements or design preferences.

Hence throwaway prototypes assist users in defining their requirements as well as letting users decide whether or not they like the design and behaviour of the system. If they dislike, or disagree with any part of it, the programmer is able to change it until it is to their satisfaction. At this point the design will be documented, the system built according to that agreed design and the prototype destroyed. This speeds up and increases the precision of the analysis and design parts of the life cycle. This model is illustrated in Figure 10.2. This approach also means that the prototype can be developed using software that is not the target software of the final system. Hence software that allows quick prototype developments with advanced presentation features may be used. For example, we have seen PowerPoint slide shows used to produce effective workflow prototypes. This approach to prototyping does not require much investment in software tools and can easily be integrated into the analysis and design stages of development. It pleases users and reduces the communication problems usually associated with solely paper-based analysis and design. Many authors see the incremental prototype as

Figure 10.2 Throwaway prototyping life cycle.

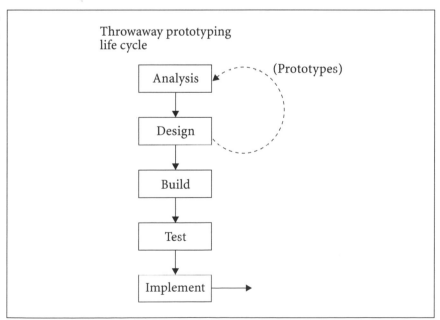

201

helping to define the requirements, which can then be properly engineered in the construction (programming) phase of systems development.

10.3.2 Evolutionary prototyping

This form of prototyping is radically different from the throwaway approach. In the evolutionary approach the prototypes are constructed in the target software and the principle is that the prototypes will be incrementally developed until they become the final product. This approach is particularly appropriate where prototypes are generated automatically from CASE tools.

At the end of the process, after the iteration of testing and amendments, the users have a real sub-system that can be used in the business instead of a mock-up illusion. The process of prototyping also incorporates the testing process so that when it is completed it is also user tested.

When each part of the system is built in this fashion it is 'bolted on' to the existing part of the system and so the testing should include integration with what has been already developed. In this way the whole system is developed and released in increments or 'evolves' through the prototyping process. This approach allows later changes in requirements to be incorporated as long as the costs and impacts of such changes are managed. Evolutionary prototyping allows the phased development of the system and is what is envisaged in the FC plc application. In such an approach each prototype is essentially a fully engineered product. The progressive delivery of the system is very attractive to users. However, critics of the approach have questioned whether meaningful sub-systems of sufficient quality can actually be developed within the time frame of the timebox. They have also been concerned that a poor overall design might emerge from not taking the whole system scope into consideration, leading to future problems in enhancement and maintenance. Studies have shown that prototype systems often score well in functionality and usability but less well in robustness and enhancement. The ability to deliver evolutionary prototypes also depends upon the organisation's willingness to invest in relatively expensive software. Some RAD protagonists only perceive that it is possible with investment in advanced program-generating CASE tools.

The life cycle for evolutionary prototyping is shown in Figure 10.3.

The two approaches to prototyping are not mutually exclusive. Throwaway prototyping could be used for the development of a usable system, then evolutionary prototyping for its refinement.

10.4 Prototyping tools

Throwaway prototyping can be carried out relatively cheaply using spreadsheets; presentation software and other PC-based products. Microsoft Access is often used to produce analysis and design prototypes.

Figure 10.3 Evolutionary
prototyping life cycle.

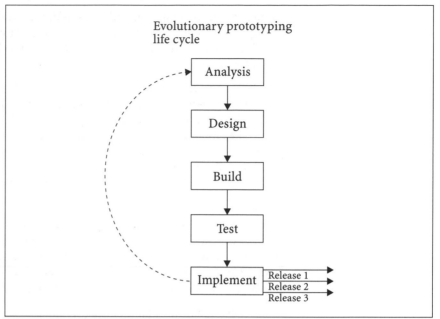

Standard application packages may be used as demonstration systems
with the user identifying problems, possibilities and opportunities using
the package as a yardstick. It is often easier to say what is inadequate
about, say a production control package, than it is to define requirements
in the abstract. In this instance the package is not seen as a solution; it is
thrown away once requirements have been elicited.

Evolutionary prototyping, however, places greater demands on the
software. Listed below are some generic tools that are used to develop
these forms of prototype.

▶ Program generators

Program generators have been available for a number of years and a
variety of different types may be identified. One sort uses a question and
answer English dialogue to produce the program logic, which it then
encodes in a high-level language such as BASIC or COBOL. A different
type adopts a screen-based approach where the designer effectively paints
the screen they wish to be displayed by typing directly on to it. Once
satisfied with the display, the program generator may be invoked, which
automatically produces the code required for the screen. It may also
produce validation routines stopping only to request what type and range
of data is required in a certain field and what error message should
appear when the user makes a mistake. These may be produced directly if
the Program generator has access to a data dictionary.

▶ Reusable code

Many systems are conceptually similar. Tasks frequently reappear –
menu design, password protection, print routines, date checking etc. It is
possible to build up a library of well-proven, well-documented routines,
which may be plugged together to make up a system. The content, not the

logic, will need changing, and some patching will be required to make a complete system. However, access to a store of well-tested standard modules and classes should ease prototype development and maintenance.

▶ Object and library sets

PC development languages increasingly have published object and library sets, which can be purchased and plugged into a specific tailored system. Examples include generic facilities, such as calculators and browsers and application objects, such as invoices and despatch notes. Shippable business objects (order, invoice, shipment, delivery etc.), often in defined frameworks, should hasten the construction phase of the project.

▶ CASE tools

It is with CASE tools that prototyping becomes particularly effective. The facility of some CASE tools to generate code means that the maintenance of the software is provided through the models, not through the code itself. Hence code and models are always compatible. This is a key advantage. CASE tools are considered in more detail in the next section.

▶ Fourth Generation Languages (4GLs)

Languages may be seen as passing through three previous generations:

- First Generation: machine code – instructing the machine through direct binary code. Closely associated with the architecture of the host processor. Complex to write, read and debug.
- Second Generation: assembler languages – use symbolic codes. Machine instructions are given by mnemonic alphabetic codes. Easier to understand, although still closely allied to machine architecture.
- Third Generation: high-level languages such as FORTRAN, COBOL, PL/1 and BASIC. Written in procedural code. Largely independent of the hardware architecture permitting portability. Much easier to use.

There is no agreed definition on what constitutes a Fourth Generation Language, but a checklist might include:

- Database facilities.
- Links to other proprietary databases and other non-database files. This will permit gradual transition to the new development strategy.
- Integrated and active data dictionary.
- Simple query language. May use a syntactical structure and/or a query by forms.
- Integrated screen design tool.
- Dialogue design tool. Including generation and manipulation of business graphics.
- Report generator.

- Procedural coding facility. This may be done directly through a conventional language (say COBOL) or indirectly via a code design aid (such as an action diagrammer).
- Non-procedural programming code.
- Spreadsheets and graphics.
- Integrated test tools.

If a 4GL is to provide a complete development facility for the professional programmer, analyst and end user, it must clearly have a range of tools to accommodate disparate requirements and skill levels. It must also dovetail with the past development strategy of the organisation and the systems developed under that strategy. 4GLs that require massive rewrites of current operational systems are likely to extend the development backlog, not reduce it.

10.5 Computer-Aided Software Engineering (CASE)

CASE tools support the analysis and development of information systems. CASE tools contain:

▶ Diagramming tools to describe the system using logical models such as class models, data flow diagrams, statecharts and entity life histories. Indeed, the models of Chapters 6, 7, 8 and 9 could all be diagrammed with a CASE tool. Diagrams produced using such CASE tools may be edited and reprinted much more quickly than manually drawn equivalents.

▶ A data dictionary that contains documentation to support the graphical models. This is a repository for the vast amount of information gathered during analysis.

▶ Diagramming rules to ensure that models are technically correct. For example, on a data flow diagram the CASE tool will not allow the user to create a flow between an external entity and a data store.

▶ Consistency checking between models to ensure a common view of the system. Hence the different views of the system may be reconciled.

▶ A prototyping facility for inputs and outputs based on the logical data contents defined in the data dictionary entry supporting the logical data flows.

▶ A program and data generator converting logical process definitions into programs and entities into physical files, tables or databases.

A graphical representation of the structure of a CASE tool is shown in Figure 10.4.

Consistency checking
Consistency is an essential feature of CASE. In the context of a data flow diagram this might answer such questions as:

▶ Are there any data flows specified without a source or destination?

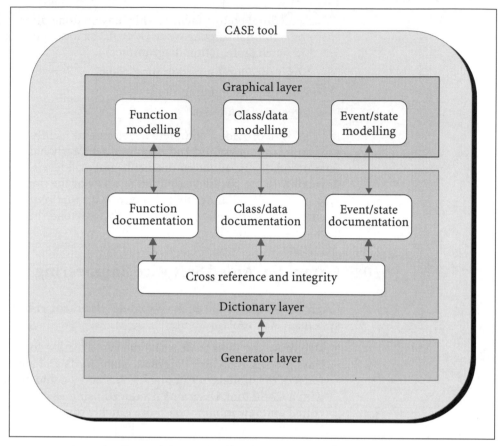

Figure 10.4 Graphical representation of a CASE tool.

▶ Are there any data elements specified in any data stores that have no way of getting there, as they are not present in any of the incoming data flows?

▶ Does a process definition demand a data element that does not enter that process?

▶ Are there data elements in any data flows entering processes that are not used in the process or do not appear in the output?

▶ Are the lower level DFDs consistent with their parents?

The automation of consistency checking eliminates a considerable amount of desk checking. It will help identify missing and irrelevant data items and incomplete processes. Consequently, the CASE tool not only ensures the validity of the design but also identifies and justifies the role of each data element. Thus it is possible to demonstrate why data is collected and where and how it is used.

Coding
In most CASE tools the description of the data structures in the data dictionary should be detailed enough for the generation of data

descriptions in the host language or Data Manipulation Language (DML) through a pre-compilation pass of the dictionary. In fact, some CASE tools are offered by the vendors of Database Management Systems (DBMS) to permit the definition of data files through a diagramming front end.

If the CASE tools hold information on the logical sequence in which data is used by processes then automatic program code definition is feasible. CASE tools which offer this facility can give significant productivity gains, not only because of the speed with which code is produced, but also because of the quality of that code. Program testing should not be necessary. A review of four early users of Information Engineering Facility (a CASE tool) revealed systems with six million lines of COBOL code going into production without a single failure. Some commercial CASE tools use Action Diagrams (see Chapter 8) to generate program code.

Change

Tracing the effects of changes through the system is a time-consuming and difficult task. Impact analysis is the term given to the analysis of the effect of proposed program and system changes. The recording of the associations that exist between the various classes should allow the effects of addition, amendment or deletion of a particular class to be predicted throughout the whole system. Thus the system and resource implications of a change can be completely understood before they are implemented.

In active data dictionaries it may be possible to generate many changes automatically. This is particularly true of data validation changes, where the rules for validation (format, length, value ranges etc.) are maintained in the dictionary rather than the program code. Thus changes are only being defined in one place (the dictionary entry), not in all the programs that access that data.

Where the system has been automatically generated from a CASE tool, changes are applied to the models. After checking for completeness and consistency, the whole system is regenerated.

Reporting and documentation

CASE tools usually have flexible and comprehensive reporting facilities. In fully integrated CASE tools the documentation is central, because that is where the code originates and where it is tested and maintained. The documentation is the system.

10.6 Requirements gathering

Chapter 5 described a number of requirements-gathering techniques. Because of time constraints and the nature of many RAD developments, only a few are applicable to this approach.

10.6.1 Workshops

There are two forms of workshop used in RAD projects: Joint Requirements Planning (JRP) and Joint Application Development (JAD).

Many organisations have their own terms for these forms of workshop – the name is less important than the principles that apply to each.

JRP

As described in Chapter 5, this workshop takes place at the beginning of the RAD process. Its purpose is to identify and prioritise the business requirements. Participants will be high-level users (management, supervisors), including the project sponsor, who can take decisions concerning the relative priority of requirements.

The workshop will identify the functionality of the new system. It will state simply *what* the system will achieve. This may be Critical Success Factor analysis, simple brainstorming or a 'talking wall' exercise. The workshop may also develop an outline class model.

JAD

This is a workshop in which an end user, analyst, programmers with a prototyping tool, a scribe and a team leader work on finer grained requirements for the agreed functions. The programmers are sometimes known as a SWAT (Skilled With Advanced Tools) team. The outcome of these workshops is an agreed detailed description of *how* the function will operate. This workshop will probably also use a facilitator, but on many occasions the JAD will simply be the way the systems are developed.

The JAD will identify the detailed data needed for the functions to be performed and so build up a class or data model, which can then be implemented in an appropriate database.

Techniques such as use cases, scenario analysis and task modelling will be used in the workshop to describe the functionality of the system. The SWAT will develop prototypes to test these scenarios or task models and submit them to the user member for acceptance. The prototype will usually go through three or four iterations, each one refining or clarifying the functional requirements.

During this process, the non-functional requirements (response times, privacy and security considerations, usability stipulations) will also emerge and be specified and tested.

By the nature of the development and because of the tight time constraints, standard interviewing and observation techniques are seldom applicable to RAD projects. The intensity and pressure of these developments mean that the workshops and iterative development with the user membership of the design team provide the best way to extract and meet the users' requirements with the lowest risk of misunderstanding or omission.

10.7 Suitable cases for RAD

A UK standard for RAD is Dynamic Systems Development Method (DSDM). The DSDM manual proposes a 'suitability filter' for projects to judge whether or not RAD is an appropriate method of conducting a project.

The filter includes the following aspects of a development:

▶ **The divisibility and visibility of the system**
The system has to be divisible into components and each of these must have a visible interface (screens, reports, file prints), which can be demonstrated to the end user. If the system cannot be reasonably divided up for prototyping and the correctness of the prototype assessed easily by the user then RAD is probably unsuitable. Much of the processing of process control/real-time applications is not particularly visible to the end user and hence is less suitable for RAD.

▶ **Are the user roles easily identified?**
It is important that the whole range of end users is involved or at least represented in the project. The essence of this participative approach is that it is the users on the team who make design decisions and who test each stage of the development and who thus have a sense of ownership and commitment to the finished product. RAD projects work where senior user managers are committed to significant end user participation.

▶ **How tight are the time constraints on the project?**
If the deadlines are artificially or arbitrarily imposed by management, then there is always a temptation to allow them to slip and RAD becomes unnecessary. If there is a clear business need, such as FC's launch date, then RAD is a very useful approach to maintaining the discipline of deadlines. When deadlines are arbitrary the temptation for users to demand that all requirements are met, rather than a subset, is stronger. To trade off functionality against deadlines is no longer an important part of the development.

▶ **Are the requirements flexible and incomplete?**
If the requirements specification is complete in all details and signed off as being complete there is no scope for prototyping to elicit the finer-grained detail. The development can still be carried out in a quasi-RAD manner with incremental delivery, generated by a 4GL, but there is no evolution of the system and the design is constrained by the analysis previously carried out. RAD is best carried out in applications where requirements are incomplete and difficult to articulate.

▶ **Application environment**
The exhaustive validation and verification activities required for safety-critical systems make them less suitable for iterative development. In such systems the full requirements should be defined in advance and the program coding subject to tight quality assurance procedures and testing. However, throwaway prototyping may still be applicable in the analysis and design stages.

10.8 Summary

This chapter has described Rapid Application Development (RAD). RAD depends upon a number of conditions. These are:

▶ Design teams are made up of both IT developers and end users. All are equal members of the team and share in the decision making.

▶ Design and delivery are carried out in timeboxes of predetermined length. The deadlines for these deliveries are sacrosanct; quality and cost are subordinate goals to delivery.

▶ The development work is done by prototyping rather than by programming from a complete design. CASE tool support ensures that the implemented system is derived from the analysis and design models and therefore is complete and correct.

▶ Implementation of the system is iterative. Successive implementations of the system should lead to improved user motivation. The phased implementation increases familiarity with the system and reduces training time.

▶ In circumstances where RAD is inappropriate or (because of absence of tools) impossible, the preferred approach is to perform a more complete analysis – using the techniques and models in Chapters 5–9, before undertaking much of the work usually associated with the construction phase.

EXERCISES

A clothes wholesaler with branches across the UK and Ireland, plans to introduce new information systems for the following functions.

▶ Batch data entry for customer orders (Sales)

▶ Offline invoice generation (Invoicing)

▶ Creating Purchase Orders (Purchasing)

▶ Recording Deliveries (Goods-In)

▶ Stock Recording (Stores Manager)

▶ Recording new customer leads (Marketing)

▶ Aggregating sales returns from each branch (Head Office Sales Director)

▶ Handling Customer complaints and Queries (Customer Services)

▶ Building a Help Desk for system users (IT Support)

1. It has been decided that some of these systems will be developed using RAD, and others will be developed using an approach based more on prior specification. Identify which of the above functions are best suited to RAD. Explain why each of the ones you have *not* selected is unsuitable for RAD.

2. Evaluate the usefulness of the following requirements gathering techniques for RAD projects:

   ▶ Document searching

   ▶ Ethnographic studies

   ▶ Workshops

- ▶ Interviews
- ▶ Questionnaires
- ▶ Scenario analysis

3. Describe the elements that distinguish RAD from JDI.

4. Some users are uncertain about what is expected from them in the prototyping sessions. Explain their involvement in:

- ▶ Rapid prototyping sessions
- ▶ Evolutionary prototyping sessions

5. Evaluate the possible application of RAD to the Woodland Transport scenario.

6. An examination body usually distributes its examination results by surface mail. The candidates normally receive their results three days after they have been posted. There are approximately 100,000 examination results for each six-month sitting of the examination. The examination body is now considering allowing candidates direct access to their results held on the examination body's mainframe computer system.

   Explain how RAD might be used in assessing the feasibility of this application

References

Martin, J. (1991). *Rapid Application Development*. New York: Macmillan.

McConnell, S. (1996). *Rapid Development*. Redmond, WA: Microsoft Press.

Stapleton, J. (1997). *DSDM Dynamic Systems Development Method*. New York, John Wiley.

Designing, assuring and implementing requirements

The final part of this book looks at a number of issues concerning the design, quality assurance and implementation of information systems.

The focus of this book is on external design. These are the elements of the constructed system that are experienced by the end user, represented here by the inputs, outputs and interface (Chapter 11) and by system controls (Chapter 12). The internal aspects of construction – program and data design – are not considered here, although the models developed in the second part of the book form a good basis for such internal design. For example, the class model or ELHs could provide the basis for a construction that uses an object-oriented language and object-oriented database. The ERM could form the basis of a relational database design, with the data action diagrams providing detailed specifications for programs that access and write to that database.

Chapter 11 focuses on usability, with particular emphasis on input and output design. Chapter 12 switches the emphasis to security and controls. Some of the models introduced in Part 2 are seen in a new light, providing detailed test scripts that anticipate the requirements of testing (Chapter 13). Chapter 12 also reviews two elements of important information systems legislation: the Data Protection Act and the Computer Misuse Act.

Chapter 13 looks at quality assurance and testing throughout systems development and reinforces the need for careful and unambiguous requirement specification – the theme of Part 2. In many respects this chapter underpins the whole book, because careful verification is important in both the inception and elaboration phases. However, this chapter also provides some insight into the testing phases that will be required before the constructed system is formally signed off and accepted by the users.

One of the main reasons for this book's focus on external, rather than internal, design is the fact that many organisations now construct their information systems requirements with a software package, rather than building a bespoke solution. Chapters 14 and 15 give an in-depth look at software package selection, looking at its advantages and disadvantages as well as suggesting an approach to effective selection. The models required for such an approach are also considered.

Finally, Chapter 16 looks at implementation tasks and strategies. A number of important tasks are required in this stage (file conversion, training, documentation) as well as the selection of an appropriate implementation strategy. These tasks have to be meticulously planned and performed or else the careful work of the previous stages of systems development can be undone or undermined. This chapter represents our look at the transition phase of the systems development process.

External design

CHAPTER OVERVIEW

In this chapter you will learn about:

▶ Output design and technology
▶ Input design and technology
▶ Dialogue structures
▶ Usability checklists
▶ Prototyping external design

11.1 Introduction

A distinction is often made between internal and external design. Internal design concerns the detailed implementation of files, databases and programs and is largely beyond the scope of this book. However, external design is the design experienced by the users of the software. In general, users are not concerned with the detailed design of processes (as long as they are correct) or files and databases. They expect the system to be easy to use and it is this usability that forms the focus of this chapter. It begins by looking at input, output and dialogue structures before examining some general issues of usability. The chapter concludes with a brief review of the benefits to the user and the developer of prototyping the user interface.

11.2 Output design

The need to produce certain outputs (whether they are documents, reports or files) is the main reason why many computer systems are developed. These outputs will have been defined and specified in requirements analysis (see Chapter 5) and the developer will now be concerned with the detailed design and flexibility of those outputs.

Output design has to follow many of the 'rules' of usability defined in the checklist presented later in this chapter. In particular, outputs must be consistently presented through the system following an appropriate Style Guide, while overall appearance and aesthetics will also be

Table 11.1 Standards in a Style Guide.

Standard	Guideline
Heading	The report must have a self-explanatory title.
Reference	The report must include a reference code to allow unique identification. This is particularly useful to the Help desk dealing with any problems arising from a report. Many reports have very similar names (headings), so a unique reference code allows easy identification of the report in question.
Page number	Defined as n of N.
Print time and date	In certain circumstances this allows users to identify the actual date (and time) the report values refer to, as well as allowing them to identify the most up-to-date printout of the report.
Effective dates	In certain circumstances the report refers to data values between two specified dates.
Font size	
Page break	The rule for breaking a page (for example, on department).
No data	How the report should work if no data can be found to fulfil the report's criteria.
End of report	A message showing that the report has ended.

important. For output reports, the standards shown in Table 11.1 might be defined in a Style Guide.

Examples of required Woodland Transport outputs were given in Chapter 1. These can now be elaborated to follow these guidelines; see Figure 11.1.

Using the sequence of the data to emphasise its message can also enhance the effectiveness of reports. Information generally has to be presented in some specified order; for example numerical, chronological or alphabetical. This sequence allows easy searching and browsing, particularly if the report extends over several pages. Reading lengthy listings is easier if the importance of the data items is reflected in the order of presentation. A report showing debtors in declining size of debt is more immediate than one given in alphabetical order. For example, the Last Known Trailer Location report identified in the Requirements Analysis for Woodland Transport could be more effectively presented in date rather than trailer number sequence. This would highlight the trailers that have been at certain locations for the longest period of time.

Output reports and documents may also have legal requirements (for example, VAT number has to be shown on an invoice) as well as rules for filing, distribution and destruction. Consideration should also be paid to any

Figure 11.1 Woodland Transport – delay type report.

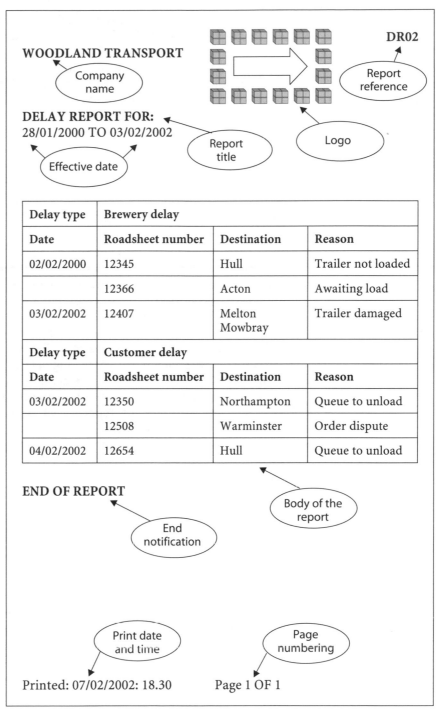

proposed manual filing. Space should be left at the top or the left of the page to prevent data being lost through holes being punched in the printed data or hidden in binder margins. Output documents (such as Despatch Notes and Invoices) may also include the company name, logo and terms of business.

Draft layouts of outputs can be made on special paper charts or directly on a screen using some form of screen painting and formatting software. The latter is much more effective as the user can quickly appreciate the contents and aesthetics of the displayed information because it is in the medium that will be used in the final system. It also permits much easier amendment of layouts, and this is particularly useful if the user is present and able to discuss fine details of position and vocabulary.

Many systems have important management reporting requirements. However, within these requirements, different types of report may be identified and defined.

▶ On demand reports

These are usually produced to satisfy *ad hoc* queries about data stored in the system. These may be fulfilled in a number of ways. One option is to ask the Information Systems (IS) department to write a bespoke program to extract data and produce the report. However, this may be costly and is unlikely to provide immediate results, so alternatively the users may produce their own *ad hoc* reports using a Report Generator. This type of software usually guides the user through a set of questions, such as what fields are required on the report (for example, forename, second name, gender and age) and the selection values (gender = Female AND age > 17) that are to be applied. Such Report Generators allow the user to experiment with the system, extracting data that fulfils different criteria. Unfortunately their use can impose great demand on the computer system and consequently create performance problems in operational systems. Hence such *ad hoc* reports are often executed on *extracted data* that perhaps reflect last night's figures. In such circumstances the information is downloaded into a separate system and the users run their reports on the extracted data of this separate system.

▶ Summary reports

Some reports only give the totals from the detailed listings of individual data records. Such reports may be produced at specific intervals and so may not be up to date when used near the due date of the next generation. Again, most of these summary reports are produced from extracted data. These reports are particularly acceptable in circumstances where the user does not need to access completely up-to-date information.

▶ Exception reports

These reports assist decision making by including only data items which are extraordinary in some way. Their purpose is to prompt some action or procedure. Many data values can be considered normal, acceptable or predictable and the inclusion of such values in a report only confuses the recipient. Exception reports only show data items that have passed a defined limit (for example, below a stock reorder level), or are unexpected in a way that demands investigation or action. For example, the Last Known Trailer Location report identified for Woodland Transport may be best presented as an exception report, only showing equipment which has been at a location for more than a certain number of days.

▶ **Internal reports**

Some reports contain detailed information but are not used outside the organisation, so promotion of the company image is not important. Some outputs act as files for answering queries by those who cannot access the data directly; for example a price list.

▶ **Archival reports**

Some reports are produced when the appropriate data is no longer required on the system. For example the details of a dead person's medical records may be output on paper or microfiche for research purposes. Similarly, reports of historical financial transactions may be required for company taxation purposes.

Many organisations now attempt to create large data repositories or warehouses that are independent of the main operational systems of the company. These data warehouses take information from the operational systems, but organise and optimise it specifically to support the reporting requirements and decision-making processes of the organisation. Reporting from such repositories is efficient and accurate and avoids the performance impact caused by the heavy demands of management reporting on live operational systems and databases. The tools that access these repositories or warehouses are often called Business Intelligence software, giving access to corporate-wide data with a range of extraction and presentation options.

11.2.1 Output technology

The most common output technologies are monochrome or colour visual display screens for transient display of information and printers (inkjet and laser) for permanent 'hard copy' output. Some systems need the output of graphical information and therefore require the use of very high-resolution visual display units or plotters. Voice, music and video are also candidate technologies for applications such as office automation, electronic conferencing, knowledge transfer and other specialised applications.

In applications where the output is to be used as subsequent input the data may be produced in a format suitable for direct entry. This may be in a human readable form (for example, a document in an Optical Character Recognition font) or in a medium suitable for machine reading (tape, disk, CD etc.). Other output technologies include mobile telephones (particularly for text messages) and emails (sent to recipients once a certain event has taken place).

Many outputs are now electronic (for example, purchase orders) and are communicated to the recipient through Electronic Data Interchange (EDI) standards.

The chosen output technology will reflect:

▶ **The application**

For example, periodic management reports required at board meetings will demand hard copy output from a high-quality printer.

▶ **Volumes and frequency**

For example, a printed stock report produced at the start of the trading period may be sufficient for certain users. However, an order clerk responsible for accepting and allocating stock to customer orders will require the immediate display of up-to-date information about stock levels. An historic order report does not provide the information needed for the clerk to do the job successfully.

▶ **Circumstances**

User and environmental constraints also influence the selection of the output device. Visually impaired people will require special consideration and sound or touch devices may be needed. The location of the information requirement may demand output devices that have certain security features, are tolerant to dirt and dust or which are mobile and can be wheeled freely around the factory floor.

▶ **Cost**

The boundary of the application and the technology used for output will have to reflect cost–benefit issues. Sophisticated data plotters may be difficult to justify given the perceived benefits of the application.

In general, the boundary of output design is changing. Many organisations are replacing outputs to customers (whether printed or verbal) with allowing customers to have direct access to data held within the supplying organisation. For example, most parcel courier companies will allow customers to track their deliveries through the Internet so that they can see the current location and status of their delivery. This service was only available before through ringing the courier and asking an internal member of staff to provide this information. This was time-consuming and most customers did not use this facility. Opening up the boundary of the system allows the courier to provide a better service to customers as well as releasing internal staff from the tracking information task.

This type of opportunity is open to Woodland Transport. The Delivery Report is primarily meant for Kronenhalle Brewery. Giving the brewery access to the internal Woodland Transport system could provide such information (together with the status of all other Delivery Notes).

11.3 Input design

Input design will also have to consider many of the issues of usability defined later in this chapter. In many systems, the capture and preparation of data for input is often considered as an afterthought to the actual processing of data, but a system's design cannot be considered complete unless proper attention has been given to data entry. There is a wide variety of methods of recording input data, and the choice between them depends on the application involved, the overall system timing requirements, the volumes of data to be processed and equipment costs and benefits. In some systems, the design of the input method is the most critical part of the external design.

The input methods must be reconciled with the operating requirements of the user, so that inappropriate suggestions are not made. For example, the workplace may be dirty and noisy, and this must be taken into account in the selection of the appropriate technology. Furthermore, the provision of input and receipt of output may be the only contact that the majority of employees in a company have with the computer system. If the provision of input is seen as a tedious and unrewarding activity, it is likely that the quality of the information provided will suffer. This will lead to the fulfilment of the acronym GIGO (Garbage In, Garbage Out). Every effort should be made to make data capture as unobtrusive as possible, a by-product of the data provider's normal activity rather than an irritating distraction from 'real work'. The overall objective of data capture is to collect and convert the data into machine-readable form with the minimum delay, minimum introduction of errors and at minimum cost.

Depending upon the method of data capture and preparation that is adopted, some or all of the stages defined in Table 11.2 will be involved, although the sequence may vary across applications.

To encourage accuracy and save time, there should be as few stages as possible and the following design guidelines should assist. The selection of an appropriate input technology should be influenced by three design guidelines.

1. Seek to minimise data transcription

Every time that data is transcribed or copied the chance of error and delay is increased. Data preparation staff transcribing data from a survey form (human-readable) to disk (machine-readable) incur cost and delay. There will also be transcription errors as the data is copied, so procedures will have to be designed to locate these errors. This leads to further expense and delay.

2. Attempt to minimise data transmission or communication

In data capture procedures each transmission, whether by word of mouth, surface post or telephone line, incurs cost, delay and an increased

Table 11.2 Stages of data capture and preparation.

Original recording	An event takes place, which the organisation wishes to record information about.
Transmission	Details about that event are sent to some location.
Transcription	Details about that event are entered into a computer system.
Verification	The entered details are verified to ensure that the information has been entered accurately.
Validation	The entered details are validated against rules and values held in the computer system to check that the entered information is acceptable.
Storage	The entered details are stored in the system.

chance of error. The cost of transmitting data along telephone lines may be an important consideration in the design of a computer-based system. If the cost is significant it may be advantageous to place processors at a number of locations with only limited interaction between these local processors and the organisation's main computer. For example, summaries of stock transactions may be transmitted weekly rather than posting individual transactions to a geographically remote computer.

3. Strive to minimise the amount of data recorded

Designers should use their prior knowledge of the characteristics of the system to reduce the burden placed on the data provider. A request, for example, for payment of water rates can print or code data about the user's name, address, postal code, property reference and payment required. The data provider's only action is to pay the bill! The same principle applies to a bank cheque transaction, where the data concerning branch, account and cheque number is already recorded in a sequence of codes and the only data collection required is the date, the payee and the amount of the cheque – the only variable data. The opportunity to code or print known data items varies from system to system, but the designer should seek such opportunities because every additional data item required from the data provider increases the chance of error in the collected data. The use of turnaround documents (where the printed output document is used as an input into the system) greatly reduces input errors and volumes.

11.3.1 Input technology

Full advantage should be taken of information already available within existing computer systems. If input can be completely avoided by importing extracted data from other systems, then important sources of error, cost and delay will have been eliminated. Data held within computer systems is likely to have already been validated. Much of the data required by government agencies can be provided to them on computer media, which may be imported directly into an application. For example, employment payments and payment details may be sent directly to the Inland Revenue on tape.

Input devices fall into two distinct categories. One uses keyboard transcription where data is transferred from 'human readable' to 'machine-readable' form by keyboard input; the other is concerned with direct input into the computer.

Keyboard transcription includes the traditional task of data preparation, where the operator takes clerical documents and transcribes data on to a suitable computer medium. This medium is usually some kind of secondary storage – tape, disk or CD. Data entered in this way must be subjected to some kind of verification and validation. Verification is usually achieved by transcribing the data twice and investigating any discrepancies. Validation is likely to be the task of a specially written data validation program that examines incoming data and rejects entries that do not conform to an expected value range or format (see Chapter 12).

Devices that permit direct entry of data into the computer eliminate transcription completely. Developers may wish to look for the opportunity of using such technologies in their application.

▶ Voice transmission. Voice recognition software is cheap and becoming more accurate, and provides an alternative data entry method for those who are unfamiliar with the layout of the keyboard.

▶ Handwriting and printing. Two options are available for entering handwritten and printed information.

– Optical Character Recognition (OCR). The technique is widely used in insurance premium notices, public utility billing and hire purchase agreements. The OCR reader reads and stores the entered data.

– Magnetic Ink Character Recognition (MICR) is used mainly in the banking industry, with the characteristic font found in every cheque book. This font is read directly by the MICR reader.

▶ Human/computer marks. Optical Mark Recognition (OMR) readers recognise hand- or machine-printed marks on forms. Current devices are not limited to pencil marks but can interpret any dense mark: ballpoint pen, typewriter etc. OMR is widely used in examinations, surveys and lottery systems. The latter is an example of a system where the input method (and the subsequent fast printing of a ticket) is a vital part of the system's development.

▶ There are numerous badges, tags, cards and similar devices which may be used for specialised data capture requirements. Bar codes are extensively used in retailing, allowing the collection and analysis of sales information with the minimum of transcription.

The relative expense and specialist nature of the direct entry technologies and the problems of keyboard dexterity have led to other possible options designed to ease interaction with the computer. These include touch screens, where the operator selects the required option by touching it with a finger; joysticks, where a handle is used to move the screen cursor in an appropriate direction; or pointing with a mouse. These devices may be used to 'draw' input directly on the screen, as well as being used as a selection pointer.

Designers must be familiar with a wide range of technologies. Furthermore, the Internet provides a good example of how changing the boundary of the system changes the input task. Many Internet sites allow users to purchase goods and services over the Internet. The significance of this to the input design is that it transfers a significant amount of the cost of data entry to the customers (rather than the supplier). Hence the purchaser becomes responsible for data entry, verification and any errors they make!

Finally, the design must be appropriate to the situation. For example, contrast a Health Visitor recording system with a patient drug administration system in a hospital.

Health Visitor statistical returns may be collated, batched together and entered on some intermediate medium before being transmitted to the main computer system at a convenient time. In this instance the data capture and data preparation does not tie up the resources of the main computer. Clearly in such circumstances an on-line facility would be wasteful and not reflect the needs of the system. In contrast, fast data capture facilities may be required in a system monitoring patient health. Information concerning drugs administered by one clinician on a ward round must be entered quickly into the system so that the patient's profile is quickly updated. This prevents a second clinician ordering treatment incompatible with the administered drugs. Slow data entry via an intermediate medium would be unacceptable in these circumstances.

Thus the data capture solution must fit the requirements of the system. The input technologies considered at Woodland Transport appear to be relatively conventional, envisaging the input of data by administrative staff. However, the designer may wish to explore the following opportunities:

▶ The replacement of the printed roadsheet with information entered and displayed inside the driver's tractor.

▶ Recording of hours driven and miles travelled through a tachometer-related system.

▶ Monitoring of tractor and trailer locations through satellite tracking.

11.4 Dialogue structures

A human–computer dialogue may be defined as (Coats and Vlaeminke, 1988):

> an exchange of information governed by agreed conventions which takes place between a computer-based system and its users via an interactive terminal.

A dialogue consists of a set of procedures for the exchange of information between the user and the computer. The appropriate commands and responses provide the mechanism for executing the processes provided by the system and required by the user. The structure of the dialogue will control the interaction between the user and computer and determine how information is presented and received. A dialogue may vary in this degree of control, from user-initiated (where the user is in command) to computer-initiated (where the user simply responds to the requests of the system).

To most users the dialogue is the system! Ambiguities and difficulties in the dialogue cause problems in training and operation and lead to systems underperforming. For example, a clerk who has problems entering data because of a poor screen design is likely to make more transcription errors. Similarly, a manager who wishes to display the latest sales forecasts may be frustrated by problems in obtaining that information (through poor menu design) and confused by the results that appear (due to a complicated screen layout). The clerk will have to tolerate such poor design features but will perform the task inefficiently. However, the manager is a discretionary user of the system and the lack of his or her support and use of the system will reduce the chances of achieving a successful implementation.

To be effective a dialogue has to be both functional and usable.

▶ Functionality is concerned with ensuring that all the required data has a mechanism for input and output.

▶ Usability should reinforce functionality. Operators of the system should be given a dialogue that is 'user-friendly'.

11.4.1 Dialogue types

There are a number of ways of structuring the dialogue. Some of these are briefly considered in this section.

Menus
Menus present a selection of the possible options at certain stages in the dialogue. Users select a particular option by giving the **appropriate letter or number** or by selecting an **icon** with a keyboard highlight or a mouse. Many systems use permanently displayed drop-down menus within a dialogue. A distinction can be made between a drop-down menu, where the menu option appears in the menu bar of the application window, and a pop-up menu, which is a floating menu that appears when specifically invoked by the user. The items displayed on the menu depend on where the pointer was located when the button was pressed. Menus may have sub-menus (cascading menus) and standards are usually defined for showing the presence of and access to such sub-menus.

The main advantage of this style of interface is that it requires few keyboard skills and hence is ideal for the inexperienced or infrequent user. It is also applicable to circumstances where no specialised knowledge or training can be given or assumed. Error rates with menu dialogues are generally low and the system is effective even if the user is frequently interrupted or distracted.

However, menus may be intolerably slow for experienced users. Consequently, the design of the menus should offer flexible paths around the system and so provide short-cuts to normal routes. This can cut down the irritation of experienced users.

Form filling
In a 'form-filling' dialogue, input data is entered on screens that resemble a form. Areas of the screen are protected from input and the cursor is placed at relevant points to indicate where and in what order the data is to be entered.

Completion of forms is a familiar activity to many employees and systems can often be designed to match proposed or existing clerical forms. This familiarity reduces the need for training. Furthermore, a relatively large amount of data can be entered on one screen and the values of this data do not have to be predicted by the dialogue.

Buttons

Buttons are graphical controls that initiate certain actions. Users can choose options by clicking them with a mouse or by some defined keyboard alternative. A distinction can be made between command buttons and action buttons. A command button is rectangular, containing a specific label such as Save, Cancel or Amend. An option button represents a single choice in a set of mutually exclusive choices. In any group of option buttons the user can only select one at any time. Option buttons are represented by circles. When an option button choice is selected, the circle is filled; when the choice is not selected, the circle is empty.

Boxes

The interface may offer a variety of boxes. Three are described here: check boxes, list boxes and spin boxes.

Check boxes control individual choices that are either turned on or off. When the choice is turned on, the check box shows an X in it. When the choice is turned off, the check box is blank.

List boxes are used to display choices to the user. Standard lists always remain the same size: tall enough to show from three to eight choices and several spaces wider than the average width of items in the list. When the list contains an item that is too wide for the list box, a horizontal scroll bar may be placed at the bottom of the list. A drop-down single selection list is another variant of the list box. When closed, a drop-down list is only tall enough to show one item. When open, it should be able to show three to eight items, like the standard list.

A *spin box* is a specialised text box that only accepts a limited set of discrete values. It consists of a text box with a pair of arrows (one upward pointing and one downward pointing) to allow movement up and down the discrete values.

Many of these constructs are shown on the interface in Figure 11.2.

Command language

In menu and form-filling modes the user responds to a computer-initiated dialogue. However, command or direct language is user-initiated. Commands or codes which should be known to the system are directly entered from the keyboard. The system does not try to predict these commands in any way.

Command language offers little support to the user but it does provide a precise, concise dialogue that allows a considerable degree of flexibility and control. In general, command language is the least supportive dialogue structure and is most appropriate to experienced and frequent users.

In practice all the dialogue types will probably be used at different parts of the system. A menu structure might be most appropriate where the

Figure 11.2 Different types of dialogue construct.

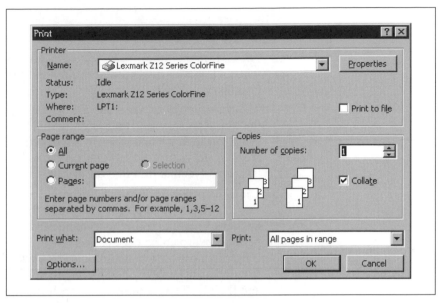

range of inputs is relatively small and all possible inputs have to be explicitly displayed. Forms are particularly suitable for input of a large set of data values taken from standard operational transactions, such as time sheets, invoices and down-time notifications. Command language is appropriate where only a few input values will be required for each process and these values are taken from a limited set of easily recalled commands. Question and answer dialogues are suitable for applications where the range of input values is too great for a menu structure, too complex for command language, or where the next question depends upon the answer to the current one.

11.4.2 User issues

Hardware and software capability
The usability issues listed below are clearly affected by the capability of the hardware and the software and so they should be assessed in that context. Not all the options (colour, pull-down lists etc.) are available to all developers. Hence the development environment may critically constrain the usability of the system.

User tasks
User tasks may vary considerably, from data entry, to report production. Usability is affected by the nature of those tasks. For example, the usability criteria of an interface for repetitive data entry by experienced users will clearly be different from one for occasional report production by a discretionary user. Hence there are few absolute truths in interface design.

Categories of user

Issues to consider here include:

▶ *The IT expertise of the user.* Do the users have basic Windows skills, so that such familiarity can be assumed in the construction of the interface?

▶ *The discretionary nature of the user's tasks.* Some users do not have to use the computer system. If the system is difficult to use then they may avoid using it as their job and tasks do not depend on it. In contrast, some users are obligatory users of the system and have to use the software as part of their jobs, whether they find the system easy to use or not.

▶ *The ability to train the user.* In some circumstances it is possible to identify all potential users of a system (both discretionary and obligatory) and to train them, hence altering their expertise and perhaps overcoming (as well as identifying) some usability issues. This is usually possible when all the users work within the company that the system has been developed for. However, in other instances the users and their skill levels cannot be predicted and neither can they be given training. Internet and extranet sites are used by people who cannot usually be identified in advance and asked to attend a training course.

11.5 Usability checklist (a 25 point approach)

Listed below are some of the usability issues that the designer/developer must consider in systems development. They are in no particular order and they may not all be relevant in all circumstances. They should certainly be viewed within the perspectives discussed in the rest of the chapter. However, they should provide a useful checklist to tackle the issues of usability and to harden the definition of *user-friendly*.

1. *Consistency*
2. *Style guides*

Users can be confused by systems that are internally inconsistent in the way they handle features and operations. Consistency is required in:

▶ Function keys

▶ Field termination

▶ Screen layout

▶ Colour

▶ Position of error messages

▶ Feature naming. For example, one package refers to the employee details as Employee Library, Employee File and Main File at different parts of the interface.

▶ Menu commands

Consistency is promoted by the development of **Internal Style Guides** that define ways that designers should implement certain features. These Internal

Style Guides are usually specific to each development environment (for example, COBOL on the mainframe or Visual BASIC on a Personal Computer). This consistency is even stronger if these Internal Style Guides follow defined industry-wide standards that are supported across systems of that type. The best example of this is the Windows Style Guide, which can be used by developers in a Windows environment to design systems that 'look and feel' like Microsoft products. The adoption of such a familiar interface shortens the learning curve of users and also provides a high degree of instant usability. Indeed, it might be claimed that it is this familiarity that makes such software 'intuitive', not the commands themselves or the icons themselves.

3. *Follows the business logic*

4. *Tab sequence*

Usable software usually follows the logical sequence of the business process. This may reflect a telephone dialogue between a business user and a customer, a standard approach described in a business process manual, or the sequence defined on a document or form. The user often enters the data in the process by using a TAB sequence to move from one input field to the next, so it is important for the designer to prove and test this sequence to ensure that it reflects the flow of fields in the system and not their build sequence.

5. *Meaningful field descriptions*

It is important that field names displayed on the screen assist the user in entering the appropriate data value. For example, the following field name in the entry of customer account details is not very helpful:

Def N/C

It could be better presented as:

Default Nominal Code

In some instances the field name on the database is often presented as the field label and this is not very helpful to the end user.

6. *Helpful format instructions*

On-screen format instructions, either within or next to the appropriate field, can assist the user in accurate data entry. For example, date fields may include formats within the field definition (DD/MM/YYYY) to assist users in entering the date in the correct format.

7. *Mandatory values*

Many systems require certain fields to be filled in by the user. For example, employee number, date of birth and start date may be mandatory fields in the entry of employee details in a payroll system. It is important that the obligatory nature of these fields is communicated to the user. This may be achieved in a number of ways:

▶ Not allowing users to skip past these fields, with a message confirming that data entry is required.

▶ Using colour, shading or some other mechanism to show that that field entry is required. For example, an asterisk is often used to indicate mandatory data entry.

8. Default values

In some instances it is possible to confidently predict the input value of a certain field. For example, suppose most products have a VAT rate of 17.5%. In such instances the computer system can populate such fields with a **default value**. This value may be confirmed (usually by tabbing over the field) or overwritten by the user. Default values improve the speed and accuracy of data entry. Default values are often used on confirmation fields (see below).

For example: **Do you wish to return to the Operating System?** Default value = **NO**

9. Confirmation messages and values

Confirmation values are used to confirm and accept a user action. They can also be used to confirm a data entry, displaying descriptive values to confirm an entered data value. For example; Customer Name and Customer Address are displayed to confirm that the correct Customer Number has been entered.

Entered data value	Confirmation fields
Customer Number	Customer Name Customer Address
Order Number	Order date
Product Code	Product Description Price

Confirmation messages are particularly significant in data saving, where users wish to be reassured that their data entry has been successful. For example, an email is often sent to confirm details of an Internet sale.

10. Clear error messages

It is important that every error message is clear, avoids technical reference and jargon, and suggests a course of action. So, for example, the error message should report the problem in business terms (opening entries do not balance) and suggest a course of action (post £1.90 to a sundries account).

> **The date you have entered is in an incorrect format. Re-enter the date in the format DD/MM/YYYY. There is no need to enter the / characters, as these will be automatically inserted by the computer system.**

This message is much more informative than a message which just says **Invalid format**. These error messages will be assessed in both system and user acceptance testing.

11. Activity during delay

Users are disconcerted if there is no clear confirmation of the action they have taken or the option they have selected. This has already been pointed out in the context of data saving. However, the issue is particularly significant when a certain action has been taken (for example, producing a report) and the system is preparing its response, but the user is not made aware of this. Consequently the user may repeat the action, leading to user frustration and potentially causing a problem in the system. For example, an output report sent five or six times to the printer can lead to a long printer queue.

Hence there needs to be some unambiguous way of showing that the system is active. Common solutions are:

▶ Displaying an appropriate icon (for example an egg-timer or a clock)

▶ Displaying a progress bar, showing percentage completion

▶ Displaying an appropriate message:

Please wait, the system is retrieving the relevant employee records

12. Response time

The issue of activity during delay raises the consideration of system response time. The response time should be appropriate for the task at hand and slow response time at the development stage must be addressed. Clearly, accurate response times will only become available when the system is being load (performance, stress) tested, so this issue may have to be revisited late in the development cycle.

Fast response time can also be a problem, as users may be unsure whether the system has actually performed the task they requested. This is where **confirmation messages** become important.

13. Clear icons

Usability in Windows software is usually enhanced by the use of icons. These are small pictures or diagrammatic representations of a feature. The icon is selected by pointing with a mouse and then clicking the mouse when the arrowhead is over the icon. The icon has to be clear and meaningful. In some instances the purpose of the icon is not self-explanatory, so its purpose is revealed when the arrow-head is placed over the icon and explanatory text is revealed. For example, the paintbrush icon in Microsoft Word is supported by the text 'Format Painter' and the pram in Pastel Payroll by 'SMP Payments'.

14. Escapability

Most people who use software have, at least once in their life, been in the position of worrying about the consequences of their next action. In such circumstances the user requires a simple and reliable way of escaping from the situation they are in to return to part of the software where they feel more comfortable. This is usually provided by using the <ESC> key or the UNDO icon. Without clear escape paths, users are liable to panic and select inappropriate options or, even more worryingly, switch the machine off in the middle of a business process, with unpredictable results.

15. *Alternative methods of data entry*

The pull-down options such as File, Edit and View in Microsoft Word may be selected by mouse pointing and clicking. However, an alternative method of data entry is to use ALT keys; for example, ALT-F will select File. Certain users may prefer keyboard entry to mouse movement. The option of alternative methods of data entry is a key issue in providing a usable system.

16. *Context-sensitive help*

Usability is enhanced by providing an on-line context-sensitive help facility. Many systems have now adopted an approach to the help system based on the one found in Microsoft software. This usually contains a list of contents and an index presented in alphabetical order. Software is available to help developers build this type of help system. An example of the QiHire Leisure help is shown in Figure 11.3 and its similarity to those of the Microsoft products is very clear. This is an example of applying the industry standards discussed earlier in this section. Users familiar with Windows, but new to the QiHire Leisure package will have little difficulty in understanding and negotiating this help system.

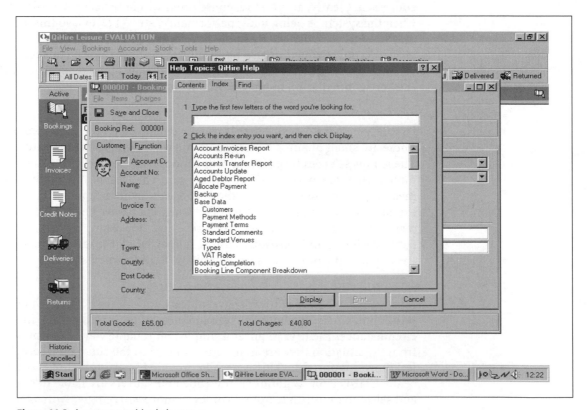

Figure 11.3 A context-sensitive help system.

17. *Use of colour*

Where available, colour is a powerful way of improving usability. However, it has to be used carefully. Three issues require particular attention:

▶ Users may be colour blind.

▶ Certain colour combinations are more effective than others, and guidelines are available.

▶ Brand colours used in marketing material may be inappropriate on a computer screen.

If colours are used for a specific purpose (for example to highlight mandatory fields), then it may be inappropriate to give users the facility to change and personalise colours.

18. *Limit options*

In some instances the field may only be populated with a limited range of data values. In this situation this limited set of values may be implemented as a pull-down list. Standards apply to how a pull-down list is implemented and how options are displayed and selected within the list.

19. *Choices displayed must be available*

Users may be confused and irritated if the system offers options which are not available at that point, or indeed at all. For example, an accounting system has a button where users can enquire about the current credit value of the customer account. This is available on all screens, including the one that creates the account in the first place. If the option is selected at that point then an error message is presented 'Customer account does not yet exist'. Instead of an error message, the system should grey it out or simply not offer this option at this point.

This usability issue is also demonstrated on many Web sites where options are presented which are no longer available or indeed do not yet exist (for example, 'this page is still under construction').

20. *Clear menu structures*

The grouping of certain options under menu headings needs great consideration. If the menu structure is unclear, then users may find it difficult to locate various options because they are not held in a logical place. This is often the case when the menus are devised by developers, rather than users. A Master File menu and its contents may seem clear to a programmer, but to a user some of these options (such as Maintain Customer Details) may logically belong elsewhere. The location of Header and Footer in the Microsoft Word menu structure (under View) could be debated. An argument could be made for it being in the Format or the Insert menu.

In character-based systems the hierarchy of the menus has to be carefully considered, so that it is not too long and narrow, creating subterranean menus with users unclear where they are and how to get back. On the other hand, menus with many options may appear cluttered and incorrectly structured. User advice is again required.

21. *Correct interdependency between fields*

Designers must ensure that fields which are dependent upon each other are properly displayed and controlled. For example, in a screen where the field **Director from date** should only be accessible if the **Director** box is ticked, the **Director from date** should be greyed out until the **Director** box is ticked, and so data entry should not be allowed in this field. Similarly, if the box is ticked and a date entered, the **Director from** box should be greyed out again as soon as the tick box is unticked and the date removed.

22. *Avoid over-functionality*

Usability is not always encouraged by technical over-elaboration. Unfortunately, some developers build in superfluous technical functions (such as pop-up calculators, calendars, and unnecessary graphics and pictures). For example, a popular accounts software package provides a pop-up calculator to enter the customer account number! Such functions can be at best annoying and, at worst, confusing. They may also compromise performance. Many web sites are slowed down by unnecessary graphics and pictures, many of which have not even loaded before the user loses interest and goes elsewhere.

23. *Language*

The interface should avoid technical jargon and, where possible, should use the business terminology of the user. This applies to error messages, screen instructions, activity messages, help screens etc. Emotional and threatening messages, such as 'Fatal Error, Abort data entry now!', 'Your system has terminated' and 'Your computer has performed an illegal operation', are stressful rather than helpful.

24. *Aesthetics*

This does include such issues as layout and colour, but may be extended to also include the general appearance of the screen and 'screen clutter'. This is usually very subjective, so the agreement of the user is important.

25. *Correct spelling*

Some developers find this difficult to accept, because they argue that it really does not matter. However, incorrect spelling gives many users a negative image of the software that they find hard to overcome, whatever the functionality of the software.

11.6 Prototyping the interface

The design and agreement of the user interface comes from a combination of the standards adopted by the organisation and the requirements of users in particular. The standards and style guides have been considered in the previous section. Prototypes give the user the chance to experience the 'look and feel' of the system and they can make detailed recommendations and changes. These alterations might be discussed in facilitated workshops, with the developer making detailed changes to the interface on the spot. If the programming language used by the developer does not support prototyping, then consideration might be given to developing a simple demonstration system in a package such as Microsoft PowerPoint. It is important to try to allow the user the opportunity to experience the interface as early as possible in systems development. Furthermore, it is difficult for users to comment on static representations of the interface, such as flow charts and screen layout documents.

11.7 Summary

This chapter has looked at key usability issues in software design. In many situations, the software is assessed as much on its usability as its functionality. The interface may also be a key issue in package selection, with one package getting the nod over another because it is easier to use and is aesthetically more pleasing. External design is a key area for end users, because to them the interface is the system. This is particularly significant where the person is a discretionary user of the system (for example, using the Internet to visit an organisation's web site to purchase goods or services). If the site is difficult to use, the person may never complete that purchase.

EXERCISES

GoodThings, a mail order company, has traditionally done business by receiving orders through the post. In this approach the orders are sent in to the company by customers using standard forms enclosed in their catalogues. Once received, the orders are entered in batches of 20 by data entry clerks, using double entry verification. There have been complaints about a high proportion of errors in the data entry process. However, on investigation, many of these errors turn out to be errors made by customers on the order forms. The fields on the order form are:

Date:
Customer No: [Optional]
Customer Title
Customer Name
Customer Address
Post-code
Customer Telephone number
Delivery Address
Delivery Post-Code

Item No
Item Description
Quantity Ordered   } Repeated
Price
Value of Quantity
Total Value of Order
Post and Packaging (Calculated by customer)
VAT
Total Due

1   Explain the principles of double entry verification. Suggest validation and consistency checks that could be made to help ensure the integrity of the data entered into the system.

2   GoodThings is introducing a system to support a new telesales operation. In this instance the telesales clerks will enter the details themselves from the telephoned order, as the customer dictates. The order details listed above will be the same, with the addition of credit/debit card details for instant payment. Suggest what measures can be taken in designing the proposed system to help reduce the risk of making errors in this new approach to data capture.

3   If a customer changes their personal details, clerks in the Customer Services Department make the amendments. A new system is being designed to help maintain the customer records. A junior designer has suggested the layout below for the clerks to use to edit the details. The screen is invoked by a menu selection. When the user enters 'Y' in the Accept box at the bottom right of the screen, they will be given

Amend Customer Details

Customer No: I118730   Date: 12/04/03

Customer Title: Mr-----   Customer Initial: S--

Customer Name: Samuals

Address: -153 Focaccia Road-----
         - Paddington Green----
         - Barnsley--------------

Post code: BA16 7LX

Telephone: 01333 99325

Account Rep SSA   Balance: £145.78-   Accept changes? Y/N the opportunity to edit another record or to exit. The clerk, during this edit, can amend all of the underlined field entry headings.

Evaluate the suggested screen.

4   Produce an improved layout for the Tractor Utilisation statistics report in the Woodland Transport case study.

5   Evaluate a software product you are familiar with using the Usability Checklist defined in this chapter.

References

Coats, R. and Vlaeminke, I. (1987). *Man–Computer Interfaces: An Introduction to Software Design and Implementation.* Oxford: Blackwell Scientific.

Hackos, J. and Redish, J. (1998). *User and Task Analysis for Interface Design.* New York: John Wiley.

Smith, A. (1997). *Human Computer Factors.* New York: McGraw-Hill.

Security and controls

In this chapter you will learn about:

▶ System controls

▶ Audit trail

▶ Clerical controls

▶ The Data Protection Act

▶ The Computer Misuse Act

12.1 Introduction

This chapter looks at issues of control and error prevention and detection. It looks at these issues from both the data and process perspective, before examining the content and implications of two important acts of legislation – the Data Protection Act and the Computer Misuse Act.

12.2 The source of errors

Most documented errors are caused by accident; the wrong input of data, incorrectly defined processing, misinterpreted output. These are due to genuine mistakes, miskeying and misunderstandings. It is the task of the system developer to design systems that minimise the chance of such errors reaching processing or system outputs. Controls will be required on data at all stages of its collection, processing, storage and retrieval. Data should be accurate and complete at all times, and its manipulation both authorised and legitimate. It is important to recognise that the necessary controls will be implemented in the clerical procedures of the system as well as in the software itself. The following controls are defined in this chapter.

▶ Controls across business objects – for example, ensuring that a roadsheet can only be allocated to one Driver. The class model (Chapter 7) will help us define these.

▶ Control within business objects – for example, ensuring that an invoice received by the company cannot be paid until it is authorised. Statechart diagrams will of use to us here (Chapter 9).

▶ Control within data items – for example, reducing the chance of entering invalid data both within each data field (only Male and Female permitted in the Gender box) and across data fields (Gender = Male and Reason for Leaving = Pregnancy).

▶ Control across business functions – for example, an invoice may not be raised until a despatch note is created.

▶ Control within business functions – for example, credit notes are processed differently from debit notes.

12.3 Class controls

The class model (see Chapter 7) defines the business rules of the enterprise and so, by default, determines some of the controls that must be implemented and tested. For example, Figure 12.1 defines the business rules for Tractor, Roadsheet and Driver.

Figure 12.1 Class model and selected business rules for Woodland Transport.

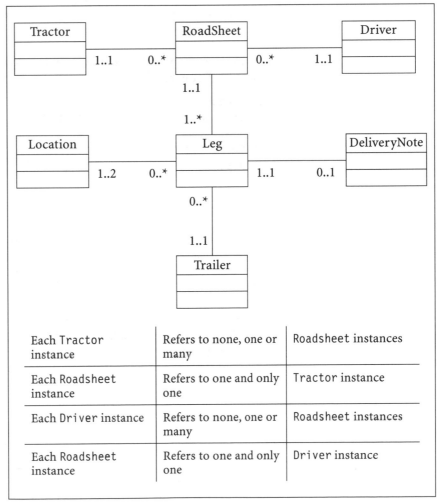

Each Tractor instance	Refers to none, one or many	Roadsheet instances
Each Roadsheet instance	Refers to one and only one	Tractor instance
Each Driver instance	Refers to none, one or many	Roadsheet instances
Each Roadsheet instance	Refers to one and only one	Driver instance

These defined relationships will form the basis of some of the business controls in the application software. For example, a Roadsheet (for example, Roadsheet Number: 0980) can only be raised for one Driver (Driver Number: 34) and appropriate testing (trying to allocate that Roadsheet to more than one Driver) will verify that control.

12.4 Data controls

Classes contain attributes and information will need to be collected about these. Typical information is type, length, format, value range, optionality and default values. Examples are shown in Figure 12.2 for three representative data items.

This information is collected by the analyst and stored in a data dictionary. The information is required for the programmer and the database designer as well as providing a basis for subsequent systems testing. In the context of the application, information about the data will be used to control data entry through validation routines. In the example, this should ensure that only correctly formatted NI (National Insurance) numbers are entered and that only valid values of gender (Male and Female) are permitted.

Control can also be imposed though defining relationships between data items. For example,

```
IF Gender is Female
Salutation must be Mrs, Miss or Ms

IF Gender is Male
Salutation must be Mr or Mister

IF Gender is Male
Reason for Discharge cannot be Pregnancy
```

Such rules again preserve the integrity of the data as well as forming the basis for subsequent system testing. It should stop some of the more ludicrous errors that can emerge, such as those quoted in Warner and Stone (1970) of one airman discharged on the grounds of pregnancy, and the award of a flying badge to a carpenter.

Code design can assist in data control. It may be feasible to implement a code design which has elements of self-checking. Thus the first facet of the code (say the first three numbers) may be split off and certain checks performed. This might include consistency checks against other parts of the code.

A code is helped by the addition of a check digit. This represents a number added to the end of the code that permits the rest of the code to be checked for transcription, transposition and random errors. One of the most common methods of allocating a check digit is the modulus 11 algorithm. This is best illustrated by example.

A company uses product numbers of six digits. 345621 is a typical example. It wishes to incorporate a check digit into the code in an

Figure 12.2 Data about attributes.

Characteristic	
Type	Fields may be of different types, for example alphanumeric, character, numeric, date or logical. A subsequent test is to enter characters into a numeric field.
Length	Fields are of a defined length. Tests will be conducted to examine what happens when oversize field values are entered.
Format	Format checks are performed to check that data always conforms to the specified format. Thus a product code designated as two letters followed by four numbers is always entered this way. Invalid entries such as A2341 or AS231 are rejected.
Value range	Range checks acknowledge that the data either lies between certain prescribed values or can only take a limited set of values. These may be set globally (e.g. Property Reference Code must be between 100 and 200) or may be more selective to identify uncommon occurrences. Thus, if 90% of all Property Reference Codes are between 100 and 110, then legitimate but infrequent codes may trigger a request for operator checking.
Mandatory	Some fields require data entry. These will be tested with no entry.
Default value	These is the value that will automatically appear in the field.

Class (for information)	Driver	Delivery Note	Driver
Characteristic	NI Number	Despatch Qty	Gender
Type	Alphanumeric	Numeric	Character
Length	9	4	6
Format	XX999999X	9999	XXXXXX
Value range	The final character must A, B, C or D	1–4999	Male Female
Mandatory	Yes	Yes	No
Default value	None	1	Male

attempt to reduce the number of clerical input errors. This will thus make a new seven-digit code.

The method of calculation is as follows:

Number	3	4	5	6	2	1
Multiplier	7	6	5	4	3	2
Product	21	24	25	24	6	2

Sum of products = 102

Divide by modulus 11:   9 remainder 3
Subtract remainder from the modulus: $11 - 3 = 8$

The remainder is appended to the code to make the new one:

3456218

Every time that the operator enters this code into the system, the software undertakes a modulus 11 check to validate the check digit. The check is performed by multiplying each number of the code by new weights and if the sum of the products is divisible by the modulus (with no remainder) then the code is accepted. For example;

Number	3	4	5	6	2	1	8
Multiplier	7	6	5	4	3	2	1
Product	21	24	25	24	6	2	8

Sum of products = 110

Which is divisible by the modulus.

The effect of a transposition error may be demonstrated.

Entered code: 3546218
Products: $21 + 30 + 20 + 24 + 6 + 2 + 8 = 111$

This is not divisible by the modulus (there is a remainder of 1), so the entered code is rejected.

It should be recognised that all these data checks should be applied together. The erroneous input 3542133 may have survived format and range checks only to be tripped up by the check digit. However, the latter is not a coding panacea. It will not prevent the mistake of a user who has a list of valid and verifiable numbers and applies the wrong one by mistake.

12.5 Event controls

Many systems have to support agreed business rules. For example, a payment may not be made until an invoice has been received; an invoice may have to be authorised before it can be paid; etc. These business rules should have been agreed and documented in the functional specification. The statechart diagram has been introduced in Chapter 9 and an example is given in Figure 12.3 for Order.

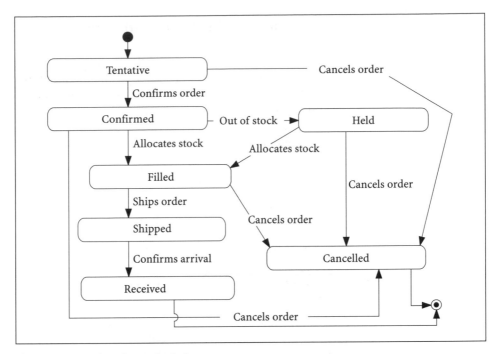

Figure 12.3 Statechart diagram for Order.

These transitions define the business controls that the system must impose. It must not be possible to cancel a shipped customer order (note the absence of a transition from Shipped Customer Order to Cancelled Customer Order) as this will cause major business problems. To ensure that such controls are imposed, they are subject to negative testing in the systems testing phase. Test scripts for transitions may be developed from these diagrams. Examples are given below.

Test Id	From	To	Expected	Actual result	Comments
1	Tentative	Confirmed	Allowed		
2	Confirmed	Filled	Allowed		
3	Tentative	Filled	Not allowed		
4	Shipped	Cancelled	Allowed		

12.6 Workflow: definitions and tests

The functional requirements of the system may be expressed in a series of business use cases that describe logically distinct business processes. Use cases were described in Chapter 6. Five possible high-level use cases in a system are given below.

Description	Comment
Arrange interviews	This function arranges interviews for the short-listed applicants.
Store applicant details	This function stores information about all applicants who apply for a particular post.
Select shortlist	The most appropriate applicants are short-listed for interview.
Record post information	This function stores information about a particular post.
Notify panel	The interview panel is notified of the applicants who have been short-listed and who are intending to attend the interview.

A workflow diagram can be constructed to describe the acceptable transitions between these use cases (Figure 12.4).

Workflow scripts can be developed from these diagrams. An example is given below, again showing transitions between use cases that should not be permitted.

Figure 12.4

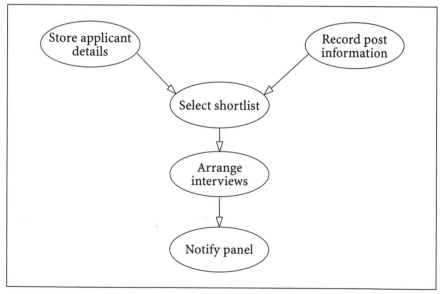

Test Id	From	To	Expected	Actual result	Comments
1	Store Applicant Details	Select Shortlist	Allowed		
2	Select Shortlist	Arrange Interviews	Allowed		
3	Store Applicant Details	Arrange Interviews	Not allowed		
4	Record Post Information	Arrange Interviews	Not allowed		

The contents of the ellipses are defined in detailed use case specification. These address control issues by the use of extensions (see Chapter 6). Hence different scenarios can be explored, including the error handling paths. An example of a use case specification for Woodland Transport is given in Figure 12.5.

The following controls are suggested for this use case.

▶ Finish Mileage must be higher than Start Mileage

▶ Finish Time must be after Start Time

▶ Delay information and action details must be entered for all legs which were not completed or were delayed.

Hence the models defined earlier in the book do, to different degrees, address the issues of control and allow the development of test scripts to examine their implementation.

12.7 Systems audit trail

Many software applications have a systems audit trail to allow the detection of fraud. Such audit trails are used to record information about significant events in the system (such as payment to a customer). The information about the transaction might include:

▶ Date of the transaction

▶ Time of the transaction

▶ User id of the person making the transaction

▶ Machine id of the terminal or PC used to make the transaction

▶ Type of transaction (such as Payment, Credit Note or Invoice)

▶ Amount of transaction

▶ Value before transaction

▶ Value after transaction

A unique sequence number usually identifies each transaction on the systems audit trail. The audit trail may be scrutinised by both internal

Figure 12.5 Use case
specification: Confirm Post-Delivery
Roadsheet.

Primary Actor	Admin Clerk
Goal	To confirm the details of a post-delivery roadsheet
Scope	Roadsheet
Level	Low level, single sitting
Stakeholders	Driver – Their pay depends upon accurate capture of their week's work
	Director – needs accurate information for his reports to the client
	Logistics – needs the data to be correct, in order to plan efficient delivery schedules for client
Preconditions	User has accessed details of correct roadsheet, and has driver's copy of roadsheet in front of him/her
Trigger/event	A driver has returned from the shift with a completed roadsheet
Success guarantees	System is updated with details of miles, delays and exceptions, fuel and oil drawn and time taken
Main success scenario	1. Admin Clerk enters start mileage and finish mileage from the driver's copy of the roadsheet
	2. Admin Clerk enters fuel drawn from the driver's copy of the roadsheet
	3. Admin Clerk enters finish time from the driver's copy of the roadsheet
	4. Admin Clerk enters oil drawn from the driver's copy of the roadsheet
	5. Admin Clerk enters the trailer number for each leg from the driver's copy of the roadsheet
	6. Admin Clerk confirms that all legs completed/not delayed
Extensions	2a Finish Mileage is lower than Start Mileage
	2a1 System rejects roadsheet details and returns to main menu
	4a Finish Time is earlier than Start Time
	4a1 System rejects roadsheet details and returns to main menu
	6a Some legs were delayed/not completed
	6a1 Admin Clerk enters delay information and action details

and external auditors looking for unusual or unbalanced transactions (for example, a Payment without an Order, a Credit Note without an Invoice).

The definition and agreement of the contents of the audit trail is a further task for the systems developer.

12.8 Clerical controls

It may be possible to implement control totals that are summed both manually and automatically. These totals are compared, and if they agree then the data is assumed to have been correctly entered by the user and the batch can be posted for processing. Such totals are particularly common in accounting systems, where the accuracy of data is paramount. Totals may be on apparently inappropriate fields such as account numbers and the nominal codes entered on the batch. These are useful accuracy checks, but clearly they have no particular significance. These meaningless sums are often termed hash totals.

Clerical controls are also of importance where source documents are posted around sections or buildings. It is very easy for forms or returns to be 'lost in transit', with the result that certain transactions, such as employee payments, do not take place. Movement control is usually enforced by the completion of batch control documents that give sufficient information for the recipient to check for the completeness of contents. Typical of data on a control sheet would be:

▶ Serial number of the batch – whether this follows the last received batch of documents. Has a whole batch gone missing in the post?

▶ Count of batch contents – the number of forms that should be in the batch.

▶ Serial numbers of forms – the serial numbers or number range(s) of the enclosed forms.

A large information processing centre will have a section dedicated to data control, responsible for checking input data, enforcing input schedules, locating errors, organising and validating output etc. They will also wish to impose standards of good housekeeping so that disks are properly and clearly labelled, unused files deleted, proper control documentation established and maintained. This is often sadly missing in personal computer (PC) installations, where disks go unlabelled (or labels are never changed), hard disks become cluttered with obliquely named files which no-one can recall creating, let alone naming, and backup procedures are ignored because 'we haven't got enough spare disks'.

12.9 The Data Protection Act

During the 1970s, the increasing use of computers, and their perceived threat to privacy and the rights of individuals, led to a demand for data protection and privacy legislation. The original UK Data Protection Act received its Royal Assent on 12 July 1984. It applied to automatically processed personal data, giving rights to individuals to access data held about them and to seek compensation for loss or damage caused by the misuse of personal data. The office of the Data Protection Registrar enforced the Act.

In 1998 the United Kingdom was required to pass a revised Data Protection Act as part of its European Union commitment under the Data Protection Directive.

The principle behind this directive was the harmonisation of data protection laws across the member states. The 1998 Act replaced the 1984 Act, modifying and extending the legislation to include manual records and virtually any form of data processing. It also banned, subject to certain exceptions, the transfer of data outside the European Economic Area.

This section briefly reviews the Act and its implications for information systems development.

12.9.1 Definitions

In the context of the 1998 Act, data means information that is:

▶ Recorded in a form in which it can be processed by equipment operating automatically in response to instructions given for that purpose.

▶ Recorded with the intention that it should be processed by means of such equipment.

▶ Recorded as part of a relevant filing system or with the intention that it should form part of a relevant filing system.

▶ Does not fall within the first three statements but forms part of an accessible record.

Accessible records are primarily concerned with health, education and other public records. This overall definition of data is much wider than the original Act, which only considered automatically processed information.

The Act defines:

Personal data as data relating to a living individual who can be identified from that information, or from other information, which is in the possession of, or is likely to come into the possession of, the data controller. This includes any expression of opinion about the individual, but not any indication of the intentions of the data controller in respect of that individual. Hence a manager's opinions about an employee are within the scope of the Act.

The data controller is a person who determines the purposes for which and the manner in which any personal data are, or are to be, processed. The individual who is the subject of personal data is called the data subject.

The data controller registers the details of the data he or she wishes to hold with the Information Commissioner. The office of Commissioner replaces the Registrar defined in the original Act.

A data subject is, given certain exemptions and conditions, able to examine what personal data the data controller is holding about him or her. The rights of individuals are specifically defined in the Act. A data subject is entitled, upon written request to the data controller, to be informed whether personal data is being processed about them. The data subject may be charged a nominal fee for this information and the data controller has a specified number of days to respond to the request. Where personal data is being processed the data subject is entitled to be given a description of:

▶ The personal data held about the individual

▶ The purposes for which this information is being processed

▶ The recipients or classes of recipients to whom this information may be disclosed

In addition, the data subject is entitled to have this information communicated to him or her in a form which can be understood. In most instances these requests for information are met by giving the data subject a copy of the information plus an explanation of any data fields which are not self-explanatory.

Any individual who suffers damage as a result of a contravention by the data controller is entitled to compensation for the distress or damage that this incorrect information has caused.

12.9.2 Principles

The UK Data Protection Act is framed within the spirit of the following principles. The actual Act uses slightly different definitions at times, with references to specific sections, but the spirit is similar.

The first principle

The information to be contained in personal data shall be obtained, and personal data shall be processed, fairly and lawfully.

Hence the information must be obtained fairly from the data subject. The data subject must be aware of what data is being collected and how it will be used. It cannot be obtained by coercion or by deception. For processing to be lawful it needs to meet at least one of the following conditions.

▶ The data subject has given his consent to the processing.

▶ Processing is necessary for the performance of a contract to which the data subject is a party, or for the taking of steps at the request of the data subject with a view to entering into a contract.

▶ The processing is necessary for compliance with any legal obligation to which the data controller is subject, other than an obligation imposed on contract.

▶ The processing is necessary in order to protect the vital interest of the data subject.

▶ The processing is necessary for the administration of justice and for other functions of a public nature exercised in the public interest by any person.

▶ Processing is necessary for the purposes of legitimate interest pursued by the data controller or by the third party or parties to whom the data are disclosed, except where the processing is unwarranted in any particular case by reason of prejudice to the rights and freedoms or legitimate interest of the data subject.

Further conditions apply in the UK legislation if the data is defined as sensitive. Sensitive data consists of information concerning

- ▶ The racial or ethnic origin of the data subject
- ▶ His political opinions
- ▶ His religious beliefs or other beliefs of a similar nature
- ▶ His membership of a trade union
- ▶ His physical or mental health or condition
- ▶ His sexual life
- ▶ The commission or alleged commission by him of any offence
- ▶ Any proceedings for any offence committed or alleged to have been committed by him, the disposal of such proceedings or the sentence of any court in such proceedings

The second principle

Personal data shall be held only for one or more specified and lawful purposes and shall not be further processed in any manner incompatible with that purpose or all those purposes.

So, for example, data cannot be stored for one purpose, such as the provision of a service (say providing electricity to a customer) and also used for marketing and offering other services (such as insurance), unless the data controller has specified these purposes. This principle applies in most data protection legislation. The information cannot be collected for one purpose and then used (unknown to the data subject) for others.

The third principle

Personal data shall be adequate, relevant and not excessive in relation to that purpose or purposes for which they are processed.

When collecting data, there is a temptation for data controllers to request more information than is actually required for the task at hand. This may contravene one of the principles of the Data Protection Act. In the UK, a number of people complained that the forms required for the payment of the 'poll tax' (Community Charge) included questions that were irrelevant to the purpose of poll tax assessment and collection. These questions were not relevant or were excessive given the purpose of the form. In general, the Data Protection Tribunal agreed with the complaints, finding that a substantial amount of property information requested was far more than necessary for the supposed purpose.

The role of the data dictionary in reinforcing this principle is worth stressing. The compilation of the dictionary should ensure that the role of every data item in the system could be explained and justified.

The fourth principle

Personal data shall be accurate and, where necessary, kept up to date.

This principle will not be breached if the data subject has actually provided the incorrect information as long as the data controller has taken reasonable steps to ensure its accuracy. However, where the data subject has told the data controller that data is inaccurate, the stored data must indicate that fact. In all cases the data controller is under an obligation to take reasonable steps to verify the accuracy of the data obtained. One of the best ways of ensuring accuracy is to ask the data subject periodically to confirm details about themselves.

The fifth principle

> Personal data held for any purpose or purposes shall not be kept for longer than is necessary for that purpose or purposes.

When the original purpose for collecting the personal data has passed, then the data should be destroyed. This may be implemented or at least suggested by software programs and prompts. For example, when a person leaves the organisation all his or her appraisal records could be automatically deleted.

The sixth principle

> Personal data shall be processed in accordance with the rights of data subjects under this Act

Data subjects have certain access rights and if these are contravened then this principle will be breached. A failure to comply with requests from the Data Protection Commissioner also comes under this principle. All data protection legislation confers rights on the data subject and this principle reasserts these rights.

The seventh principle

> Appropriate technical and organisational measures shall be taken against unauthorised or unlawful processing of personal data and against accidental loss or destruction of, or damage to, personal data.

Most data protection legislation demands that the data controllers apply appropriate security measures to take care of personal data. Such measures should be in place to prevent internal and external access by unauthorised users. This will include hardware (secure rooms, firewalls, CCTV) software (passwords, virus checkers) and organisational arrangements (internal audit, division of duties) which reduce the chance of unauthorised or unlawful use of personal data.

The eighth principle

> Personal data shall not be transferred to a country or territory outside the European Economic Area unless that country or territory ensures an adequate level of protection for the rights and freedoms of data subjects in relation to the processing of personal data.

This geographical restriction is specifically stated in the UK legislation, where it is also acknowledged that there is no restriction of movement of personal data within the European Economic Area. However, there clearly has to be an agreement and statement about which other countries provide an adequate level of protection. The UK Act appears to state that the European Commission will make such decisions and announcements.

The UK law is typical of Data Protection legislation in that it defines the geographical territory of the legislation and constraints on importing or exporting data outside that defined territory. After all, without these constraints the legislation would be less potent. Sensitive data could be exported to 'data havens', countries with little or no legislation, and manipulated from there. From a systems development perspective it is important that controls are in place to prevent unwitting transfer of data across international boundaries, leading to possible prosecution under the Data Protection Act.

12.9.3 Exemptions and offences

Data protection legislation normally also defines *exemptions* and *offences*. These exemptions may be from the Act altogether, or they may be from certain sub-sections; for example, the exemption may not allow subject access. Typical exemption areas are:

▶ Information to uphold national security

▶ Information about crime and taxation

▶ Data held for health, education and social work

▶ Payroll and accounting applications

▶ Domestic use of computers

▶ Unincorporated clubs and societies

Similarly, the offences will be defined in the Act. This will include such offences as failing to register for the Act and failing to notify changes as well as the more obvious misuse of personal data.

More information about the Act may be found at `http://www.dataprotection.gov.uk/`.

12.10 Computer Misuse Act

In 1984 two computer journalists gained unauthorised access to the British Telecom Prestel Gold system. One of the hackers left a message on one of the Duke of Edinburgh's accounts.

The journalists were apprehended and charged under the Forgery and Counterfeiting Act, 1981. The accused journalists were found guilty at a Crown Court, but the Court of Appeal quashed their convictions. It was agreed that their access amounted to a dishonest trick, but it was not (under the current legislation) a criminal offence.

Computer hacking is concerned with accessing and perhaps modifying the contents of a computer system without the express or implied permission of the owners of that system. The experience of the Duke of Edinburgh hackers suggested that hacking was a nuisance rather than a criminal activity. In the UK this led to a Law Commission Working Paper No. 110, Computer Misuse (1988) which examined the scope of the computer misuse law and proposed alternative suggestions for appropriate legal changes. The Computer Misuse Act was enacted in 1990. It did not restrict itself to computer hacking, but also dealt with issues of attempts and modification. The Act is not specifically aimed at external hackers, but is also applicable to inappropriate use by internal employees.

The Computer Misuse Act distinguishes between three type of offence:

▶ Unauthorised access to the computer
▶ Unauthorised access with intent to commit or facilitate commission of further offences
▶ Unauthorised modification of computer material

12.10.1 Unauthorised access to computer material

Under Section 1 of the Computer Misuse Act 1990, a person is guilty of an offence if:

▶ They cause a computer to perform any function with intent to secure access to any program or data held in any computer
▶ The access they intend to secure is unauthorised
▶ They know at the time when they cause the computer to perform the function that this is the case

The intent a person has to have to commit an offence under this section need not be directed at:

▶ any particular program or data
▶ a program or data of any particular kind; or
▶ a program or data in any particular computer

The Act specifies that a person found guilty of this offence shall be liable, on summary conviction, to a maximum prison sentence of six months or to a fine not exceeding level 5 on the standard scale or both.

This section of the Act is concerned with circumstances where unauthorised access is the ultimate motive. The offender wishes to see data that they are not authorised to see, but they do not wish to change this data or to use it to commit further offences. They may wish to see the data out of curiosity or to use it in such a way that is not illegal. This unauthorised access is an offence whether the motives for access were well-meaning or malicious.

This section of the Act covers the following example:

An employee has used an authorised user's password to secure unauthorised access to the payroll records, so that he can see how much one of the firm's Directors earns.

12.10.2 Unauthorised access with intent to commit or facilitate commission of further offences

A person is guilty of an offence under this section if they commit an offence under Section 1 (above) with the intent:

▶ to commit an offence to which this section applies; or

▶ to facilitate the commission of such an offence (whether by himself or by any other person)

It is immaterial for the purpose of this section whether the further offence is to be committed on the same occasion as the unauthorised access offence or on any future occasion. Furthermore, a person may be guilty of such an offence even though the facts are such that the commission of any further offences is impossible.

A person guilty of an offence under this section shall on conviction on indictment be liable to imprisonment for a term not exceeding five years or to a fine or to both.

This section is concerned with offences that are committed in order to commit (or attempt to commit) further offences, which are subject to other legislation (such as fraud and blackmail). For example:

> An employee has used an authorised user's password to secure unauthorised access to the payroll records to find information that can be used to blackmail one of the Directors of the company.

12.10.3 Unauthorised modification of material

In Section 3 of the Computer Misuse Act a person is guilty of an offence if:

▶ They perform an act which causes an unauthorised modification of the contents of any computer; and

▶ At the time when they do this act they have the requisite intent and the requisite knowledge.

In the statement above the requisite intent is an intention to cause a modification of the contents of any computer and in so doing:

▶ Impair the operation of any computer

▶ Prevent or hinder access to any program or data held in any computer

▶ Impair the operation of any such program or the reliability of any such data

Again, the intent a person has to have to commit an offence under this section need not be directed at

▶ any particular program or data

▶ a program or data of any particular kind; or

▶ a program or data in any particular computer

Table 12.1 Prosecutions under the Computer Misuse Act.

Case	Result	Commentary
R versus Pearlstone	Guilty plea	Used ex-employer's account to defraud computer-administered telephone system.
R versus Hardy	Guilty plea	IT manager added a program that encrypted incoming data and decrypted it when accessed. On a pre-set date (a month after he had left) it stopped decrypting data.
R versus Strickland and Woods	Guilty	The defendants were reported to have broken into a European Commission computer system and browsed expense accounts, caused damage to the Swedish telephone system and to the Central London Polytechnic's computer.

The Act defines that a person found guilty of this offence shall be liable on conviction to a maximum prison sentence of five years or to a fine or both.

This section of the Act is concerned with accessing and altering data. Examples of offences under this section would be deleting and modifying system files and records, introducing viruses, or deliberately generating information to cause a complete system malfunction. Modifications refer to both programs and data.

This section of the Act covers the following example:

An employee has used an authorised user's password to secure unauthorised access to the payroll records, so that he can access his own records. He alters these records so that, in subsequent months, he will be paid twice his current agreed salary.

From 1990–1995 there were at least 20 documented prosecutions under the Computer Misuse Act. Table 12.1 lists three examples.

The text of the UK Computer Misuse Act may be viewed at `http://www.hmso.gov.uk/acts/acts1990/Ukpga_19900018_en_1.htm`.

In Singapore the Computer Misuse Act resulted in 191 cases in the year 2000. The majority of these cases (157) were as a result of unauthorised use of computer services. Table 12.2 gives three example prosecutions.

12.11 Summary

This chapter has looked at security and controls from a number of perspectives. All of these perspectives have had implications for systems developers. These range from field formats and values, to implementing the requirements of the Data Protection and Computer Misuse Act. Most

Table 12.2 Singapore Computer Misuse Act – three examples.

Circumstances	Offence	Sentence
Male, age 33, desperate to complete purchase of a flat before wedding ceremony.	Sent over 7,500 messages to company selling him the flat. Convicted of 3 charges of interfering with, interrupting and obstructing the lawful use of mail servers.	Fined $10,000 with 2 months imprisonment in default of payment of the fine for each of the charges.
Male aged 29 used his ex-girlfriend's email account to read her private messages.	Used her email account to send lewd emails to her friends. Convicted of unauthorised access to an email account.	12 months imprisonment.
Male, aged 15 hacked into intranet server.	Guilty of five charges of illegal access and modifications to two computer servers.	Total fine of $15,500, in default 11 weeks in a place of detention.

of the models introduced in the earlier chapters of this book are useful in defining both controls and the scripts that will check to see if they have been implemented correctly.

EXERCISES

1   Which (if any) principles of the Data Protection Act do the following cases violate?

(a)   A man wishing to start a new club borrows a list of his company's customers to find addresses of prospective members; he also looks at their other personal details to help him decide whether or not they would be suitable members. He is conscientious about destroying the non-address details from his own system after studying them.

(b)   Customer X was unemployed when he first took out a policy with his life assurance company, but has since found a well-paid job. He sent the details of his new job to the company, but a clerk lost them before they could be entered. When he applies for a mortgage, the lender contacts the insurance company, among others, for a credit reference. When the insurance company tells them that the man is unemployed, they turn down his application.

(c)   A member of a local chess club is at the home of the membership secretary. Out of curiosity, when he is alone in the room, he accesses the membership file and looks at the details of all the members.

(d) When an employee asks to look at the data held on her by her company, she is told that it is confidential, and she is not allowed to see it.

(e) A company employs a private detective to carry out background research on a prospective senior executive that they wish to recruit. The information that the detective collects is put onto a recruitment system that they are building.

(f) A marketing company sends shopping habit questionnaires to a random selection of the general public. The questionnaire covers details such as age, gender, income, ethnic background, quantity and brands of alcohol, tobacco, tinned food, newspapers/ magazine bought, and other specific produce, such as fresh fruit and vegetables, meat and so on. It also asks questions about hobbies, about date and place of birth, about parents' dates and places of birth, and how long the respondent and their families have lived in the town where they are at the moment.

2   A security auditor from Head Office, 200 miles away from the IT installation, was able to walk out of the building housing the computer centre, with all of the previous months' backup files under his arms. Nobody was aware of this until he walked back in and returned them. Describe all the measures that the auditor is likely to recommend as a result of this exercise.

3   Explain how the analysis models that describe both persistent data and event modelling can be used to protect the business integrity of the computer systems.

4   The managers at Woodland Transport are concerned about the implications of the Data Protection Act and Computer Misuse Act for their proposed system. Draft a report for the managers explaining the implications of this legislation for the proposed system development.

5   A government department handles payments to building contractors. Each payment normally goes through the following stages:

1.   Receipt of Invoice from contractor
2.   Matching of Invoice against Order
3.   Authorisation of Payment of Invoice
4.   Raising Cheque
5.   Despatch of Cheque to Contractor

Other stages (alternatives to above)

2a   Unmatched Invoices
3a   Rejected Invoice

During this process, many contractors phone up asking about the progress of their Invoice and its subsequent Payment. Bought Ledger Clerks respond to these queries by accessing their accounts system, which identifies the current status of all Invoices and Payments. The department is now considering putting this information online so contractors can access this information via the Internet.

Define test scripts for this requirement, demonstrating both positive and negative testing.

6   Produce a test script for the use case Maintain Pay Rules in the Woodland Transport pay system.

References

Bainbridge, D. (1996). *Introduction to Computer Law*. London: Pitman.

Carey, P. *Data Protection Act – 1998*. London: Blackstone.

Warner, M. and Stone, M. (1970). *The Data Bank Society*. London: George Allen & Unwin.

Quality assurance and testing

In this chapter you will learn about:

▶ Characteristics of quality software

▶ Quality management, assurance and control

▶ Limitations of testing

▶ Testing throughout systems development

▶ Automated testing tools

13.1 Introduction

The development of high-quality systems is essential in most organisations. In some instances, this quality is needed because system failure would be catastrophic and might lead to loss of life. In other systems, failure may just lead to embarrassment and user frustration, culminating in questions about the competence of information system developers. Within the context of this book, we are primarily concerned with quality assuring the products of the systems specification and highlighting how these may be used in later stages of testing.

The need for quality assurance at the start of the project, rather than just at later testing phases, is clear when the following table is examined (Jones, 2000).

Defect origin	Percentage defects
Requirements	20
Design	25
Coding	35
Documents	12
Bad fixes	8

This suggests that 20% of the defects found in a system actually originate from errors made in specifying requirements. Many of these errors are made because the specifications are written in ambiguous English, which cannot be successfully quality assured, unlike the models and prototypes suggested in this book. These figures also show the need for vigilance in the early stages of a systems development project. It is sobering to think that almost half of the eventual defects found in a system actually originate before any serious program coding has been done.

The quality of delivered software is a major issue. There are many case histories of systems failing to deliver, of failing to deliver reliably, and of being so difficult to use that they are chronically underused. Furthermore, there are also many examples of systems that are poorly designed and coded and hence are expensive to maintain and enhance. There are a number of consequences of this:

▶ Organisations spend a considerable amount of money on maintenance. Too much of this is in fixing the errors and adding and amending functionality that should have been delivered correctly in the first place.

▶ The unreliability and inaccuracy of delivered systems seriously undermines users' confidence in information systems and information systems departments.

▶ Finally, the failure of systems to work (or to work correctly) causes business problems to the organisation. Inaccuracy may lead to it trading unprofitably and unreliable systems may lead to it not trading at all for long periods of time!

This chapter looks at some issues of quality and testing throughout the systems development process.

13.2 Quality software

Although comprehensive definitions of software quality exist, we wish to concentrate on four particular issues:

1. Conformance to functional requirements.
   The software performs the correct business functions. It does what the user specifies it should do.

2. Reliability
   The software is available for the users. It behaves reliably and does not do what it is not expected to do.

3. Usability
   The software is simple to use. Users can understand it and can use it effectively.

4. Degree of excellence
   The software exhibits elements of good build, such as maintainability, flexibility, expandability and portability.

This list is not a definition, but 'if more software products answered these legitimate concerns we would be less concerned about quality' (Hambling, 1996).

A consideration of each of the four issues listed above raises concerns about delivering software that:

▶ Does not fulfil the defined business requirements. This may cause business loss and time-consuming software changes, as the software is amended to do what it was supposed to have done in the first place.

▶ Is unreliable and has significant downtime. This may again lead to business loss (in fact, the organisation may not be able to trade at all) and urgent software changes, as the software is fixed so that it will work.

▶ Is underused, because users find it difficult to learn and use. Training is time-consuming and continuous. Users cannot confidently operate the system.

▶ Is difficult to amend and enhance. Hence the cost of changes (so-called maintenance cost) is large and contributes to high business costs and reduced profitability.

As Capers Jones (2000) has put it, 'software quality is an issue of global concern'. He sees it as critical to achieving short times to market and achieving excellent market share and profitability. Evidence supports him, because as far back as the early 1970s IBM discovered that the software projects with the lowest number of defects had the shortest development schedules and highest productivity. This is because software defect removal is actually the most expensive and time-consuming form of software work.

A number of defect removal methods exist, including:

▶ Specification and development standards

▶ Inspection and review of the specification

▶ Inspection and review of design and code

▶ Organised, methodical and documented testing – a test methodology

▶ Dedicated systems testers and user acceptance testers

▶ Production-equivalent test environment

▶ Automated testing tools

▶ Test consultants

▶ Effective project management

Some of these will be considered in this chapter.

13.3 Quality management, assurance and control

Quality itself may be delivered through a number of models.

13.3.1 Quality control

Quality control groups enforce standards by preventing defective software from being released. In this model, the quality control group can hold up the release of a questionable product until management makes the decision to release or not release it. Management must weigh up the advantages and disadvantages of releasing defective software, balancing quality against business issues. In some instances they will release questionable products (or software releases) due to economic, political or other business pressures. In such circumstances, it must be recognised that the quality control group has not lost face, they have just been overruled. There are many examples where products (not just software) have been put into the market-place against the advice of the quality control function.

13.3.2 Quality assurance (QA)

Quality assurance should take place at every stage of systems development. It is concerned with standards, review procedures and educating people into better ways of designing and delivering products. There is usually a QA group that maintains standards, promotes the quality assurance or test methodology and perhaps monitors the QA process, making sure that deliverables have been properly reviewed. However, except in certain circumstances, it is not the QA group that undertakes the quality assurance itself, it is the participants in development (business analysts, systems analysts and programmers) who perform the QA. This takes place on all the deliverables of the development life cycle (from feasibility study through to implementation) and is the responsibility of different people as it progresses through the stages of analysis, design, programming etc.

13.3.3 Testing services

Some organisations have a testing services department to provide testing services to the project manager. Such a department provides staff who will perform 'systems testing' (see later) trying to find defects and describe their effect. They may also set up and maintain a production-equivalent hardware and software environment for testing as well as maintaining and promoting the use of automated test tools. Testing services often provide the infrastructure for testing, but may do little actual testing themselves.

13.3.4 Quality management system

A quality management system brings together all functions, objectives and activities that contribute to the consistent quality of a product or service. 'Writing down these policies and procedures demonstrates how each aspect of the quality system interacts to ensure the system's success in improving the efficiency, performance and cost-effectiveness of the whole operation' (Yeates and Cadle, 1996).

Another author (Hambling, 1996) states that a quality management system has the following key components:

- Management commitment
- Defined quality assurance processes (including standards for deliverables)
- Defined responsibilities
- Definitions of key interfaces
- Verification methods to check processes
- Validation mechanisms to check products

13.4 Testing in the systems development process

The place of testing in the development process is critical. All evidence suggests that the earlier a defect is found the cheaper it is to fix. Testers often complain that they join a project too late to do much good. Although they can report the errors they find, the critical decisions about usability and reliability have already been made. The life cycle 'V' model (Figure 13.1) is commonly used to identify the relationship between the development and testing phases and ensure that quality assurance and testing takes place at the right time. The example shown below (from Hambling, 1996) uses the terms Requirements Analysis and Logical Design to describe the models defined in Chapters 6–9.

The 'V' model has three main benefits. Firstly, it provides a basis for the **test approach**, planning how testing will proceed through the project life cycle. Secondly, it introduces the idea of specifying testing requirements prior to performing the actual testing. For example, the acceptance tests are performed against a specification of requirements, rather than against some criteria dreamed up when the acceptance stage has been reached. Finally, the model provides a focus for defining the testing that will take place within each stage. For example, what testing will actually take place within 'Requirements Analysis' and within 'Unit Testing'?

The 'V' model does not assume any particular approach to systems development. Both incremental and throwaway prototyping can be accommodated within this structure. The model is a way of looking at the testing and quality requirements, not the systems development methodology.

The 'V' model demands that testing should be considered early in the life of a project. Testers can have an effect earlier in development, but only if they offer the quality improvement services appropriate to that stage, for example, assisting in the evaluation of functional requirements. Testing and fixing can be done at any stage in the life cycle. However, the cost of finding and fixing errors increases dramatically as development progresses. A key issue in this early stage of development is the testability

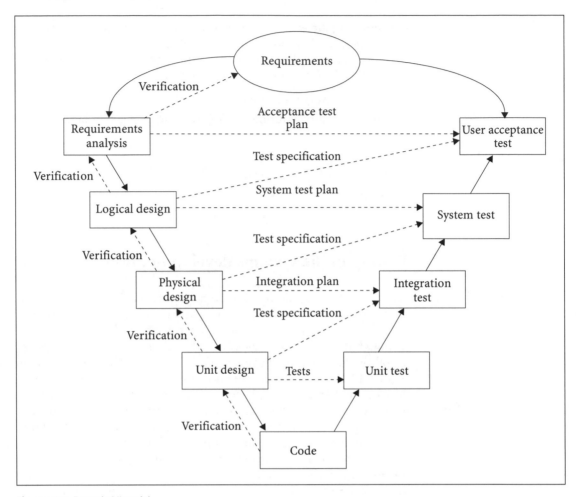

Figure 13.1 Example 'V' model.

of the functional definition. If the product is defined in loose terms then it cannot be tested. Hence the specification will be easier to quality assure if it is constructed using structured textual descriptions (such as use case specifications) and graphical models (such as class models), rather than relying on ambiguous English text. However, to illustrate the cost of impact of early error detection, if an error uncovered during design costs 1.0 monetary unit to correct, then the same error uncovered just before testing will cost 6.5 units; during testing 15 units; and after release, between 60 and 100. Hence the need for early inspection!

13.5 The limitations of testing

Many approach testing believing that a program can be fully tested, ensuring that it always works correctly. However, complete testing is impossible because there is so much variety in the inputs, paths and interfaces to make complete testing difficult to define, let alone execute.

Hence it is impossible to state that a system is completely fault-free. No matter how thorough the testing, it will never find the final bug in a system, and even if it did, nobody will know it! Experience from even the most critical computer system applications supports this view. For example, software errors still occur in space navigation systems, fly-by-wire aircraft systems and other safety-critical systems where testing has been performed more exhaustively than in a conventional business transaction system. This difficulty in supplying fault-free software is compounded by the layers of software (and hardware) often found in an application. For example, the code written by an application programmer may have to rely on error-free compilers, operating systems, embedded software and network software as well as related programs in the business application.

Because it is impossible to state for sure that systems are fault-free it is usual to supply some kind of after-sales support service. As a senior BT executive once commented, in the midst of demands for Year 2000 compliance, 'software comes with a maintenance contract, not a guarantee'. It is worth bearing this in mind. Users need to be reminded that software systems cannot be guaranteed.

The problem of providing software solutions that cannot be guaranteed is a particular difficulty for software houses. Software failure may lead to claims for consequential damages. Most recognise this in the restrictive nature of their licence agreement. An example is given below!

> Although X has tested the software and reviewed the documentation it makes no warranty or representation, either express or implied, with respect to this software or documentation, their quality, performance, merchantability or fitness for a particular purpose. This software and documentation are licensed 'as is', and you, the licensee, by making use thereof, are assuming the entire risk as to their quality and performance. In no event will X be liable for direct, indirect, special, or consequential damages arising out of the use or inability to use the software or documentation.

In practice, our inability to offer fault-free software means that:

1. Users' expectations have to be carefully managed. They cannot expect a system to be completely reliable, particularly in complex operational environments.
2. The time allocated to systems and user acceptance testing is negotiable, as at no time can testing be declared to be 'complete'.

13.6 Static and dynamic testing

Within testing, a distinction is usually made between static and dynamic testing.

Static testing techniques are used on documents; they concern reviews and inspections. They are sometimes referred to as non-execution techniques as they are applied before the software is executed. Static tests will be applied to the models described in Chapters 6–9. However, a review (walkthrough, inspection) will also be made of program code, even though this code can (and will) be dynamically tested. Static testing takes place on the downward slope of the V model.

Dynamic testing techniques are concerned with executing the software under certain test conditions. Programmers run their programs 'to make sure they work', systems and user acceptance testers put certain values into the software and predict its expected behaviour. Once the tests are run, the actual results are compared to the predicted ones. Dynamic testing takes place on the upward slope of the V model.

13.6.1 Static testing of analysis deliverables

Static testing can be examined by looking at how the deliverables of analysis (Chapters 6–9) should be quality assured. A similar approach can be applied to inspecting the accuracy and conformance of an individual program.

The analysis deliverables may be quality assured through a formal Structured Walkthrough, where the model is assessed against:

▶ *The functional requirements documented in interviews and workshops.* Here the walkthrough is considering whether the model is an accurate representation of the users' requirements.

▶ *The domain knowledge of experienced employees.* In this instance the walkthrough is looking for misunderstandings and omission suggested by experienced practitioners in the field.

▶ *The standards of the organisation or its development methodology.* Here the walkthrough is concerned with the correctness of the documentation, assessed against standards defined in the organisation or information systems department.

Walkthroughs are formal events, with participants playing a number of roles and following a number of rules.

There are three main roles associated with a walkthrough. They are the chairperson, presenter and reviewer(s).

▶ **Chairperson**
The chairperson should be a member of the project team and is responsible for the management and running of the review. To fulfil the role effectively, the chairperson should not be the presenter for that review. In order to ensure that standards are met the chairperson should have sound technical knowledge and be thoroughly familiar with the quality standards that apply to the review.

▶ **Presenter**
The presenter will normally be the author of the product. Presenting a product for review is a difficult task. The presenter should be aware of the standards that have to be achieved and must endeavour to ensure that the product meets these prior to the review. Although the presenter's

presentation skills are not actually the subject of the review, the more effective they are, the smoother the review is likely to run.

▶ **Reviewer**

The reviewers are required to help improve the product. Before the meeting they should be supplied with review checklists and details of the quality criteria that the product should meet. The review is about detecting defects. In some instances alternative solutions may be suggested, but these should not be allowed to dominate the meeting.

Each review or walkthrough should follow a pre-defined procedure. There are three steps for each review – preparation, review meeting and follow-up.

Before the walkthrough

The review should be scheduled so that the presenter has time to prepare the presentation material and the reviewer is able to read and comment on all the preliminary documentation. This is the first important principle of structured walkthroughs – *the deliverable that is to be reviewed should be developed and circulated in advance.*

The review meeting

The review meeting should last no more than two hours. When meetings last longer they become unproductive. Three further important principles of walkthroughs must be adhered to during the meeting. Firstly, the review *must be against standards* not against undocumented rules and assumptions. Secondly, the review meeting should *concentrate on the product, not the person who has developed that product.* The review meeting is not a witch-hunt. The purpose is to find defects, not to embarrass or belittle someone. Finally, the *review should concentrate on defects and omissions, not solutions.* Solutions developed on the fly are rarely successful.

After the meeting

The objective of the follow-up is to correct any errors highlighted during the review. Normally the chairperson should sign off the required actions that were specified at the review and when all the follow-up actions have been completed the chairperson signs the product off. If some errors cannot be resolved in the follow-up period he or she should report this to the project manager who may have to allocate more time for the completion of this product.

For example, a use case may be the subject of a formal review. The participants in the review will attempt to ensure that the main success scenario and extensions reflect the requirements of the Actor and other Stakeholders. They will also 'test' the use case against the standards in the organisation. Certain parts of the template may have been missed out or not correctly applied as shown in Table 13.1.

Secondly, within the use case description, the review must check that the numbering and standards of expression have been applied correctly.

Table 13.1 Some possible use case errors

Primary actor	It may be unclear who is undertaking this function.
Goal	The objective of the function is unclear or is insufficiently discrete.
Scope	The scope of the system under consideration has not been defined.
Level	The definition level of the function is unclear.
Stakeholders	Other stakeholders have not been defined.
Preconditions	Nobody has identified what must have happened before this function is invoked.
Trigger/event	The trigger for this function has been ambiguously identified.
Success guarantees	The success criteria for the function have been ambiguously defined.
Main success scenario	The main scenario cannot be completed to the required standards (see below).
Extensions	Certain extensions have not been considered.

For example, internal standards may require the sentence structure Subject... verb... direct object... prepositional phrase. A QA (quality assurance) review may be undertaken of the main scenario to ensure that it follows this defined standard.

Similar quality assurance reviews can be made of the other models defined earlier in the book.

13.6.2 Unit testing

At the bottom of the V model is program coding and unit testing. This is the construction phase of systems development and hence it is vital to build in quality processes.

Unit testing (program, component and assembly testing, white box testing) can be perceived as combining both static and dynamic testing. Static testing is performed through Formal Code Inspections, similar to the process just used on the analysis deliverables. These are enormously beneficial, as Capers Jones writes (Jones, 2000):

> It is best practice to use formal code inspections.... Formal code inspections average 65% in defect removal efficiency, and have approached 90% in some trials. There is no better method for ensuring high quality and reliability levels.

Obviously, to conduct such reviews an organisation must expend time, effort and money. However, the situation is pay now for quality or pay much more, later in the project.

Interestingly, when programmers are asked to define what is meant by program quality they define terms such as:

- Good program structure
- Modularity (however that may be defined)
- Comment density and style
- Efficiency of operation
- Adherence to company standards

Formal code inspections are effective ways of quality assuring these facets of program quality.

The programmer is also the first person to perform some dynamic tests on the software. Hence they will execute the program using certain data values to ensure that:

1. Module interfaces work correctly and that data flows correctly both into and out of the program.
2. Local data values are stored correctly and that data stored temporarily maintains its integrity during all steps in an algorithm's execution.
3. Independent paths (basis paths) through the control structure are checked to ensure that all statements in a module have been executed at least once.
4. Error-handling paths are executed and checked.
5. Boundary conditions are tested to ensure that the module operates properly at boundaries established to limit or restrict processing. For example, if a value in a field should be 1 through to 12, then it accepts 1, 6 and 12 and it rejects 0 and 13.

The scope of all of these (and any additional tests that may be considered) is defined in the exit criteria of the test phase. Once all these tests have been completed successfully and documented then the program may go on to system testing.

13.6.3 System testing

System testing is a dynamic test phase. It is usually performed by the person who established and defined the requirement (systems analyst) or by a dedicated systems tester. In either case, the tests are made against specification. It is a black box testing technique because the tester does not have access to the program code, so the way the program undertakes the function is not reviewed. The system test is concerned with what the function does, not how it does it. Indeed, this latter issue should have already been considered in the unit or white box testing.

System testing attempts to find errors in:

- **Business functionality**

The tester will perform a number of tests to ensure that the functions defined in the analysis and design stages of the 'V' model are correctly implemented in the software. The tester will not only look at the correctness and accuracy of the functions, but also determine whether certain functions are missing altogether. The models developed in Chapters 7–9 will be important inputs into this aspect of system testing.

▶ **Stability and reliability**

'Negative testing' is a key responsibility of the systems tester. The tester will try to make the system fail by performing unusual paths and entering incorrect and unacceptable data. The system should cope with this by displaying appropriate error messages. Hence the tester will apply the control tests introduced in the previous chapter.

▶ **Usability**

The tester will identify interface errors and inconsistencies. The tester will comment on the overall usability of the software as well as its adherence to local and industry standards. It is under this heading that the tester will comment on the clarity and usefulness of the displayed error messages.

▶ **Integration with other systems**

This makes sure that the software under test passes data to and receives data from other systems that it is supposed to work with. For example, a Human Resources system passes joiners' and leavers' information accurately to a payroll system.

In all instances the tester will construct detailed test scripts, showing the values they intend to test and the predicted results or outcomes. These will be compared with the actual results produced when the values are entered into the software. An example test script for a field test is shown in Table 13.2.

A decision table (Chapter 8) is a good example of a model that can be used to define appropriate test scripts. In the following example there are eight test scripts, represented by the eight columns of the table.

c1	Good payment record?	Y	Y	Y	Y	N	N	N	N
c2	Order value > £1000 p.a.?	Y	Y	N	N	Y	Y	N	N
c3	Customer > 10 years?	Y	N	Y	N	Y	N	Y	N
a1	Discount	✓	✓	✓		✓		✓	
a2	Standard price				✓		✓		✓

The predicted outcome of each path is shown in the body of the decision table. Hence the decision table is a powerful way of confirming the logic of a process (thus improving the quality of the design) as well as forming the basis for test scripts before any programming has commenced. The decision table is an excellent example of a test script because it shows the predicted outcomes before the actual tests are run.

Table 13.2 An example test script.

Field	Specification	Test type	Test value	Predicted result	Actual result
Rate per hour	99.99	Valid value	99.99	99.99	
			0.01	0.01	
			50	50	
		Invalid value	0	Error message Rate (range)	
			100	Error message Rate (range)	
		Invalid value (character)	Z9.99	Error message Invalid value	
		Negative value	–0.01	Error message Rate (range)	
		Short value	9.99	9.99	
			9.9	9.9	
		Long value	0.001	0	
		No value		Error message Rate per hour required	

This is a fundamental concept of scripting; the predicted result must be documented before the actual (dynamic) test is executed.

The use case specifications will also be a rich source of test scripts. For example, the following controls were identified in the Woodland Transport system.

▶ Finish Mileage must be higher than Start Mileage

▶ Finish Time must be after Start Time

▶ Delay information and action details must be entered for all legs which were not completed or were delayed.

Scripts will have to be constructed that test, at least, the conditions shown in Table 13.3.

System testing will also include important elements of usability testing. Aspects of creating usable systems have already been considered in Chapter 11. It is at this stage that the systems tester will review adherence to such standards and requirements, before the software is released to the intended end users. Table 13.4 summarises some of the points made in the earlier chapters and reviews the sort of issues that might arise.

Table 13.3 Conditions to be tested.

Test	Predicted Result
Finish Mileage greater than Start Mileage	Allowed
Finish Mileage less than Start Mileage	Not Allowed
Finish Mileage = Start Mileage	Not Allowed
Finish Time later than Start Time	Allowed
Finish Time before Start Time	Not Allowed
Finish Time = Start Time	Not Allowed
All Legs Completed	No Delay Information Allowed Action details cannot be completed
No legs with delay	No Delay Information Allowed Action details cannot be completed
One Leg not completed	Delay Information Allowed Action details must be completed
One Leg with delay	Delay Information Allowed Action details must be completed

13.6.4 User acceptance testing

These tests are meant to show that the software meets the user requirements as shown in the system specification. Hence these are tests against the functional business requirements defined at the start of systems development.

These tests are generally done by the users, although it is possible that the development team may be called in to help by setting up the hardware, software etc. Users generally test the system by passing through *realistic* values and seeing whether they produce the expected results. Users need to apply the same rigorous approach as testers in the rest of the process. For example, they need to predict results before running tests and they must document tests and the assumptions behind those tests. Three types of error tend to emerge at this stage and these have to be addressed.

1. Failure to meet the defined business requirements
A failure to meet a well-defined business specification is a failure of the quality assurance and testing cycle and must be addressed quickly and accurately. A failure to meet a poorly defined business requirement may lead to a review of specification methods and the quality assurance of the specification. A realisation that the business process was incorrectly

Table 13.4 Usability issues to be tested.

Usability issue	Sample usability issues
Adherence to company standards	Adheres to standard internal Style Guide?
Adherence to industry standards	Adheres to Microsoft Design Guidelines?
Consistency	Use of function keys Display of error messages Position of error messages Field termination
Clarity of on-screen instructions	Is the message 'Processing dates now' meaningful?
Clarity of screen presentation	Consideration of screen layout aesthetics
Ease of report production	Report generator facility provided?
Ease of escape and error correction	UNDO facilities
Clarity of error messages	Is the message 'Type 32 mismatch error' meaningful?
Ease of data entry	Default values Mandatory values
Clarity of icons	Universal images
Confusing feature names	Add or Save?
More than one name for the same feature	Employee file, Employee Library, Main File
Performance issues	Response time
Failure to show activity during long delays	Percentage bar, egg-timer Appropriate messages
Unclear data saving	Message required to show that Employee Details have been saved successfully
Inappropriate language and reading level	User language, not IT
Inappropriate emotional tone	Abort, fatal error, termination, illegal operation are all emotional terms
Failure to report the correct error	Error reported too late in the dialogue
Misuse of colour	Some people are colour blind Corporate colours may be inappropriate
Poor menu design	Poor grouping of options
Poor aesthetics in data layout	Screen clutter
Data entry does not match the business process	Match data entry to input forms or procedures
Excessive functionality	Pop-up calculators, calendars, gimmicks

Usability issue	Sample usability issues
Assessment of help facility	Correct and up-to-date
Assessment of user manual	Correct and up-to-date
Choices displayed that cannot be taken	Inaccessible options should be clear 'This page under construction' is unhelpful
Undocumented features	Gimmicks and old releases

Table 13.4 (continued)

specified will lead to re-specification under the auspices of the change control procedures of the company. This re-specification will lead to the testing cycle beginning again.

2. Usability problems

It may not have been possible to identify all real-world problems during usability testing. Hence problems may emerge that have to be addressed by:

▶ Restructuring the user interface or amending screen messages

▶ Redefining the sequence of fields or screens within the software

▶ Retraining staff

▶ Redefining the business process

3. Compatibility and performance problems

Unforeseen compatibility problems may emerge at this stage as users perform the tests on hardware with unpredicted coexisting software such as screensavers, or with previous releases of supporting software or with slightly different hardware configurations to those defined at the start of the project. Because of the difficulty of performing load testing, it may be at user acceptance testing that performance problems emerge as the system is used within the business and hardware constraints of the target environment.

The target of the Information Systems department is to prevent users finding any errors at all during user acceptance testing. Many departments set up specialised test centres or Model Offices designed to mimic the users and to basically perform usability and functional testing prior to its delivery to the end users for formal acceptance testing.

13.6.5 Stress testing

Volume, load or performance testing concerns testing every documented limit on the behaviour of the software. In general it is testing the software:

▶ With the number of users the software is expected to support

▶ With the size of data files the software is expected to generate and maintain

▶ With the proposed hardware and software activity and location the software is expected to work within

▶ With the expected speed and volume of network devices and traffic

Load testing checks the size of files the system can work with, the number of printers it can drive, and the number of terminals, modems and bytes of memory that it can manage and support.

Load testing is essentially boundary condition testing. Tests should be run which the software should be able to pass (such as maximum number of terminals) and other tests that the software should fail (one too many terminals). Limits should be tested in combination because the software may not be able to cope with more than one limiting case at once.

It is very difficult to perform adequate load testing without the use of specialised computer-based tools, and these are discussed below.

13.7 Automated testing

This section reviews the application of automated testing tools against different stages in the quality assurance and testing process.

13.7.1 Requirements definition and design

Computer-Aided Software Engineering (CASE) tools can assist the quality assurance of the pictures and diagrams typically used in structured and object-oriented methods. These tools will ensure that the diagrams follow the agreed conventions and, to a certain degree, will also assist in defining the completeness of a particular model. CASE tools usually have a data dictionary that provides a repository of information about data items and data fields, some of which can be used in data value definition in later systems testing.

13.7.2 White box testing (unit testing)

Programmers have a number of tools to help them produce error-free code. The compiler itself may have a debugging facility that identifies and displays suspected errors. However, there are also a number of software products that can be used to explore and test the structure of a program. For example, it is possible to automate the path testing, with tools that automatically identify, draw and highlight the different paths through a program.

13.7.3 Black box testing (system testing)

Many automated testing tools belong to a set of dynamic testing tools called capture/playback tools. In capture mode, the tool records all the information entered into the system. This includes data entry, mouse movements, icon selections and output screens and reports. In playback mode, the system repeats all input, mouse movement etc. and executes as it did in the original, captured session. Most of these tools also allow data entry from previously created values, usually held in a spreadsheet. These values are selected to represent the boundary and equivalence classes defined by the systems tester and they are entered, by the tool, into the software under test as if they had been input from the keyboard. The expected outcome of each of these tests can be specified in advance and the testing tool can compare the actual outcome with the expected one. Tests that fail may be identified displayed and documented by the software. This takes most of the drudgery out of the field value testing in the systems testing stage of the development life cycle. An example of a capture/playback tool with sophisticated diagnostics is WinRunner.

13.7.4 Load testing

The point has already been made that load or stress testing is extremely difficult to do manually. Many such tests are quite unsystematic, for example all employees in the company are asked to perform certain keystrokes at a given time, and are almost impossible to repeat. Furthermore, it is difficult to conduct tests across a sufficient variety of hardware loading, network traffic, coexisting software and use of parallel applications. Software testing tools that allow hardware, network and software loading to be simulated are extremely valuable. In such tools it is possible to see how key areas of the system operate under different configurations and usage. For example, it is possible to simulate a defined number of users undertaking different software functions in different hardware environments with varying network traffic. The information given by such tools is essential in large system, client server environments where poor system performance would make the software unusable. An example of a stress management tool is LoadRunner.

13.7.5 Test management

Test management tools are used to control and coordinate quality assurance and software testing throughout the life cycle. The tool acts as a repository for all information from initial requirement analysis to user acceptance testing. All documentation may be under the control of the test manager; for example, walkthrough reports may be filed here. Many of these test management tools have a facility to record faults and errors and to provide an analysis of these. An example of a test management tool is TestDirector.

13.8 Summary

This chapter has explored the important quality assurance and testing requirements of systems development. It began by looking at quality criteria and the implications of delivering poor quality software. The 'V' model was then presented as a structure for looking at quality assurance and testing. The products of the left-hand side of the model need to be quality assured in structured walkthroughs. The precision of such walkthroughs is improved if the models that have to be quality assured have been constructed to some defined standard. This is typical of the models produced earlier in the book. These models on the left-hand side of the 'V' model provide a basis for the later dynamic testing that takes place on the right-hand side of the model. These phases of testing have been introduced, together with a review of the tools to automate these tasks.

EXERCISES

1   Explain the meaning and significance of the assertion: 'Software comes with a maintenance contract, not a guarantee'.

2   The development of the new membership system for 'Instant Help', a motorway vehicle recovery contractor, is nearly complete. The senior programmer is comfortable with the accuracy of the code, as he has developed similar systems for other companies in the recent past. However, the project is in danger of overrunning, as the design and hardware procurement phases both overran significantly. In order to achieve the project deadline, a member of the analysis team has made the following suggestions:

   (a)   Miss out the module testing, static and dynamic, as the programmer has already written similar programs that were checked successfully.
   (b)   Miss out the usability testing, as the users helped with the early prototypes so the interface should suit them.
   (c)   Do the full system test with live data to show that the system works with real data.

   Respond to each of these suggestions.

3   Explain the difference between Quality Assurance and Quality Control

4   Considering the large proportion of errors that are made at the requirements stage of many projects (see Section 13.1), suggest three ways that these can be trapped before coding begins.

5   Quality assure the following use case specification:

Primary actor	Admin Clerk Payroll clerk.
Goal	Enter order details on to the system.
Scope	Order handling system.
Level	Low level, single sitting.
Stakeholders	*Sales Manager* *Customer.*

Preconditions	User has accessed correct part of the interface.
Trigger/event	An order has been received.
Success guarantees	On order is stored on the system. Number of orders-year-to-date incremented.
Main success scenario	1. Payroll Clerk enters order handling part of the interface 2 System provides next order number 3. System enters order date and customer address details 4. Payroll Clerk enters product code and order quantity into the system 5. System calculates the line price (price × order quantity) 6. System calculates an order total 7. Payroll Clerk enters the VAT code for this order 8. System calculates a VAT amount for this order total 9. System confirms that the order details have been stored and orders-year-to-date incremented on the Customer file
Extensions	1a. Payroll Clerk does not have access rights 1a1. Transaction is terminated 9a. Order details have not been stored 9a1. Transaction is terminated

6   Research and classify automated tools for supporting the following aspects of the V model:

▶ Requirements analysis

▶ Coding

▶ Unit testing

▶ System testing

▶ Load testing

References

Hambling, B. (1996). *Managing Software Quality*. New York: McGraw-Hill.

Jones, C. (2000). *Software Assessments, Benchmarks and Best Practices*. Reading, MA: Addison-Wesley.

Yeates, D. and Cadle, J (1996). *Project Management for Information Systems*. Harlow: Pearson.

Software package approach

CHAPTER OVERVIEW

In this chapter you will learn about:

▶ The software package approach

▶ Advantages and disadvantages of the software package approach

▶ Package evaluation matrices

▶ Imperatives in software package selection

14.1 Introduction

There is a strong tradition of bespoke systems development in information systems delivery, where 'in-house' analysts and programmers develop systems to meet the specific requirements of an application. In bespoke systems development the models of Chapters 7–9 are turned into a physical design with programs and databases implemented by systems developers. In the formative years of computing there was little alternative to this approach because generalised software packages did not exist and the fragmentation of the hardware market reduced the viability of such an approach. For many years the market-place was:

▶ Supported by the notion that systems developers had to be part of the company (like production staff, catering staff and cleaners) and located in an identifiable IT department.

▶ Dominated by mainframe and minicomputer manufacturers delivering expensive and non-standardised technology. The hardware spend (both for purchase and maintenance) dominated the IT department's budget.

▶ Restricted to a limited set of software packages, usually framed to follow legislative requirements (such as integrated accounts) and only available on a restricted number of hardware platforms.

However, in the intervening years, a number of trends have affected this perception of the market-place.

▶ The recognition that IT may be best organised as a procurement, rather than development, department. There has been a trend towards outsourcing as companies have downsized to concentrate on their core business. Consequently, the number of developers left to produce the in-house solutions has decreased significantly. IT is not the only function to be affected in this way. Cleaning and catering, once provided by local employed labour, has now been outsourced by many companies.

▶ The reduced cost and standardisation of hardware has meant that fewer organisations are tied into a manufacturer's strategy. Software is available across a limited set of dominant platforms and the cost of moving from one platform to another has considerably reduced. Software (or more accurately the people who develop it) is now the most expensive part of systems development. As a result, the cost of software production is closely monitored.

▶ Finally, the passage of time has led to more software products being made available. This has strengthened particular market sectors (for example, there are many integrated accounts packages available in the market) as well as broadening the scope of package solutions. There are packages for golf club administration, patient records, marketing, family tree construction etc.

As a result, many organisations have focused more on fulfilling their requirements through the purchase of an appropriate software package. The perception is that this is a cheaper, faster and more reliable approach to systems development. Hence the task is to find a package that fulfils user requirements or to differentiate between computing packages that all appear to do the job. This chapter begins by looking at some of the perceived advantages and disadvantages of the software package approach to information systems delivery.

14.2 Perceived advantages of the software package approach

14.2.1 Cost savings

The most quoted advantage of the software package approach is reduced cost. The purchase of a software package is perceived as significantly cheaper than developing a bespoke alternative. In a bespoke system the cost of systems development is borne completely by the organisation commissioning the system. In a software package solution, the cost of the systems development is spread across all the potential purchasers of the system. For example, a building company estimating, accounting and job control system that currently costs £2,000 to purchase actually cost £600,000 to develop. This cheapness is usually an important factor in deciding to pursue the software package approach.

14.2.2 Time savings

The bespoke systems development needs to be tightly specified, designed, programmed and tested. This part of the life cycle is very time-consuming and during this period requirements may change, so complicating the process even further. The software package is a product that already exists. It can be purchased and implemented almost immediately. There is no requirement for design, programming, or unit and system testing.

14.2.3 Quality benefits

A further perceived advantage of the software package solution is hinted at in the previous point – the absence of unit and system testing. The software package is a proven product that has undergone system testing (in development) and user acceptance testing (by the users who have already bought and used the package). Hence the product should be relatively error-free, as well as fulfilling most of the functional requirements of the application. The implementation should not be affected by the programming errors and misconceptions that can bedevil bespoke systems development.

14.2.4 Available documentation and training

In the software package approach the documentation can be inspected and evaluated before purchasing the product. The documents (such as user manuals and help systems) are usually of high quality because they represent an important part of the selling process. In contrast, the documentation supporting a bespoke systems development is not available until very late in the life cycle, and is often subcontracted to users who do not have the time to do the job properly.

A similar principle applies to training. Prospective purchasers can attend a course prior to buying the product and so further evaluate the suitability of the package. Similarly, economies of scale allow the software vendors to produce and provide high-quality training courses, supported by professional trainers, at a relatively cheap price.

14.2.5 Organised maintenance and enhancement

Software products are usually supported by a formal maintenance agreement. Although this agreement costs money, it usually provides:

- ▶ unlimited access to a Help desk, where experts can sort out user problems
- ▶ upgrades to the software that correct known faults and also include new functionality defined and agreed with the user community

The cost of this support and enhancement is again spread across a number of users and so can be offered relatively cheaply to each individual customer. The cost of providing such services would be extremely expensive if it were borne completely by an organisation commissioning a bespoke development. The upgrade issue is particularly significant to organisations purchasing accounts and payroll packages. The functionality of such systems is affected by legislative changes made by government. These changes are frequent and unpredictable. It is comforting for the customer to know that all amendments are covered by the agreed software contract.

14.2.6 Try before you buy

This is perhaps the most significant advantage of the software package approach – the ability to examine the product in detail before purchasing it. This is clearly not possible in the bespoke approach to systems development where the product is not ready until the end of the project. The evaluation of the package can be assisted if it can be borrowed (or rented) for a trial period and used in the target hardware and software environment. This can be supplemented by visits to actual users (reference sites) where the operation of the package can be observed and user comments and experiences documented.

However, it must be recognised that the ability to 'try before you buy' places the initiative with the user – not the supplier. Hence the fit to user requirements must be ascertained and confirmed by the customer – not the supplier.

14.3 Perceived disadvantages of the software package approach

14.3.1 Ownership

In the bespoke systems development approach, the ownership of the software usually resides with the purchaser – the customer, not the supplier. This is particularly clear if the development is undertaken 'in-house', where the ownership of the code clearly resides with the organisation, not the IT department or individual programmers. Even if an external software house produces the code, the contract usually specifies that the source code belongs to the commissioning agent (the customer) and not the supplier.

In the software package approach, the ownership of the software usually remains with the supplier. Customers are licensed to use the product, but they never own it. This ownership issue has three implications:

1. The supplier decides the future development of the package. Hence future functionality is not in the control of the customer – although of course they can lobby for certain features to be included in future releases.
2. The software supplier can make decisions about the ownership and support of the product. These decisions may have far reaching effects

on current customers. For example, the software supplier may decide to withdraw support from earlier versions of the package. Hence customers may be forced into unnecessary (and potentially expensive) upgrades. These may involve hardware upgrades.

3. The software supplier may decide to sell their product to a third party. Individual customers may be unnerved or inconvenienced by such a move. For example, a few years ago a popular package was sold to a large industry player with a reputation for aggressive customer relations. Many customers of the package were worried by this move (despite assurances from the new owner) because they were more comfortable with the 'laid-back' approach of the former owner. Some began to make plans to move their systems to a rival product.

The key issue here is that the software purchaser has little control over the future direction and ownership of the product they are buying. This is not the case with bespoke development.

14.3.2 Financial stability of the supplier

Internal Information Systems (IS) departments do not go out of business. However, external software suppliers are subject to the vagaries of management and the markets. There is a risk that they may go out of business, or experience financial problems that affect the quality of their support and development services. It is possible to reduce these risks (through escrow agreements; see later), but the disruption likely to accompany the enactment of such an agreement should not be underestimated.

14.3.3 Competitive edge

Many organisations claim that they use (or wish to use) IT and IS as a competitive edge in the market-place. They develop bespoke systems to give them that edge. In the software package approach, the software solution (or product) is open to all competitors and potential competitors. It is difficult to see how such a solution can provide a competitive edge, as all potential competitors have access to that solution.

14.3.4 Failure to fit requirements

One of the most commonly claimed disadvantages of the software package approach is the inability of the product to fit all the users' requirements. This means that either:

1. Users have to make compromises and accept that they will not get all the functionality they require, or
2. Tailored amendments will have to be made to the software product to deliver the required functionality.

Whichever way is chosen, it is clear that most software packages do not fulfil all the user requirements defined for a particular application. Furthermore, they often include facilities and functions not required by a particular user, which only serves to confuse when the product is implemented in the organisation. In contrast, the bespoke solution should completely fulfil all the user's requirements and, if it does not, will be amended until it does.

14.3.5 Legal redress

In a bespoke development, the ultimate failure of the system to fulfil the user's functional requirements can be resolved (usually in favour of the customer) by law. Clearly this last resort is inappropriate if the system has been developed by an internal IS department, but it is an option if the system has been developed by an external software house. Legal redress is well documented in a number of high-profile cases.

However, the legal responsibilities of a software package provider are more complex. The licensing agreement is defined in favour of the supplier. In that agreement there is usually a clause that states that the package may not support the functional requirements of the customer – and it is the customer's responsibility to ensure that it does. Unfortunately, many customers do not take that responsibility seriously and are unable to properly assess whether a particular package supports their needs – or 80% of their functional requirements – whatever 80% means!

14.3.6 The changing nature of requirements

There is plenty of evidence to show that requirements change during the lifetime of a system. These changes are due to a number of factors:

▶ Users change. New managers arrive who have a different perception of requirements and the business process. They demand new output reports to support their particular management information requirements.
▶ The business changes. The business may decide that it wants to operate in a different way. This may be led by new product and marketing initiatives or may simply be a reaction to changes in the business environment that force the company to rethink its organisation, products and services.

Changes are due to:

▶ Actual experience – using the software may lead to a realisation that the functional requirements were not quite correct.
▶ Emergent hardware and software technologies – bespoke systems can usually be amended to reflect these changes. However, software packages may or may not. The problem is still one of control. It is not possible for the software supplier to predict or to cope with changes in

a particular business implementation. Some of the changes may be incorporated into a future release, but at the outset there is no guarantee of this.

The main point is that users normally evaluate potential packages against the current requirements of current users, and this may lead to products quickly becoming inappropriate in dynamic organisations and market-places.

In summary, organisations now have the opportunity to fulfil most of their information system requirements through software packages, rather than building bespoke solutions. The advantages of this approach, particularly the perceived cost and time savings, appear self-evident. However, there are disadvantages, which must be carefully understood and evaluated before selecting and purchasing a software package. The organisation must also be aware that it is probably entering a long-term commercial relationship with a supplier. It may be costly and difficult to end such a relationship, as converting data from one product to another may be prohibitively expensive. Hence the risks of the software package approach must be identified and appropriate risk avoidance and mitigation actions developed.

14.4 High-level evaluation matrix

If the organisation wishes to adopt the software package approach, it might begin by establishing a high-level evaluation matrix, which considers five categories of customer need. The first stage in the approach is to allocate the relative importance, to the customer, of each of these categories. It is important to initially quantify this relative importance, but it must also be stressed that these weightings may be reconsidered right through to finally placing the order for a particular product. The weightings of the categories also give some assistance in defining how much time should be spent investigating each of these requirements.

	Category	Relative importance
1	Current requirements	
2	Product requirements	
3	Supplier requirements	
4	Implementation requirements	
5	Cost and time constraints	
	Total	100

For example, Woodland Transport is considering a software package approach to the Recording Vehicle Movements project. The initial project workshop has identified the following weights in the high-level evaluation matrix:

	Category	Relative importance
1	Current requirements	40
2	Product requirements	10
3	Supplier requirements	20
4	Implementation requirements	10
5	Cost and time constraints	20
	Total	100

It is also possible to produce a more sensitive breakdown by subdividing each category, creating the ten-category matrix defined below. Each of these categories will be examined in detail in Section 14.5.

	Category	Relative importance
1.1	Functional requirements	30
1.2	Non-functional requirements	10
2.1	Technical requirements	8
2.2	Design requirements	2
3.1	Supplier stability requirements	18
3.2	Supplier citizenship requirements	2
4.1	Initial implementation requirements	8
4.2	Operability requirements	2
5.1	Cost constraints	18
5.2	Time constraints	2
	Total	100

14.4.1 Imperatives

Imperatives are a fundamental part of software package selection. They are requirements the software package must definitely provide for it to be considered in the selection process. If an *Imperative* is not supported then the package is excluded from the selection. Because of the draconian nature of the *Imperative* it must be used wisely and sparingly. *Imperatives* may be particularly identified in technical, supplier and cost requirements. Examples of each are given below.

Technical requirements
This is a significant area for *Imperatives* because the IT infrastructure or IS strategy of the organisation may define particular constraints. These constraints may concern, for example:

- Hardware
- Operating systems
- Programming languages
- Network protocols
- Co-resident software
- Available memory
- Disk space

Supplier stability requirements
Imperatives might state that the supplier must have three years of audited accounts, or that it is, for example, a Microsoft Certified Solution Provider.

Cost constraints
Cost is usually a very important *Imperative*. There is no point in receiving tenders from suppliers offering products that are considerably above the agreed budget. There are two distinct ways of tackling this *Imperative*:

- Stating the agreed budget in the Invitation to Tender
- Pre-selecting suppliers whose products seem to fall within +15% of the agreed budget

This latter consideration allows for hard negotiation at contract time!

Time constraints
Imposed time constraints and deadlines are another source of important *Imperatives*.

14.5 Functional and non-functional requirements

These are the first two categories in the evaluation matrix and are usually given a large weighting by users. Functional requirements concern the required business functionality of the package. This includes requirements that are supported by the current system (for example, producing a payslip) as well as future requirements, which can be anticipated and articulated (for example, identifying staff competency gaps). In conventional terms, the definition of functional requirements is the product of analysis, culminating in a Requirements Specification signed off by the user. The functional requirements will be suggested by the operations of the current system (whether it is clerical or computer-based) and current managers and employees will identify the anticipated future requirements.

Non-functional requirements are requirements the package must support but that are not directly related to the business or organisational functions it performs; for example:

- Performance requirements
- Security and audit requirements

▶ Legal compliance

▶ Interfaces with other systems

▶ Archiving, backup and recovery

Functional requirements are defined using the models explained earlier in the book. However, because there is no ultimate need to construct a bespoke design from these models, the level of detail and method of expression, needs consideration.

In the first part of software package evaluation the process model can be explored with use cases, but the results can be converted into a checklist approach, with each element of this checklist being allocated a priority or company need. For example, consider again the use case for confirming the details of a post-delivery roadsheet (Figure 14.1).

Figure 14.1 Use case for Confirm Roadsheet.

Primary actor	Admin Clerk
Goal	To confirm the details of a post-delivery roadsheet
Scope	Roadsheet
Level	Low level, single sitting
Stakeholders	*Driver* – Their pay depends upon accurate capture of their week's work *Director* – needs accurate information for his reports to the client *Logistics* – needs the data to be correct, in order to plan efficient delivery schedules for client
Preconditions	User has accessed details of correct roadsheet, and has driver's copy of roadsheet in front of him/her
Trigger/event	A driver has returned from the shift with a completed roadsheet
Success guarantees	System is updated with details of miles, delays and exceptions, fuel and oil drawn and time taken
Main success scenario	1. Admin Clerk enters start mileage and finish mileage from the driver's copy of the roadsheet 2. Admin Clerk enters fuel drawn from the driver's copy of the roadsheet 3. Admin Clerk enters finish time from the driver's copy of the roadsheet 4. Admin Clerk enters oil drawn from the driver's copy of the roadsheet 5. Admin Clerk enters the trailer number for each leg from the driver's copy of the roadsheet 6. Admin Clerk confirms that all legs completed/not delayed
Extensions	2a Finish Mileage is lower than Start Mileage 2a1 System rejects roadsheet details and returns to main menu 4a Finish Time is earlier than Start Time 4a1 System rejects roadsheet details and returns to main menu 6a Some legs were delayed/not completed 6a1 Admin Clerk enters delay information and action details

This use case may be converted into a checklist of requirements with each requirement given a value from a simple scale. This allocation of a numeric value is adopted to allow the calculation of weighted values in the subsequent matrices.

Company need	Scale
High	8–10
Medium	4–7
Low	1–3
Not needed	0

Applying these to the Confirm Roadsheet use case results in the following table:

From Confirm Roadsheet	Company need
Enter mileage details	10
Enter fuel details	10
Enter time details	7
Enter oil details	5
Enter trailer details	10
Enter delay details	10
Validation of time details	6
Validation of fuel details	6

The static class model (see Chapter 7) remains a powerful tool in analysing functional requirements. It is suggested that this continue to be an important part of the analysis, because it will identify important requirements that cannot be expressed in a textual checklist. However, it is unlikely that Sequence Diagrams (Chapter 8), Data Flow Diagrams (Chapter 8) and Entity Life Histories (Chapter 9) will have any role in the software package approach. The key models are likely to be use cases, class diagrams and statechart diagrams (Chapter 9).

Further information can be held about classes and this may include volume data (for example, 80 roadsheets are issued every shift) and retention and deletion rules. Information can also be held against attributes (for example, roadsheet number). This might include field lengths, default values and mandatory/optionality rules. The analyst can determine the level of detail in the context of the project.

In some instances it may be essential that the system support certain lengths and formats of particular data items, as it is not possible for the company to change these. For example, a company-wide product coding system may be an *Imperative* in software package selection. If this is missed in the analysis stage, then the consequences can be very embarrassing. For example, Woodland Transport may wish to store Kronenhalle information on its system. The format and length of such information is outside Woodland Transport's control, so it must ensure that any software package they purchase supports these format and length requirements as they cannot change the structure of the data items to fit the package.

Non-functional requirements will also be established through conventional analysis. Seven potential categories are listed in the table below. However, these are generic headings and can be converted into specific requirements in a particular project. The ratings given below are for the Woodland Transport system.

Non-functional requirements	Need	Rating
Performance requirements	High	9
Interfaces with other systems	Medium	5
Security and audit issues	Low	3
Legal issues	Low	3
Archiving, backup and recovery	Low	1
User interface requirements	Medium	4
Reporting	Low	2

14.6 Product requirements

This may be divided into two sections: technical and design requirements. The Invitation To Tender (ITT) will include a number of questions concerning the use and structure of the product. This will include the size and distribution of the current user base, licence agreements for the product, a description of the product and (where relevant) the modules of the product and how they fit together.

14.6.1 Technical requirements

In some instances the software package has to be evaluated against certain technical requirements. For example, there may be preferences about the operating system or the programming language used to write the software. There may also be a preferred hardware platform. Some of these technical requirements may become *Imperatives*.

Technical issues that may have to be addressed include:

▶ **Hardware platform and available hardware resources**
This needs to be included in the evaluation if the hardware platform is not an *Imperative*. At Woodland Transport there may be some flexibility in the selected hardware but the company has certain preferences and wants these to be included in the evaluation.

▶ **Software development language and database preferences**
In general, the software development language and the supporting database should not be an important issue. However, the customer may have certain preferences, perhaps concerning future maintainability, portability and flexibility, that need to be considered. Development using popular and well-established products may be an important part of the evaluation. In principle, software developed using a Relational Database Management System (RDBMS) and Object-Oriented Programming languages (OOPs) are to be preferred.

▶ **The operating system the software package supports**
This may again be an *Imperative*; for example, the software must run under Windows NT. However, where there is some flexibility it should be included in the evaluation. Preference may be given to non-proprietary operating systems (such as Unix) over operating systems that are developed and owned by one computer manufacturer.

▶ **Network and other communications issues**
It may be desirable for the software to support standard communication protocols.

14.6.2 Design requirements

It is clearly impossible to be sure if the software will fulfil requirements that have not yet been established. However, it has to be recognised that businesses alter their requirements and priorities to reflect changes in the organisational environment, new business strategies and changes in managers and their priorities. Part of the evaluation may be an assessment of how well the product is designed to provide future flexibility. The stability of the application under consideration is clearly very important. Some business applications are relatively stable (payroll, accounts); others are more volatile (HR systems, MIS applications).

Design requirements are rarely *Imperatives* but they may play an important role in the evaluation. Issues that may need considering are:

▶ **Architecture**
In many instances it is still difficult to assemble systems from components selected from several manufacturers. However, several vendors have formed the Open Applications Group (OAG) in order to set standards for an open application architecture with the aim of allowing their components to be linked seamlessly together into a comprehensive solution. Adherence to the principles of open architecture and open systems may be an important issue in the evaluation of competing solutions.

▶ **Internal design**
The way the software has been designed influences its future flexibility. In general, the data design (files, tables, databases etc.) should lend itself to flexibility, maintainability and expandability. The program design should be modular and structured with program modules displaying high cohesion and loose coupling. Complex code

leads to high error rates, difficulties in defect identification and removal, and expensive maintenance. There are well-established code complexity measures that help avoid such problems (such as McCabe's Cyclomatic Complexity Number). It may be useful to include such measures in the evaluation to see whether the software vendor uses such measures in the program design. At least one major company does not permit program modules to be released with a Cyclomatic Complexity value of more than 15.

▶ **Configurability**

Configurability is about how the software package may be tailored to the customer's requirements, without resorting to changes in source code. In the context of the approach defined in this chapter, alterations and additions to source code are called *Modifications* and should be avoided at all cost. In contrast, configuration can be performed by a non-programmer and is concerned with setting parameters and creating records that make the application appropriate to the customer's environment.

These issues may be summarised on a product requirements matrix, using the classification system introduced earlier in the chapter. The ratings given below are for the Woodland Transport System.

Product requirements	Need	Rating
Hardware requirements	Low	3
Software requirements	Medium	5
Operating system requirements	Low	3
Networks and communications	Low	1
Architecture	Low	1
Internal design	High	9
Configurability	High	9

14.7 Supplier requirements

14.7.1 Supplier stability requirements

Stability requirements are concerned with evaluating the experience, stability and financial robustness of competing suppliers. Most companies wish to buy products from companies that they perceive as being respected, stable and established and so will be able to offer software support and development for the foreseeable future.

Size and location
The Invitation To Tender (ITT) will request certain simple administrative information from the supplier (name, address, contact names etc.) and

some of these may find their way into the supplier evaluation matrix. For example, the customer may prefer to deal with suppliers who are geographically close, perhaps within walking distance of their main office. Questions may also be asked about the size of the company (number of sites, departments, employees) and this again may form part of the evaluation. However, it should be acknowledged that large, significant suppliers might not always be desirable. A relatively small customer may be happier dealing with a smaller supplier where they perceive that their account will be valued and given more attention.

Financial stability

Clearly the ITT will request a range of accounting reports. It is normal to ask for audited accounts and annual reports for the last three years. Management accounts may also be requested for the period since the last audited accounts. However, as well as requesting this information, some thought has to be given as to how it will be evaluated. For example, how important is it that the company has been profitable for the last three years? It may also be important that the software vendor has a turnover above a certain amount, for example £1.5 million per annum. There may also be *Imperatives* in the assessment of the financial stability of the vendor. For example, products supplied by companies with less than two years trading may not be considered at all.

Market-place knowledge

Most customers are happier dealing with suppliers who are well established in the market-place, have a good reputation and have a deep understanding of the issues, jargon and preoccupations of the industry. Hence some weighting may be given for duration and expertise in the marketplace. This is unlikely to be an *Imperative*, but may be included in the supplier evaluation matrix.

Ownership and structure

The ownership and structure of the company is usually requested in the ITT. The aim is to see whether the company is part of a larger group (which may itself be subject to further financial investigation) and to identify significant shareholders. Many customers feel reassured if they can identify major institutions among the shareholders. The structure of the company will include its legal status. There are a number of possibilities (sole trader, partnership, limited partnership, private limited company, public limited company). There may be certain preferences. For example, the customer may be wary of dealing with sole traders and partnerships because of their unlimited liability. Certain details about the company (such as company registration number) will be required for the investigations that will be conducted as part of the evaluation. Certain *Imperatives* may be identified within this sub-section; for example, the supplier must be a limited company.

Accreditation

It may be important that the supplier is an accredited provider of certain hardware and software products. Other accreditations may be more general and relate to the industry as a whole, for example International Organization for Standardization (ISO) and TickIT accreditations. Again, some of these accreditations may be *Imperatives*, but in other instances they will need to be considered during the evaluation of the supplier.

Quality assurance procedures

The customer may wish to identify and preferably inspect the quality assurance procedures of the vendor. It may be important that certain structural components of quality assurance (such as project quality plans and test methodologies) are in place and are adhered to. The Software Engineering Institute's Capability Maturity Model (CMM) is an indication of the development maturity of the supplier. It may be important, for example to request that vendors have reached at least level four (managed) in the CMM hierarchy and to show evidence of this.

Automated tools

The use of CASE tools and program generators may again be an indicator of the maturity of the supplier, the robustness of the software package and the ability of the supplier to respond quickly and reliably to requests for software changes. Questions about the use of such tools may be included in the ITT and they may also be part of the evaluation. Some authors make a particular point of evaluating the use of CASE tools in the evaluation matrix, but it is unlikely that use of CASE tools will be an *Imperative*.

Insurance

The customer may have to satisfy him or herself that the vendors have adequate insurance cover. This may include employer's liability insurance, public liability insurance and professional indemnity insurance. Again, some of these requirements may be *Imperatives*, while in other circumstances they should be defined within the evaluation process.

Procedures for handling disputes

The supplier needs to be asked how disputes between the vendor and the customer will be settled. It is unlikely that this will be an *Imperative*, but it may have some weighting in the supplier evaluation matrix.

Outstanding issues

Outstanding issues may include questions about current litigation, arbitration, or the involvement of directors in receivership action in other companies. Outstanding organisational issues may concern such things as merger discussions or proposed restructuring or sale of the company.

14.7.2 Supplier citizenship requirements

In certain instances the supplier may also be evaluated in terms of its good citizenship. This might consider, for example, its policies towards its employees; the environment; working conditions; race and gender issues in the workforce; and its trading policies with other nations.

Questions about such issues are particularly common in public sector ITTs, although some thought has to be given as to how the responses will be evaluated. Listed below are some potential subheadings that may be included in the evaluation.

- ▶ Equal opportunities policy
- ▶ Race relations policy
- ▶ Health and safety policy
- ▶ Trade union policy
- ▶ Charity and donations policy

Overall responsiveness
Responsiveness will not be directly assessed within the ITT, but the matrix needs somewhere to record the impressions and recommendations of reference sites, user groups and other customers. The need for an evaluation copy of the software and possible arrangements for a 'trial use' of the software might also be recorded in this section. This part of the matrix will be revisited in the later stages of the software evaluation process.

Using the classification principles already introduced in this chapter, the following matrix might be defined for Woodland Transport.

Supplier requirements	Need	Rating
Size and location	Medium	5
Financial stability	High	9
Marketplace knowledge	Medium	6
Ownership and structure	Medium	6
Accreditation	High	8
Quality assurance procedures	High	9
Automated tools	No need	0
Insurance	High	9
Procedures for handling disputes	Low	1
Outstanding issues	Low	3
Equal opportunities policy	Low	3
Race relations policy	Low	3
Trade union policy	No need	0
Charity and donations policy	No need	0
Overall responsiveness	High	9

14.8 Implementation requirements

14.8.1 Initial implementation requirements

The initial acceptance and implementation of the software package is a critical stage. This category lists requirements concerning the creation of files, file conversion, initial training and, where necessary, hardware installation.

File creation and conversion
Although software packages include all the programs required for a solution, they do not have the data required to make the system instantly usable. Hence the user has to enter details about customers, departments, accounts, transactions etc. If the system is to hold no historical data (that is, all transactions will only be held from the first day of the software's use) then the task is one of data and file creation. This is often the case in a payroll or accounts system. However, if the task of file creation is daunting (say 100,000 customer accounts records have to be established) or if the system is to report on past transactions, then data and file conversion becomes a major issue in package selection. This will involve data mapping between current and proposed file structures, writing programs to do the conversion, testing those programs, planning the timing of conversion and executing that conversion. Hence the implementation evaluation matrix may include questions on the issues of data conversion and the help the supplier might provide during this process. Assistance in data conversion may be an *Imperative*, as there may be no in-house expertise to perform this vital task.

Installation
Installation has both hardware and software facets. For example, it may be important that the supplier attends the site, installs the software, tests the success of the implementation and provide hands-on guidance in the initial use of the software. There may also be issues of hardware installation and it may be useful if the supplier handles both, to prevent the software supplier blaming a hardware fault (and supplier), and vice versa, for errors and failures in the application.

Implementation
Implementation concerns how the software will be introduced into the organisation. The two clear-cut alternatives are direct conversion/ changeover and parallel running. Both of these may demand support from the supplier. Direct conversion may require special hotline support or the attendance of staff during the first few days of the new process. Parallel running, with its heavy demands on employees, may require the provision of extra staff during the parallel running process and suppliers might be able to supply such resources.

Training

The ITT will also pose a number of questions about the training offered by the supplier. For example, does the supplier offer on-site courses or do employees have to attend standard courses at the supplier's premises? Is it possible to tailor courses to the requirements of a particular company, both in content and delivery days? Can third-party trainers be used? Finally, is it possible for training to be delivered in Computer-Based Tuition (CBT) packages or using some other technology (Internet, video etc.)? These issues may need to be addressed on the implementation evaluation matrix.

14.8.2 Operability requirements

These are continuous implementation requirements concerning such issues as the quality of the supporting documentation, the types and methods of training and how support is organised and when it is available.

Documentation

Documentation will include user manuals, technical documentation, help facilities and crib sheets. The way the documentation is structured will have a major impact on the usability of the software, so an assessment of the clarity and usability of the documentation may be included in the implementation worksheet.

Support structures and policy

Support structures include the technical support hotline (and its hours of operation), agreed response times for solving support problems and policies towards supporting previous releases of the software. These may all be significant issues in the evaluation of the package.

Upgrade policy

The upgrade policy not only includes the likely cost of upgrades, but also the frequency of the upgrade and the process by which the upgrade is distributed. The upgrade policy should also include alterations in documentation.

Legal protection

Legal protection is primarily concerned with what happens if the supplier goes out of business. There is usually some agreement about lodging the source code with a third party (an escrow agreement).

So, again using the classification approach, the implementation requirements for the Woodland Transport system might be:

Implementation requirements	Need	Rating
File creation and conversion	High	10
Implementation	Medium	6
Installation	Medium	6
Training	Medium	6
Documentation	Low	2
Support structure and policy	High	9
Upgrade policy	High	9
Legal protection	High	9

14.9 Cost and time requirements

14.9.1 Cost requirements

This category does not consider cost *Imperatives*; these are examined elsewhere. However, it provides an opportunity to weight cost against other issues in the software selection. For example, although the budget may be £450,000, it may be feasible to select a package for £50,000 that provides 75% of the recorded requirements. This may be acceptable to the organisation, so the remaining £400,000 may be spent (or not spent!) elsewhere in the company.

If cost is not an issue (as long as it is below or on budget then the package is acceptable) this section may be omitted from the evaluation matrix. It is essentially an *Imperative* and the task becomes to buy the best money can buy for the budget. There is no trading off of cost against functionality.

14.9.2 Time requirements

Again, this category does not consider *Imperatives* but rather the relative value of time in the selection process. If the software package has to be implemented by a certain time then this is an *Imperative*. However, if this is not the case then it can be weighted using the normal classification.

The rating given below is for the Woodland Transport System.

Cost and time requirements	Need	Rating
Time constraints	Medium	5

14.10 Summary

Many organisations now choose to implement their information systems requirements using an off-the-shelf software package. This chapter has considered the advantages and disadvantages of such an approach and suggested a framework for software package selection. The next chapter looks at finding packages that may fulfil the company's requirements and evaluating these in a structured way.

EXERCISES

See the exercises for Chapter 15.

References

Hollander, N. (2000). *Software Package Evaluation and Selection*. New York: Amacon.

Software package selection

In this chapter you will learn about:

▶ Invitations To Tender
▶ First-pass software package selection
▶ Second-pass software package selection
▶ Implementation and the long-term relationship

15.1 Introduction

The previous chapter has established a framework for software package selection. The requirements for a particular project have now been defined and classified. This chapter looks at identifying products and their suppliers who may fulfil the requirements of Woodland Transport. Competing products are evaluated in a matrix-based two-stage approach to find an eventual 'winner'.

15.2 Identifying suppliers

One approach to identifying suppliers is to invite them to identify themselves. This may be done by placing an advertisement in the trade press (usually *Computing* or *Computer Weekly* in the United Kingdom). A broad outline of the system requirement is provided (often only a title) and potential suppliers are asked to send for further details. Suppliers who respond are then sent the Invitation To Tender document and are asked to submit their bid within a certain time.

The potential suppliers may be asked:

▶ To pay a fee for the tender document as a charge, of say £100, tends to deter marginal suppliers.

▶ To return the tender document, whether they respond to the tender or not. This prevents the document from passing into general use or into competitor's hands, or from being used to the benefit of the supplier (for example, as a basis for package design). A confidentiality clause may also be needed to support this requirement.

This approach to potential supplier identification may be required by law (Local Authorities may have to run an open-tendering system where all potential suppliers are able to respond), but there can be problems because:

▶ Certain qualifying suppliers may fail to tender because they did not see the advertisement.

▶ A large number of responses could result, each of which has to be carefully considered before drawing up a shortlist.

An alternative approach is to identify potential suppliers and then, after initial research or discussion, invite them to tender for the work. This means that the number of organisations invited to submit tenders is under greater control (and hence can be restricted to a manageable number, say 7–10) and some initial assessment of the company and the product can be undertaken before the formal tender is requested.

Potential sources of suppliers are:

▶ Sells Products and Services Directory

▶ Dun and Bradstreet

▶ Kompass Company Information Register

▶ Software Users Yearbook

▶ Trade magazines

▶ Trade shows

▶ General business magazines

▶ Hardware and database vendors

▶ Internet searches

The first three of these, at least, should be found in the local library as well as on their respective Internet sites. This Internet approach is very significant because it allows a company to research both the organisation and their product range without coming into personal contact with staff of the supplying organisation.

15.3 Invitations To Tender (ITT)

Invitations To Tender are formal documents requesting a response from a potential supplier. They usually contain the following sections.

Information about the tender itself
This includes when the tender should be returned, whom it should be returned to, how it should be returned. This may also include certain aspects of the tendering process. For example:

▶ Who will answer questions about the contents of the tender during the tendering process.

▶ Disqualification procedures and circumstances for anybody offering inducements during the tendering process.

The tendering process may also include a Bidder's Conference where vendors can ask questions and tour the facilities and hear the questions posed by other companies. The tender should be confidential and the vendor and customer may agree to exchange letters of confidentiality.

The organisation issuing the tender
There is usually a brief section about the organisation itself. This may include its purpose (for a non-profit-making organisation) and/or products (particularly for a commercial company) and information about any subsidiaries or holding companies. This general information about the organisation should be supported with details about the departments concerned with this particular project and how those departments relate to other parts of the company. An organisation chart may be helpful.

The project
This is a brief description of the objectives and scope of the project that is the subject of the tendering process. It is useful (but not always essential) for the potential supplier to know:

▶ **Objectives** – why the project is being commissioned and what benefits are being sought.
▶ **Scope** – the boundary of the project and what may be outside the scope at this stage.
▶ **Constraints** – any constraints that may apply. These are the *Imperatives* of the application and might include:
    – budget
    – time
    – standards
    – interfaces with other systems
    – hardware platforms
    – supporting software
    – operating systems
▶ **Authority** – defining the user in the customer organisation who will define the agreed requirements and sign-off the suitability of the package.
▶ **Resources** – defining the resources in the customer organisation available to support the supplier. Key factors will include:
    – access to users
    – resources available from the customer, in particular for user acceptance testing
    – access to hardware
    – access to current software

Format of the response

The analysis of competing vendors is easier if the suppliers are using a standard format. If possible, the suppliers should enter information electronically into the ITT and its associated spreadsheets. This will allow easy pasting of data into the evaluation spreadsheets.

Requirements

The requirements documentation reflects the structure defined in the previous chapter and will include a formal restatement of the *Imperatives*. The structure of the requirements part of the document reflects the high-level matrix structure developed in the previous chapter. The table below shows this.

	Requirements
1.1	Functional requirements
1.2	Non-functional requirements
2.1	Technical requirements
2.2	Design requirements
3.1	Supplier stability requirements
3.2	Supplier citizenship requirements
4.1	Initial implementation requirements
4.2	Operability requirements
5.1	Cost constraints
5.2	Time constraints

Project procedures

The approach applied within the supplier organisation to manage the delivery, enhancement and maintenance of their product.

Evaluation procedures

This is an explanation of the approach that will be taken to evaluating the suppliers and their products. This helps the suppliers formulate their response, as they gain some insight into the criteria their submission will be evaluated against.

Table 15.7, at the end of this chapter, contains a high-level checklist of information that might be requested from a potential supplier. However, many companies have their own detailed checklists that may include information requirements particular to those organisations. For example, purchasing managers or legal and financial departments often request that certain information is formally requested in the ITT.

Once the Invitation To Tender has been issued then the customer must await the responses.

Woodland Transport decided to approach six potential suppliers directly. However, it also placed a small advertisement in *Logistics Management Today*, and as a result of this five other potential suppliers were added to the list. Consequently, 11 potential solutions were evaluated in the first-pass evaluation.

15.4 Assessing the responses to the ITT

15.4.1 Functional match

In the first instance it is easier if the suppliers provide an assessment of the functional match of the package against the textual list of functions. At this stage, it is their perception of the fit between their package and the requirements. They provide the raw scores against the requirement list. The approach used here is to ask them how long it would take them to amend their software to fit the requirement. The score may be supplemented by an actual price for the change (for scores 1–3), which may be used in the evaluation if the customer decides to tailor the software.

Score	
4	The package supports this function without modification
3	One or ess than one staff-day of work is required to modify the package to support this function
2	Two to five staff-days of work are required to modify the package to support this function
1	Six to ten staff-days of work are required to modify the package to support this function
0	More than ten staff-days are required to modify the package to support this function

Each of these scores is changed into a weighted score by multiplying by the rating.

Once the weighted scores have been added for each package, they are expressed as a percentage of the theoretical maximum (sum of ratings × 4) and this value will now be carried on to the high-level evaluation matrix. Table 15.1 reflects the functionality of five representative functions from the Woodland Transport system. Only two competing packages are shown in this matrix. In reality, the number of competing packages assessed at this stage would be much greater. For example, Woodland Transport will have a matrix for 11 products. Two of these, ADMini (Package A) and Btrack (Package B), are shown in the analysis.

Table 15.1 Functional requirements matrix: Woodland Transport.

Function	Rating	Package A	Package B	Weighted A	Weighted B	Weighted maximum
Function 1	9	4	4	36	36	36
Function 2	5	3	4	15	20	20
Function 3	8	3	0	24	0	32
Function 4	5	4	2	20	10	20
Function 5	3	0	1	0	3	12
Total				95	69	120
Functional fit				79.17%	57.50%	

15.4.2 Non-functional match

The suppliers again provide the match between the software package and the requirements. The principles are as for the functional match (see above), except that an optional weighting column has been added. This is to allow the non-functional requirements to be given relative importance to compensate for too many relatively unimportant requirements. The total weighting value is calculated by multiplying the number of non-functional requirements by 4. So, for example, in the example below, this is 40 (10 non-functional requirements × 4). If each requirement is equally important, then a weight of 4 is given to each requirement. However, if some are more important than others, then the relative weights may be altered, with the proviso that the total weighted score remains at 40. The total rating score is equal to the sum of the ratings × the weight. In Table 15.2, a further example, the CLocate software product (Package C), has also been included.

The inclusion of the weighting column allows some interesting 'What if?' experiments. For example, changing values in Table 15.2 leads to:

Requirement	Package A: weighting		Package B: weighting	
Roadsheet produced in 2 minutes	7	4	7	4
Download facility to Excel	1	4	1	4
Percentage coverage	82.92%	82.02%	84.17%	76.75%

Once the weighted scores have been added for each package, they are expressed as a percentage of the theoretical maximum (sum of ratings × 4) and this value will now be carried on to the high-level evaluation matrix.

Table 15.2 Calculating a non-functional match.

Non-functional requirements	Rate	Weight	Raw scores			Weighted scores		
			A	B	C	A	B	C
Roadsheet produced in 2 minutes	9	4	4	4	4	144	144	144
Download facility to Excel	5	4	4	0	4	80	0	80
User specified passwords	6	4	4	4	4	96	96	96
Read only passwords available	6	4	4	1	4	96	24	96
Supports data protection legislation	9	4	4	4	4	144	144	144
Software audit trail facility	7	4	1	4	1	28	112	28
Back up from within the package	2	4	4	4	0	32	32	0
Archiving facility provided	5	4	0	1	4	0	20	80
Standard Windows interface	6	4	4	4	0	96	96	0
Easy to use report generator	2	4	4	4	0	32	32	0
		40	33	30	25	748	700	668
Total score	912	40	Percentage			82.02%	76.75%	73.25%

15.4.3 Product requirements

The scores for these requirements may be determined directly from suppliers or from interpreting the responses to the ITT. It is likely that the results will be more polarised in this section; after all, the software is either developed in Visual Basic or it is not, and it can hardly be tailored for a particular client! The basis of this evaluation (Table 15.3) is exactly the same as that for non-functional requirements.

15.4.4 Supplier requirements

Some of these scores may be allocated directly from the supplier's response to the Invitation To Tender, others will require a subjective assessment on the five point scale (0–4). These assessments should take place in a facilitated workshop. One approach is to allocate the company with the strongest position a value of 4 and then place the others relative to them. Alternatively, a scale of assessment may be devised. An example is given for dispute handling.

Table 15.3 Calculating products requirements.

Product requirements			Raw scores			Weighted scores		
	Rating	Weight	A	B	C	A	B	C
Hardware requirements	3	4	4	4	0	48	48	0
Software requirements	5	4	4	4	0	80	80	0
Operating systems	3	4	4	0	0	48	0	0
Network and communications	0	4	4	0	4	0	0	0
Architecture	1	4	4	0	0	16	0	0
Design requirements	9	2	1	4	4	18	72	72
Configurability	9	6	1	4	4	54	216	216
		28	22	16	12	264	416	288
Total score	480	28	Percentage			55.00%	86.67%	60.0%

Score	Dispute handling
4	Procedure in place with comprehensive evidence
3	Procedure in place, but little evidence provided
2	Procedure in place but no evidence provided
1	Brief textual statement of procedure
0	No procedures for handling disputes

The overall responsiveness score may be preliminary at this stage, derived from a few telephone calls to reference sites. The basis of this evaluation (Table 15.4) is exactly the same as that for non-functional requirements.

15.4.5 Implementation requirements

Some of these scores may be allocated directly from the supplier's response to the Invitation To Tender; others will require a subjective assessment on the five-point scale (0–4). These assessments should take place in a facilitated workshop. The basis of this evaluation (Table 15.5) is exactly the same as that for non-functional requirements.

15.4.6 Cost

If all the package solutions are within budget, then cheaper packages may be given a rating here. There are a number of approaches to this. One

Table 15.4 Calculating supplier requirements.

Supplier requirements	Rating	Weight	Raw scores			Weighted scores		
			A	B	C	A	B	C
Size and location	5	1	0	0	4	0	0	20
Financial stability	10	7	1	1	4	70	70	280
Market-place knowledge	9	7	1	1	4	63	63	252
Ownership and structure	5	4	4	4	4	80	80	80
Accreditation	5	2	0	1	4	0	10	40
Quality assurance procedures	7	2	1	4	4	14	56	56
Insurance	7	1	1	4	4	7	28	28
Dispute handling	7	4	4	4	1	112	112	28
Outstanding issues	9	5	0	4	4	0	180	180
Equal opportunities policy	5	4	2	2	4	40	40	80
Health and safety policy	5	4	4	4	4	80	80	80
Overall responsiveness	10	7	3	4	4	210	280	280
	84	48	21	33	45	676	999	1404
Total score	1488	48	Percentage			45.43%	67.14%	94.35%

approach is to take the cheapest solution and to rate all other packages relative to that cost. The cheapest solution is given 100%, and all other packages are given a lower value, based on some agreed formula. One possible solution is to rate the variance from the cheapest cost as a percentage. For example:

1 – (Cost of Package – Cheapest Cost of Package)/
Cost of Cheapest Package

The application of this principle is shown below:

	Cost	Variance	Adjusted
Cost of Package A	39,000	0.00%	100%
Cost of Package B	41,000	5.13%	94.87%
Cost of Package C	45,000	15.38%	84.62%

This approach can also be used if there is no budget limit.

Table 15.5 Calculating implementation requirements.

Implementation requirements			Raw scores			Weighted scores		
	Rating	Weight	A	B	C	A	B	C
File creation and conversion	10	4	4	4	4	160	160	160
Implementation assistance	5	4	4	4	4	80	80	80
Installation – software	8	4	4	4	4	128	128	128
Installation – hardware	5	4	0	0	4	0	0	80
Training	8	4	4	4	4	128	128	128
Documentation	5	4	0	0	4	0	0	80
Support	9	4	0	2	2	0	72	72
File structures provided	9	4	1	2	4	36	72	144
Legal protection	9	4	0	4	4	0	144	144
	68	36	17	24	34	532	784	1016
Total score	1088	36	Percentage			48.90%	72.06%	93.38%

The finalised high-level evaluation matrix is shown in Table 15.6.

The matrices devised above have been shown for three competing packages. In reality, they may be developed for many competing products and are used as a basis for narrowing the field down to two or three packages that can now be subjected to a final evaluation. In this limited example, Woodland Transport would carry Packages B and C through to the second stage evaluation.

15.5 Second-stage evaluation

The actual gap between the software and the requirements can now be investigated in detail for the two or three packages that have been selected from the evaluation described in the previous section.

There are essentially two distinct ways of defining the size of this gap. The first is the scripted demonstration, where the vendor is asked to run through a number of scenarios defined from the specified use cases. The script is essentially a set of detailed instructions defining exactly what the vendor should do at the demonstration. Users will be asked to attend the demonstration and score each function accordingly. These scores will be compared and a composite value agreed. This value will replace the value provided by the supplier in the original matrix.

Table 15.6 The high-level eva

	High level matrix		Raw scores			Weighted scores		
	Category	Rating	Package A	Package B	Package C	Package A	Package B	Package C
1.1	Functional requirements*	30	81.36	83.90	72.88	2440.80	2517.00	2186.40
1.2	Non-functional*	10	82.92	84.17	74.58	829.20	841.70	745.80
2.0	Product requirements	10	55.00	86.67	60.00	550.00	866.70	600.00
3.0	Supplier requirements	18	45.43	67.14	94.35	817.74	1208.52	1698.30
4.0	Implementation	12	48.90	72.06	93.38	586.80	864.72	1120.56
5.1	Cost constraints	18	100.00	94.87	84.62	1800.00	1707.66	1523.16
5.2	Time constraints	2	100.00	100.00	100.00	200.00	200.00	200.00
	Total	100	513.61	588.81	579.81	7224.54	8206.30	8074.22
			Percentage fit			72.25%	82.06%	80.74%

*These values reflect the complete analysis of functional and non-functional requirements.

However, such demonstrations take the vendor at least a week to prepare and it may be uneconomic for them to do this. Hence an alternative is for two or three representatives of the customer to learn the package (using a trial version) and construct their own version of the demonstration. There are two advantages to this:

▶ It allows an assessment of the usability of the package.
▶ It allows the construction of an object class model of the package, exposing weaknesses that may have not been apparent from a vendor-led presentation.

15.5.1 Evaluation of the suppliers

The final evaluation of the suppliers will mainly concern reference sites and detailed financial investigation.

Reference sites
These sites will have been provided by the supplier in their response to the Invitation To Tender (ITT). It is now necessary to phone or visit these sites to gain relevant information.
The following provides a checklist of information that could be used:

▶ Your purpose for phoning or visiting the reference site. The type of business you are in and the confidential nature of all information revealed during the call or visit.

▶ The type of industry, size and structure of the reference site, what version and modules of the software they are using and how long they have been using them.

▶ The information systems structure of the company and how the software package fits into their software strategy.

▶ The hardware used by the reference site, the number of users supported and the communications protocols and physical distances involved.

▶ Confirmation of the cost of the product and the annual maintenance fee.

▶ The relationship of the reference site to the supplier and whether they are being paid to provide a reference and on what basis this payment is made.

▶ Reasons for selecting the package in the first place and why that package was preferred to alternative solutions.

▶ Whether the package was modified in any way and the scope of these modifications.

▶ Whether the package has lived up to expectations, what benefits it has brought and the reaction of users to the package.

▶ Whether the package is reliable and free from defects and, if faults have been found, how quickly a new release was provided.

▶ The performance and response times of the package given the number of users and the hardware platform, the communications protocols and the software mix.

▶ Problems encountered in the implementation and use of the package, the reasons for those problems and (where necessary) how the vendor reacted and solved those problems.

▶ Specific issues concerning file creation, conversion and implementation. What problems were encountered during this stage and how did the vendor react to these?

▶ General questions about the way the vendor conducts business and whether there was any indication of financial or morale problems at the company.

▶ Issues arising from the training courses and documentation supplied by the customer.

▶ Issues arising from the support offered by the vendor; for example from the Help desk.

▶ Specific issues that arose in contract negotiation and any advice they may offer when negotiating terms with this vendor.

▶ Questions concerning the role and usefulness of the User Group (if it exists).

The answers to some of these questions will lead to changes in rating on the supplier and implementation evaluation matrices; for example, dispute-handling procedures, implementation assistance, and file creation and conversion. It is also at this stage that a more reliable value can be placed on overall responsiveness of the vendor (in the supplier requirements matrix). If the product has a User Group, then it is useful to contact active members in this group and request past documentation from meetings and conferences. It may also be possible to attend these events during the evaluation exercise. Again, information gleaned from these meetings may be fed back into the relevant evaluation matrix.

Financial information

Although standard information has been provided by the vendor in their response to the Invitation To Tender, it is useful to make a number of covert enquiries. In the United Kingdom a primary source is Companies House, and other potential sources are companies specialising in providing credit information on suppliers.

Once this information has been gathered, relevant parts of the supplier matrix may be updated, in particular the assessment of financial position. It may also lead to certain *Imperatives* not being met (undisclosed by the vendor) and hence the elimination of that package from the whole process.

Once the matrices have been updated, the final workshop may be held to select the winner and to place the contract.

15.6 Implementation considerations

Implementation usually concerns testing, training, documentation, and file conversion and creation (see Chapter 16). In the software package approach, testing is largely irrelevant. Program and system testing should have already been performed by the supplier and need not be undertaken by the customer. It could be argued that user acceptance testing is required, but this again has largely been undertaken in the package selection. If the software does not support the user's functional requirements then it should not have been selected in the first place. However, some elements of user acceptance systems testing might be prudent, for example:

▶ Volume testing
▶ Testing interfaces with other systems
▶ Final usability checks

Standard documentation will be provided with the package, although there may be a need to create a limited set of documents to assist the use of the package within the specific environment of the organisation. This may include both manual and automated operations. For example, how the package (to produce Purchase Orders) fits into the complete

Purchase Ordering process of the organisation itself. Similarly, the vendor will provide training courses and it is the responsibility of the customer to ensure that users attend relevant courses at the most appropriate time. Training may have to be supplemented by courses in the complete business process; for example, processing a Purchase Order Form from a request to completion, rather than just producing it from the package.

However, it is with file creation and conversion that many major issues emerge. The selection of the package should have taken file conversion into consideration and the cost and time of this conversion should be reflected in the evaluation.

The detailed work of conversion should:

▶ Ensure that the physical conversion of data is possible.

▶ Undertake a data mapping between the files and databases of the current system and the data structures of the proposed system. Problems (such as shorter length data items) should be noted and addressed.

▶ Specify, develop and test programs to undertake the conversion. The results of the conversion must be verified before the conversion programmes are applied to the live operational data.

▶ Finally, undertake the live conversion at a convenient time. It may also be necessary to enter values for data items required in the new system that were not held in the current one.

In some applications, the software vendor will undertake file conversions at, or below, cost, because they realise that it can be a significant reason for selecting their product in the first place. In such instances it is important that the customer assures itself of the process (and QA procedures) accompanying the file conversion requirements.

15.7 Managing the long-term relationship

One of the significant disadvantages of the software package approach is that the lack of control (over business direction, software functionality and version control) of the customer over the supplier leads to significant risks. This risk needs to be managed.

The customer should at all times:

▶ Strive to maintain good relationships with the supplier and seek to achieve compromises rather than escalate conflict.

▶ Maintain a watching brief on the performance of the supplier, looking for evidence of problems. Many supplier evaluations only take place at the time of first purchase, rather than throughout the whole relationship.

▶ Develop and maintain a contingency plan for moving from the vendor's system to an alternative.

▶ Maintain an escrow agreement with the supplier.

15.8 Tailoring software package solutions

Tailoring the software package is often suggested when the package fails to completely meet all the user's requirements. There are a number of approaches to this. The first option is to ask the software house to make the changes and to pay accordingly. However, this begins to reduce the advantages of the package. It incurs cost and delay and, because it involves program specification, design and testing, it can also reduce the quality of the product. It also removes the 'try before you buy' element from part of the product and it is unlikely that bespoke documentation and training will be produced.

This approach also assumes that the software house is willing to tailor the product to meet an organisation's specific requirements. In many instances the software house is not prepared to make such amendments. The reason for this is that the company wishes to offer a standard product. Tailoring a particular implementation creates specification, programming and testing problems and costs and it is unlikely to be very profitable. However, their reluctance is primarily due to the problems of controlling releases and ensuring that future upgrades (containing new functionality and fault fixes) work properly with both standard and tailored releases. This latter issue is a major problem because most software houses want to reduce the number of versions they support, not increase them. Changes are controlled more easily if they can be rolled into the standard version of the software.

An alternative to software house amendment is the purchasing and amendment of source code by the customer. In this approach, the customer buys the source code of the product at a certain point in time and then undertakes all subsequent amendments and upgrades himself. This removes most of the advantages of the software package approach. The product now becomes a bespoke solution – but a solution where internal developers are (at the outset) unfamiliar with the construction and operation of the programs and data structures. Consequently, there is a large learning curve in the early stages of source code acquisition. Two other problems must be recognised and they both concern support:

▶ Errors due to coding are no longer fixed under a support contract, even if those errors occur in code unaffected by bespoke changes.

▶ Future upgrades of the native software package cannot be reliably integrated into the bespoke solution. The specification of the changes may be used in producing bespoke amendments.

The purchasing of source code may reduce programming effort, but the time taken to confidently understand the operation of the software often means that such time (and cost) savings are marginal. There is also no guarantee that the underlying design is flexible enough to support the changes that are likely to be required in the future.

In general, tailoring (changing the source code) the software package is not good practice and the alternative (changing the business practice to reflect the package) is cheaper and more reliable.

15.9 Summary

This chapter has provided an approach for comparing competing software packages. The framework is based largely on a supplier-based assessment for a first pass, which is subsequently confirmed by the customer as a second pass. This second pass updates the relevant matrices and a final selection is made. The chapter concluded with some issues about contractual terms, implementation and managing the long-term relationship with the supplier. This approach to information systems development still requires a successful inception phase, but the elaboration phase is probably reduced in detail, perhaps using the models of Chapters 5, 6 and 7 but not Chapters 8 and 9. The construction phase is replaced completely, but transition, the implementation phase (see next chapter) remains.

Table 15.7 ITT checklist.

Supplier information
Full name of the company
Registered address of the company
Address for correspondence concerning this tender (if different from above)
Telephone number, fax, email numbers and addresses
Contact name for this tender (extension number, direct line)
Trading status (sole trader, partnership, private limited company, public limited company)
For a partnership – name of partners; for a limited company – names of directors
Partners/directors and their recent involvement (if any) in receivership
Partners/directors and their relationship to the customer – whether through employment or supply/current supply of goods and services
For a limited company – give registration number and details (if appropriate) of group structure and any ultimate holding company
Contact name for financial information (extension number, direct line)
Name and address of bank
Audited accounts and annual reports for the last three years to include:
Balance sheet, detailed profit and loss account
Full notes to the accounts
Director's report or equivalent
Auditor's report
Management accounts relating to the period since the last audited accounts
Employer's liability insurance – insurer, policy number, extent of cover, expiry date
Public liability insurance – insurer, policy number, extent of cover, expiry date
Professional indemnity insurance – insurer, policy number, extent of cover, expiry date

Table 15.7
(*continued*).

Details of outstanding litigation or arbitration

Details of outstanding taxation disputes

Guarantor – providing a performance bond for the contract

Statement of equal opportunities

Prescribed questions on race relations

Contact name for health and safety policy (extension number, direct line)

Prescribed questions on health and safety

Trade union policy

Strategic aims and objectives

Number of employees (and their distribution by country, department etc.)

Current organisational issues (merger discussions, restructuring etc.)

Product information

Full name of the product

Brief description of the product – functionality

Historical perspective and version release

Modular structure (if appropriate)

Defined interfaces with other products

Current user base for the product (and, where appropriate, modules, versions and related products). User base may be split by UK/Europe/ Rest of world

Licence arrangements for the product

Cost of the product and discount structure (options for rental and leasing)

Required hardware configuration (both minimum and recommended)

Required software configuration

Supporting software products required (name, version and cost)

Operating system requirements (minimum and recommended)

Arrangements for evaluation copies of the product

Arrangements for a 'trial use' of the product

Proposed development of the product with proposed release dates for new versions and new modules

Reference sites for the product

Sample contracts

Termination agreement

Product quality assurance

Quality standards and accreditations

Product development methodology and QA procedures

Testing strategy (including Model Office) and release procedures

Change control procedures

Automated tools to support release, testing and change control

Automated tools to support product development (e.g. CASE tools)

Staff recruitment policies (and key CVs)

Staff numbers and general level of expertise in development, support, help desk

Table 15.7
(*continued*)

Support hours, defined response times and logging procedures

Handling complaints and problems

Design documentation for the product. Minimum: normalised data model supported by entity descriptions

Product services

Maintenance/support contracts. Content and cost

Training services and cost

Documentation – user manuals, technical documentation etc.

Installation procedures

Policy concerning the support of previous versions of the software

Supporting services and products

Defined links of the product with other commercial software

Integration with standard Microsoft products such as Word and Excel

Suitability for use with established data mining tools

Technical compliance (for example, ODBC compliance)

Internet, Intranet and email facilities

Document production and distribution to large data sets

Electronic exchange of data

Arrangements and cost for file conversion from current systems

Import and export formats

Consultancy and programming support

Project procedures

Agreed constraints (budget*, time, standard etc.)

Supplier contact (accounts manager)

Customer contacts (including the authority)

Restrictions concerning canvassing

Deadlines for quotation, date of delivery and mechanism of delivery

Project initiation and control procedures

Supporting project management tools

Implementation plan

Sign-off procedures for deliverables

Agreed invoicing terms and procedures**

Arrangements for settling disputes

*For example, a recent ITT contained the phrase 'the value of agreements entered into over this period is not expected to exceed £200,000'

**'Invoicing and deliverable acceptance should be kept separate. A recent contract included the phrase 'payment of any invoices does not imply acceptance of the software (or any part thereof) has been provided to the satisfaction of the customer'.

Table 15.7
(continued)

Costing worksheet (high-level)	
	Cost
One-off costs	
Software (analysed by modules)	
Implementation	
Hardware	
Installation	
Training	
Documentation	
Other costs	
Total	
Recurring costs	
Software maintenance costs	
Hardware maintenance costs	
Other costs	
Total	
Support services	
Consultancy	
Programming	
Telephone support	

EXERCISES

In the context of the Woodland Transport project:

1   What would be the relative advantages and disadvantages for Woodland Transport of adopting the software package approach to information systems development?

2   Use the ITT list to construct (as far as you can) an ITT for the Woodland Transport project.

3 Using the recommended sources, identify potential suppliers and packages for the Woodland Transport project.

4 Examine and research contracts for software package provision ready to advise the Woodland Transport management about their legal position should they wish to pursue the software package approach.

EATWELL, a catering company, wishes to replace its inventory control systems. It has decided to purchase a packaged software solution, rather than have a bespoke system built. The software will run on the same hardware as the current system. Four suppliers have responded to the Invitation To Tender, and their proposals are due to be evaluated over the next four weeks, before the decision is made.

5 What factors might have influenced EATWELL's decision to opt for a packaged solution rather than a bespoke system?

6 Describe five issues that EATWELL will consider in evaluating the four packages. Explain the importance of each of these issues.

7 If, after the evaluation, it is found that none of the packages fits the requirements perfectly, how else could EATWELL assess the strengths and weaknesses of each, in order to make the best selection?

References

Richard, S. (1991). *Package Evaluation*. Aldershot: Avebury Technical.

Systems implementation

In this chapter you will learn about:

▶ File conversion
▶ Documentation
▶ Training
▶ Implementation strategies

16.1 Introduction

This chapter looks at some of the issues that the developer will need to consider as the proposed solution becomes clearer. The first of these is file conversion and creation. The specification will become clear for this as soon as a solution is commissioned (in the case of a bespoke solution) or purchased (in the case of a software package application). At this stage the analysts can begin to map the difference between the data structures of the current and proposed system and so start to plan the conversion of data and the entry of data that is not held in the current system. It is at this stage that user documentation and training can also be planned. Finally, this chapter looks at the common implementation strategies that the development team might use to put their system in place. Overall, this chapter is concerned with the transition phase of the systems development process. Some of the issues concerned in this stage have already been considered in the previous chapter in the context of software package selection.

16.2 File conversion

Most systems require an established set of files if they are to be immediately operational. Thus an order entry system will need such files as customer data, outstanding orders, products etc. This may demand a large file conversion task (when moving from one computer system to another) or a large, one-off data entry when systems are being computerised for the first time. This conversion leads to both programming and management tasks.

If the files are currently held on a computer system then it should be possible to move the data from the present implementation to the target hardware and software. The first stage in such a conversion process is to make sure that it is technically possible to move the data, created and stored by one software package, language or database management system, to the proposed solution, which may use completely different hardware and software platforms. If it is technically possible, then the analyst must perform a data mapping between the files of the current system and the data structures of the new.

This data mapping explicitly identifies the links between the fields of the current system and the fields of the proposed system. Differences in field type, length, format and validation must be documented and the issues that such differences pose must be resolved.

For example, the new `Customer` file may have the data fields `customer-no`, `customer-firstname`, `customer-secondname`, `sex` and `Date of birth`. The current system may contain the fields `customer-no`, `customer-name` and `sex`. The data mapping exercise could highlight the following:

Proposed system field	Field length	Current system field	Field length	Comments
Customer-no	999999	Customer-no	999999	
Customer-firstname	X(30)	Customer-name	X(50)	Customer name will have to be spilt into two fields
Customer-secondname	X(30)			
Sex	X	Sex	X	
Date of birth	dd/mm/yyyy			This is not supported in the current system

Hence an approach will have to be developed to cope with the splitting of the customer-name field. One of the solutions considered may be the development of a program to search the entries on the old field and split them up using some standard algorithm (for example, all text before the first space is put into Customer-firstname, the rest goes in Customer-secondname). However, this may not work due to ethnic and cultural variations. Alternatively, all current entries may be printed out and manually re-entered into the two new fields using a data entry routine.

Furthermore, some decision will have to be made about what to do about the date of birth field for current customers, because that information is not currently available.

Programs will need to be designed, written and tested to take the data from the old system and store it in the new. These programs may also perform validation routines on the data to ensure that invalid data that has somehow made its way into the old system is not transferred to the new. Data entry programs will also have to be written for data that is to be collected for the first time. The designer may be able to use the data input routines of the proposed system for entering current information into the computer. However, it is more likely that a certain amount of historical data will also be required, and this facility will not be available in the normal input routine. For example, a system for recording customer orders stored the date of last order for each customer. In normal operations this was picked up from the order entry routine. However, at the start of live running, this field was blank in every (converted) customer record. This meant that reports running off this field were likely to be of little use until the second or third year of the system's use. Consequently a special file creation program had to be written to capture the date of last order together with other historical information required by the system.

The task of organising the creation of files must also be approached with meticulous detail. Entering 50,000 customer records is a daunting, not to say boring, task. The clerical resources of the department may not be sufficient, or willing, to undertake such activities on top of their daily work. It may be possible to phase the file creation by entering established records over a period of time, in parallel with the running of the operational system. This requires a certain discipline to ensure that the completion of data entry does not stretch too far into the future and, in addition, it has the disadvantage of the system operating for some considerable time with incomplete files.

In summary, file creation and conversion creates important technical and operational requirements that have to be anticipated and planned for by the developer.

16.3 Preparation of documentation

Documentation is a constant task in system development. The development methods introduced in this book have produced documentation that has been useful in both understanding and communicating problems and requirements.

However, the latter stages of a project give the opportunity to tidy up this system documentation and to ensure that it actually does reflect the proposed physical system.

Three further types of documentation are associated with the implementation itself:

▶ **Training documentation**
Training documentation provides detailed tuition on the operation of the proposed system. There is still a tendency to believe that the functions of the system can be learned from large technical user manuals. This is very unlikely. Most of these manuals are too long, present all the information at the same level of detail, and describe operations rather than explaining them. It is very unlikely that users will have either the time or the

motivation to work systematically through a large user manual. Even if they did, it is uncertain whether they could successfully place the information in the context of their own application and roles and hence separate the important (to them) from the trivial. These large manuals fail to recognise the distinction between learning and reference.

Documentation for learning will typically set objectives, explain concepts and commands relevant to those objectives, and then test the mastery of these commands to examine whether the objectives have been achieved. Such documentation may use conventional media and methods – handouts, lectures, tests – in the traditional setting of a training course. Alternatively, Computer-Based Training (CBT) may be considered, particularly where the users are geographically spread and cannot be spared from their everyday tasks. Certainly CBT has particular relevance in computer systems training, as the medium of that training is also the objective. Many organisations now used CBT and computer-aided assessment in the delivery of their training.

▶ User documentation

The point has already been made that user manuals should be reference rather than learning documents. Such manuals will need to reflect the expertise and vocabulary of the users involved in the system. It is preferable to write a series of small documents aimed at different types of users rather than one all-encompassing manual whose size ensures that it will seldom be used. Manuals should concentrate on business functions and issues and how to correct errors. For example, there may be small manuals or worksheets on 'How to raise a purchase order', 'How to raise an invoice' and 'What to do if you make an error in invoice posting', which provide the user with specific guidance for the task or problem at hand.

▶ Operations documentation

The operational details are obviously very important. The system may produce the payslips successfully, but someone must have responsibility for loading the paper at a certain time, readying the printer and collating and distributing the output in accordance with a defined timetable. Operators need training and documentation. They will also need to know the normal operating procedures and how to respond to errors.

16.4 Training

Training will cover the retraining of current staff and the recruitment of new personnel. The latter will involve job specification, advertising, salary advice and interviewing. Retraining will require planning and coordination.

For training to be effective, it must be clear what it is trying to achieve. This may be clarified through the setting of objectives. Three levels of objective can be distinguished. The first type demands the recall of facts – thus objectives are defined in terms of specific facts that have to be recalled. Comprehension is a different type of objective. In this instance the trainee should be able to both recall the facts and describe or illustrate them using words, actions or examples that are different from those the instructor used. Finally, objectives might be defined in terms of application, where the trainee has to use his or her knowledge in different situations of the same general type. In practice, the objectives of the training course are likely to be a mixture of recall, comprehension and application.

The setting of objectives for training will suggest ways of delivering the training. The objectives might suggest a combination of media, an approach demonstrated by the Open University who combine video, audio, tutorial texts, conventional books, case studies, practicals, lectures and CBT in the delivery of their courses.

Once the training material has been delivered, the attainment of the trainee and the effectiveness of the training methods can be assessed. The evaluation of the trainee might be through an end of course test, a subjective assessment, a statistical report from the authoring language used to produce the CBT material or some combination of all three. Similarly, the effectiveness of the trainer and of the training materials should be assessed, perhaps through an end-of-course questionnaire, and appropriate action taken.

Unfortunately, much training is poorly planned and presented at the wrong level, failing to take the expertise and expectations of staff into consideration. To compound this, the management are often reluctant to give training sessions the time or resources they require. This often manifests itself in the underfunding of training or not releasing staff for sufficient time from their daily duties. As a result, many systems are implemented with users and operators who do not fully understand their tasks and roles and this greatly reduces the effectiveness of the system.

It should be clear that the tasks of implementation – system testing, file conversion, documentation and training all require careful planning and coordination. Certain tasks must not be left too late (rushed user manuals are usually unimpressive), done too early (operator training months before the system will go live) or in the wrong sequence. Implementation is a project in its own right and will benefit from controls that are applicable to any project. There is sometimes a tendency to relax during implementation, believing that all the hard work has been done. This is false confidence; lack of control and planning in implementation can undo months of good system and programming work.

16.5 Implementation strategies

The changeover from the old to the new system can be arranged once the computer system is tested and approved. Three possible strategies are available.

16.5.1 Parallel running

In this method the old and new systems are run simultaneously for an agreed period of time and results from the two systems are compared.

Once the user has complete confidence in the system the old system is abandoned and transactions are only passed through the new one. Parallel running places a large administrative overhead on the user department because every transaction has to be effectively done twice – once through the established procedures and then again through the new computer system. Results have to be cross-checked and the source of errors located. This will lead to system modifications if problems are discovered in the computer system.

This method does have the advantage of having a 'fail-safe' system to fall back on should the new system crash for some reason. System problems can then be sorted out and the parallel run resumed. However, the duplication of effort can be something of a mixed blessing. Many operators and users still tend to rely on the established system, so some problems never appear until this has been abandoned. In addition, it may be difficult to justify a parallel run for the whole cycle of processing. Problems may only appear at, say, the end of the financial year, months after the 'fail-safe' manual system has been phased out.

16.5.2 Pilot implementation

Two different possibilities exist. The first may be seen as a sort of retrospective parallel running. This takes historical data, say the last three months' invoices, and the output produced is compared with the known results. This is only, in effect, a large set of test data, and although this is not a bad thing in itself it does not really give the users and operators the experience and urgency of live processing.

The second type of pilot implementation does use live operations. Instead of all the transactions being passed through the new system, as in parallel running, only a limited number are entered into the computer system. This may be on a sample basis (say 1 in every 10) if this still facilitates cross-checking or, perhaps more realistically, by entering only certain sections, departments or accounts. This gives practice in live processing and reduces the overheads of duplicated entry. It is less rigorous in its testing than parallel running because only a limited set of transactions is used. However, experience suggests that the transaction that causes the system to crash is in the transactions not included in the sample or in another department; a fact that is only found out when the existing system is abandoned and full live running commences.

16.5.3 Direct changeover

The final strategy is to implement the new system completely and withdraw the old without any sort of parallel running at all. Thus processing of the current system may end on a Friday night and all transactions pass through the new computer system from Monday morning onwards. There is no 'fail-safe' system at all. Direct changeover has none of the cost and time overheads of the previous two methods. Neither does it permit the old loyalty to the replaced system to influence the relative performance of the two systems. It clearly demands very thorough testing and planned file creation and training strategies. All operations of the system must be understood at the moment of going live because the opportunity for gradual training and further testing does not exist. Thus direct changeover is the quickest and most complete of our three implementation strategies, but it is probably the riskiest.

In certain instances there is no real alternative to this method. This tends to be:

▶ Where there is little similarity between the old and the replacement system so that cross-checking is not possible.

▶ Where the cost of parallel running is so prohibitive that it is cheaper to pay for the mistakes found in a direct changeover.

Where possible, direct changeovers should occur in slack periods and take advantage of natural breaks in the operations of the organisation, such as industrial holidays.

16.6 Summary

Systems implementation is a key issue in successful systems development. There are many things that can go wrong if the issues identified in this chapter are not tackled effectively. For example:

▶ Insufficient time and budget is allocated to data conversion

▶ Documentation is ineffective or misleading

▶ Training is delivered too early and is inappropriately delivered and assessed

▶ Insufficient budget is available to employ the preferred implementation method

Some of these issues should have been considered at the feasibility stage. Although they are presented in the final chapter of the book, they should be considered right at the start of the systems development.

EXERCISES

A company has recently installed a new order processing system, using parallel running. Six months after implementation, most of the old system has been switched off and the majority of the new system is accepted. However, the invoicing function is still being run in parallel, as the invoicing manager is unhappy with the accuracy of the output.

The IT manager wishes to switch off the old system completely and amend the Invoicing function as it runs.

The Sales Manager wishes to keep the two systems running in parallel until the output is satisfactory.

The Invoicing Manager wishes to switch off the new system and just run the old system until the new can be fixed once and for all.

1   Suggest reasons why this situation may have arisen in the first place.

2   Assess each of the three managers' positions, and say which of the three options you would recommend. Explain your choice.

BUY-IT-HERE is a small chain of six general stores located around a major metropolitan area in the Midlands. A large store group has recently bought it. The new owner wishes to implement a point of sale (POS) system in all of its new stores with links to its central computer system. The BUY-IT-HERE stores all currently use their own standalone cash registers.

You have been asked to assist in the conversion to the new POS system. To help in the implementation, produce:

3   A description and evaluation of the various implementation strategies.

4   A checklist, in sequence, of the activities likely to be carried out before and during implementation.

5   Suggestions as to how the new system might be evaluated after three months of operational use.

A company is changing its payroll package, and has selected a popular standard commercial package to run on a standalone PC. One difficulty with the package, though, is that the employee data is kept in a different format from that currently used. The name and address fields are currently single fields, while the new package separates out the Title, Forename and Family names into their own separate fields. Similarly, the Address in the new system is now stored in four separate fields, to cover Road and Number, District, Town and County. The number of characters for these fields is more than is currently held.

The current employee file is split into reference data and pay data. The reference data consists of: Employee No, Name, Address, Telephone No, Marital status, Next of Kin, Date Joined, Job Title, Grade, Department, Section, Rate of pay, Allowances and Deductions. The pay data refers to each week of the year, the weekly pay entitlements are entered: Hours worked, Gross pay, Income tax, NI contributions and Net pay.

The new package has the same data, but the order is slightly different: the reference section shows the data item Date Joined coming between Employee No and Name. Allowances and deductions are in the pay data sections of the record, not in the reference data section.

6   Describe how the conversion from the old system to the new can be successfully carried out.

7   Specify what checks need to be incorporated into the process, to ensure that the new system data is complete and accurate before implementation.

8   The implementation is expected to take place in the middle of the financial year. What are the implications of this decision for conversion and operation?

References

Pinto, J. and Millet, I. (1999). *Successful Information Systems Implementation: The Human Side*. Newtown Square, PA: Project Management Institute.

Poore, A. and Thomas, G. (2002). *Successful IS Acquisition and Implementation*. Aldershot: Gower.

Systems Development

This book concentrates on the techniques, issues and diagrammatic models of systems development. It is less concerned with how these are organised into a framework for systems development. However, possible frameworks have been encountered a number of times in the book and these need revisiting and putting into context. The first framework of **inception**, **elaboration**, **construction** and **transition** was introduced in the Preface and Chapter 1 as a useful basis for positioning the contents of this book.

Chapters 3 and 4 are firmly in the inception stage of systems development and would be required whether the organisation was producing a complex bespoke system, a set of rapidly produced systems to fulfil local needs or adopting a software package approach. Similarly, the concerns of Chapter 2 would also have to be addressed in all environments. How to source and account for information systems activity is something that is constantly taxing managers of organisations and about which they seem to be always changing their minds!

The techniques, conventions and diagrammatic models introduced in Part 2 largely belong to the elaboration stage, although the extent to which they would be used would depend upon the requirements of the project.

In some applications the stages of **elaboration** and **construction** are combined with more emphasis on prototyping. This usually reflects the need for a more incremental approach to development. The chapter on Rapid Application Development (Chapter 10) puts this into perspective. In this approach **inception** is perceived as complete and **transition** (implementation) is still required.

Finally, the 'V' model (Chapter 13) is a particularly useful way of looking at testing. The model again assumes that **inception** is complete and **transition** is required. Requirement analysis and logical design are essentially to do with **elaboration**. The distinction is that requirement analysis forms the text and models that the user is able to sign off and so is the basis of user acceptance testing. The logical design is the deliverables of the whole of the elaboration stage. Physical design and unit design refers to the **construction** stage. The elements and degree of testing that are appropriate have to be looked at within each project and are usually enshrined in a test strategy for that project.

In *Introducing Systems Design*, one of the predecessors of this book, the reason for not adopting a proprietary methodology (SSADM was very prevalent at the time) was explained in four points. These still remain valid and are elaborated below.

1. None of the methodologies is demonstrably applicable in all development environments. They tend to be more relevant to large organisations with significant computer resources undertaking complex projects.

    This is increasingly true today. Consider the following environments (all of which we have encountered in the last year).

A development of a large centralised system for financial monitoring
In a large bespoke development of a critical (perhaps even safety-critical) system, the developers may elect to undertake a complete analysis first, producing a specification comprising many of the models defined in Chapters 6–9. This will be particularly appropriate if the construction phase of the system is to be put out to competitive tender. In the financial monitoring example, the organisation produced a complete specification (elaboration) of the requirements and is now asking software houses to bid for the construction. Security (Chapter 13) is an important consideration in the development of this system.

A series of small 'speedboat' projects developed in Lotus Notes for local offices
These systems had to be produced quickly with little concern for future maintenance costs. In such instances RAD is clearly more appropriate, supported by selected models from the elaboration stage. In fact, the teams developing the projects used use case diagrams and use case descriptions (specifications). Emphasis was placed on usability (Chapter 11). In smaller rapid developments a subset of models might be selected or applied to only certain parts of the requirement.

The implementation of standard software packages throughout the organisation to support payroll and human resource management
In the software package approach only a subset of the models would be required. The minimum requirement is probably for a use case diagram and a set of use case descriptions for the functional view and an appropriate persistent model (class or data model). The material in Chapters 14 and 15 is most relevant to this situation. Because of the nature of the contract between the customer and supplier, the organisation spent a considerable amount of time in requirement analysis, using most of the fact-gathering techniques described in Chapter 5.

Cancellation of all projects due to financial pressure and concentration on maintaining and enhancing current systems
Much of the work in real systems development is concerned with maintaining and enhancing current computerised systems. Analysts undertaking this work need tools to help them define partial solutions and to understand exactly how the often undocumented system actually works. Such techniques as Structured English may be particularly helpful in specification. Class and data models might be

useful ways of re-engineering the software so that it can be better understood.

2. Methodologies tend to make development over-technical, presenting it as a series of increasingly complex models where the skill of manipulating the model can overwhelm the real-life business application. One writer (Kimmerley, 1984) stated that 'due in part to the legacy of various structured revolutions creativity has not only been comprehensively de-emphasised, but has come to be regarded as something to be avoided altogether'. Methodologies have tended to de-humanise analysis and design.

3. An absence of acceptable metrics and a seeming reluctance to undertake empirical research means that there is little quantitative evidence to support the efficiency claims of proprietary development methodologies.

4. The adoption of a proprietary methodology is not appropriate for introductory analysis and design training. Methodologies are essentially a second step after the developer has mastered the basic skills and is in a better position to appreciate and evaluate the presented methodology.

As stated before, the principle of Part 2 was to provide a selection of fact-gathering and modelling techniques which could be applied as required to different situations.

Hence the approach of this book has been to identify techniques as the basis of a set of tools that can be selected to suit different circumstances. The toolkit approach seeks to recognise the variety and richness of all real-world applications. This variety manifests itself along three axes (see Figure 17.1).

Figure 17.1 Axes of variety.

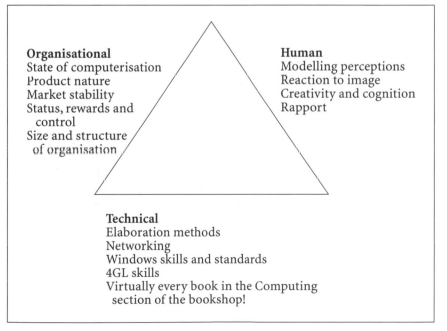

Organisational
State of computerisation
Product nature
Market stability
Status, rewards and
  control
Size and structure
  of organisation

Human
Modelling perceptions
Reaction to image
Creativity and cognition
Rapport

Technical
Elaboration methods
Networking
Windows skills and standards
4GL skills
Virtually every book in the Computing
  section of the bookshop!

Technical

This concerns itself with the technical skills of the developer and with his or her technological knowledge. The mastery of the various techniques of systems development lies along this axis. So do other learning and training skills (network management, COBOL programming, hardware maintenance). Bookshops are full of technical training books.

Organisational

The size and structure of the organisation, its products, services and geographical distribution, will affect the technical solution. It will also be affected by the personalities and skills of the managers concerned and the organisational norms of status, control and reward. Deciding the appropriate technology is not an easy matter. There are plenty of examples where information systems failure has been caused by the selection of too complex a solution and still others where lack of ambition has led to the under-use of technology. The analyst must be sensitive to the organisational context of the work, understanding that different skills and solutions will be required in what may, at first sight, appear to be familiar territory. The great variety of organisational contexts makes us nervous about recommending a 'one best way' approach to systems development.

Human

People model reality in a number of ways. It seems clear that individuals find certain techniques more appealing and comfortable to use. They come to perfectly acceptable solutions by concentrating upon a particular perspective. This is probably most marked in the distinction between the persistent (class and data models) and dynamic perspective (use cases and data flow diagrams) of the organisation. Some practitioners are more at home with the former and use it to drive their analysis work, while others prefer to concentrate upon the latter. Analysts should not exclude tools from their toolkit (after all, they never know when they will need them), but they should recognise and exploit their own modelling preferences and abilities. The toolkit approach stresses sensitivity to the organisational and human issues that confront an analyst. It recognises that a heavy methodological hammer is not required to crack every project nut.

> Of course, systems have been built using single strategies or even no formal one. However, there are several arguments that strongly suggest that the quality of applications and the application development process is highest when methods representing several strategies are used together in a balanced way. (Zimmerman, 1983)

References

Kimmerley, W. (1984). Restricted vision. *Datamation*, pp. 152–160.
Zimmerman, R. (1983). Phases, methods and tools – a triad of systems development. In *Entity-Relationship approach to Software Engineering* (eds. Davis, C. G. *et al.*). New York, Elsevier.

Index